THE COMPLETELY
SUPERIOR PERSON'S
BOOK OF WORDS

THE COMPLETELY SUPERIOR PERSON'S BOOK OF WORDS

PETER BOWLER

BLOOMSBURY

LONDON · NEW DELHI · NEW YORK · SYDNEY

First published in Great Britain 2009

Copyright © 1979, 1982, 1992, 2001 by Peter Bowler
Illustrations © 2001, 2003, 2004 Roderick Mills

Originally published as three separate volumes, *The Superior Person's Book of Words*, *The Superior Person's Second Book of Words* and *The Superior Person's Third Book of Words*

First published in the US by David R. Godine, Publisher, Inc. 1985, 1992, 2001
First published in the UK 2002, 2003 and 2004

Published by arrangement with David R. Godine, Publisher, Inc.
9 Hamilton Place, Boston, Massachusetts 02108

Bloomsbury Publishing Plc
50 Bedford Square, London WC1B 3DP

www.bloomsbury.com

Bloomsbury Publishing, London, New Delhi, New York and Sydney

A CIP catalogue record for this book is available from the British Library

ISBN 978 1 4088 0635 7

10 9 8 7

Typeset by Dorchester Typesetting
Printed and bound in Great Britain by CPI Group (UK) Ltd, Croydon CR0 4YY

To Di, with love

Acknowledgements

Acknowledgments

My sources are, naturally, impeccable (q.v.). They are far too numerous to list in full, but I must acknowledge my major, my most-often-referred-to, and in cases of doubts my ultimate authority – the Australasian edition of *Webster's New International Dictionary of the English Language* (Merriam, Springfield and Sydney, 1912), which has not only 2,662 pages and all the dirty words but also a colored supplement of the flags of the world. (Note: for the American edition of this book, we have depended on *The American Heritage Dictionary. – Ed.*)

More importantly, I cannot let these definitions go before the public without acknowledging the contribution made by Dr. Ernest Foot, of The Chambers, Cheltenham, who worked with me on the manuscript and wrote several of the definitions. To me should go much of the credit for whatever virtues this book possesses; the odium for any faults must rest entirely with him.

Ex-odium

To a reader as discerning as yourself, the following probably goes without saying, but just to leave no doubt at all in anyone's mind: The personal names appearing in this book are not those of real people, but are mere figments of the author's fevered imagination, dredged up from his resupinate subconscious for illustrative purposes only.

Prolegomena

Words are not only tools; they are also weapons. The first object of this book is to provide the ordinary man in the street with new and better verbal weapons – words which until now have been available only to philologists, lexicographers, and art critics. Hitherto, the man who has known the precise meaning of *egregious, pejorative, exigent, pusillanimous* and *usufruct* has been able to enjoy a position of unfair advantage over the rest of us. We yield to him in debate, not because his arguments are more cogent, but because they are less intelligible. We accept him as a Superior Person because his vocabulary is a badge of rank as compelling as a top hat or a painted forehead.

Society may confine the ownership of top hats or painted foreheads to a favored few; but words are free, and available to all who aspire to them. There is nothing to prevent the butcher, the baker, or the candlestick maker from larding his speech with as many *pejoratives* as the Professor of English. All that is required is the simple effort of learning a mere hundred or so of those impressive words that lie just beyond the boundary of the average person's vocabulary – words that all of us have occasionally seen or heard without ever being quite sure exactly what they mean. And very little extra effort is needed to learn a further hundred or so words that are even less familiar – in some cases, virtually unheard of, but genuine and usable words nonetheless.

Over a thousand such words are now brought together in this book. Learn them; use them; and by their use you may become a Completely Superior Person.

Of course, there have been other books devoted to the listing and explaining of hard words. But this book goes beyond that. It offers, for the first time, practical guidance on how best to use these words in real-life situations. Thus the reader will learn not only the meaning of *aprosexia* but also how best to use it when filling in his sick-leave application form. Sample sentences are given for many words, showing how they can be used to confuse, deter, embarrass, humiliate, puzzle, deceive, disconcert, alarm, insult, intrigue, or even compliment – and all with relative impunity. Incoherent rage need no longer be the reader's only response when offended in public by an errant motorist, a noisy juvenile, or a *noisome alliaphage*; instead he will be able to smile sweetly and inform the offender that he or she is a *rebarbative oligophreniac* who deserves a *vapulation*. This is the Insult Concealed, of which there are many examples in this book – as there are of the Insult Apparent, the Compliment Questionable, and the Suggestion Surreptitious, as well as all sorts of other ways of using unusual words to gain one's ends, whatever they may be.

But if words are weapons, they are also toys. They are fun to play with. And here the author confesses to having indulged himself somewhat. Several of the words appearing in this book do so simply because he could not resist the temptation to revive a pleasing archaism or to reveal some little bizarrerie that had caught his fancy.

Pronunciations are not given, except for a very few special cases where the nature of the word positively requires it. The reader who genuinely wishes to equip himself with the vocabulary of a Superior Person should be prepared to submit to the intellectual discipline of finding out the pronunciations for himself.

Finally, a special message for any lexicographers or philologists into whose hands this book falls: the author may or may not have incorporated into the text, as a stimulus and a challenge to your perspicacity, one or more deliberate errors.

A

AASVOGEL *n.* A vulture. Ideal term for oral insults, the sound being even more offensive than the meaning, which no one will know anyway.

ABA *n.* A sleeveless garment of camel or goat hair, worn in the Middle East. Pronounced 'arbor,' and therefore useless for labored Abba puns, but a nicely confusing name for your husband's tank tops, or, as such garments are sometimes risibly called, 'muscle tops.'

ABACISCUS *n.* A square tile in a mosaic floor. 'Ooh,' you exclaim with a wince, on entering your host's palatial foyer, 'I think I've just trodden on an abaciscus!'

ABDABS OR HABDABS *n.* A state of extreme nervousness. The jitters. One of those marvelous, naturally expressive terms which the dictionaries don't even try to etymologize. 'Hoo-ha' is another. 'All this hoo-ha is giving me the abdabs.'

ABECEDARIAN *a.* (i) Arranged in alphabetical order; (ii) elementary, devoid of sophistication. The present book may be considered by some to fit both applications. For a more interesting meaning, see *unbeliever's defense, the*.

ABECEDARIAN INSULT, AN *phr.* 'Sir, you are an apogenous, bovaristic, coprolalial, dasypygal, excerebrose, facinorous, gnathonic, hircine, ithyphallic, jumentous, kyphotic, labrose, mephitic, napiform, oligophrenial, papuliferous, quisquilian, rebarbative, saponaceous, thersitical, unguinous, ventripotent, wlatsome, xylocephalous, yirning zoophyte.' Translation: 'Sir, you are an impotent, conceited, obscene, hairy-buttocked, brainless, wicked, toadying, goatish, indecent, stable-smelling, hunchbacked, thick-lipped, stinking, turnip-shaped, feeble-minded, pimply, trashy, repellent, smarmy, foul-mouthed, greasy, gluttonous, loathsome, wooden-headed, whining, extremely low form of animal life.'

ABJURATION *n.* The act of renouncing, forswearing or repudiating. 'At what part of the service does the abjuration take place?', you innocently ask the vicar during his little talk with you and your fiancée about the forthcoming wedding ceremony.

ABLIGURITION *n.* Extravagance in cooking and serving. 'So wise of you to have chosen Mabel, Reginald. Abligurition is such a comforting thing in a fiancée.'

ABNEGATE *v.* Deny oneself. Not in itself a word of great usefulness. Included in this book because it is vital that the Superior Person not allow himself to be

2

confused by the similarity between it and *abrogate* (repeal), *derogate* (detract), *abdicate* (renounce), and *arrogate* (claim). Note in particular that *abrogate* is not, despite appearances, the antonym of *arrogate*. The use of these words is advisable only for pipe-smokers, whose mid-sentence inhalations may afford sufficient time for the mental gymnastics necessary to ensure that the proper term is selected. Also recommended for pipe-smokers is *antimony* (q.v.).

ABSQUATULATE *v.* To leave in a hurry, suddenly, and/or in secret. 'No problems, Mr. Burbage; just make the check out to cash – I'm doing the accounts tonight and you can rely on me to absquatulate first thing in the morning.'

ABSTRICT *v.* To set free spores by constriction of the stalk. Not a common activity, in the literal sense, but the term has obvious figurative possibilities.

ABSUMPTION *n.* The process of being wasted away or consumed, e.g., as food scraps in a compost heap, flesh in the grave, etc. 'So this is your twentieth year in the civil service, Jeremy? You must be qualified for absumption by now.'

ACEPHALOUS *a.* Without a head. Condition of a 'Project Team' in a government department which is implementing an 'Industrial Democracy Mission Statement.' Also that of a decapitated fowl.

ACEREBRAL *a.* Without a brain. A word for which there would at first sight appear to be no use, since no entity to which there would be any point in applying the term could in fact possess this attribute. (There would be no point in speaking of an acerebral windowsill.) However, recent researches into the central nervous system of the wire-haired terrier have conclusively demonstrated the need for such a word.

ACESCENT *a.* Turning sour. 'It's a rather wonderful thing, darling, but as we grow old together it seems to me that you are, if possible, even more acescent than ever.'

ACETABULUM *n.* The cup-shaped sucker of a cuttlefish or similar marine tentacle-flourisher. 'Get home before midnight, don't crash the car, and don't let that superannuated pinball parlor groupie friend of yours get her acetabula on your already over-extended credit cards!'

ACMEISM *n.* A movement against symbolism, and in favour of lucidity and definiteness in poetry, begun in Russia in 1910. 'Don't talk to me about the ineffable lightness of being, Jarrod, just because you want to go to this overnight party. I'm an acmeist, remember. Just tell me: will there or will there not be adult supervision?'

ACORPORAL *a.* Without a body. In response to a remark by Samuel Rogers that in moments of extreme danger it was very desirable to have presence of mind, the Reverend Sydney Smith replied that he would rather have absence of body. This was said on the very same night that Smith, dining at Rogers' home, was asked for his opinion of a new lighting system installed by Rogers in the dining room, in such a

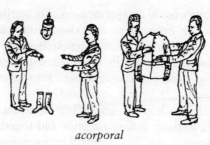

acorporal

way that the light was directed at the ceiling, leaving the table below in subdued lighting. Smith replied that he did not like the new system at all, 'for all is light above, and all below is darkness and gnashing of teeth'.

ACQUITMENT *n.* You think this is an accounting term, but more importantly it is a word used by stage and close-up magicians. For them, an acquitment is a series of moves designed to convince the audience that both the magician's hands are empty. The essence of the acquitment is that an object is secretly passed from hand to hand, one hand and then the other being shown to be empty. 'I know you don't like me associating with Leroy, Mom, just because he works at the race track; but I'm learning a lot from him. Today he showed me all about acquitments.'

ACROAMA *n.* A dramatic recitation during a meal; a lecture to the initiated. 'Mother, I have agreed to sit down at the dinner table and not to eat my food with my fingers. Is that not enough? Must I submit to acroama as well?'

5

ADJURATION *n.* A formula used in the conjuring of evil spirits, in order to compel them to do or say whatever you demand. Unfortunately there is no formula for compelling members of the opposite sex to do or say whatever you demand. You could try it on, of course. 'I adjure you, Melissa, to . . .'; but if the maiden merely says, 'What did you say?' you could always claim that the word you used was 'implore'.

ADULATION *n.* Extravagant praise. An interesting example of a word whose usage is largely confined to the noun form, even though the verb form is readily available. Thus it would seem only natural for the author of this work to receive, on its publication, the adulation of an admiring public; whereas the notion of his being adulated by the public somehow conjures up a picture of his being submitted to some kind of indelicate physical process.

ADUMBRATE *v.* To foreshadow in general terms; to sketch out what you intend to do, or what you expect to happen. 'Allow me to adumbrate in general terms the consequences of your continuing to block my driveway . . .'

ADVENTITIOUS *a.* Accidentally intruding from an unexpected quarter. 'How adventitious, madam, that you should reverse your car into the very space occupied by my own!'

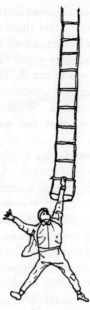

adventitious

ADVISEDLY *adv.* Deliberately, with conscious intent (of words or phrases so used). Odd that it should have this meaning, since words used advisedly are almost invariably used not on the basis of the advice of others but on the basis of one's own convictions.

ADVOWSON *n.* The right to identify the clergyman who will hold a particular benefice, or church living. The nearest thing today to this quintessentially eighteenth-century Episcopalian power would be that of our party political power-brokers in the preselection of electoral candidates and the pasturing out of faithful party hacks to the available sinecures.

AEAEAE *a.* Magic. As in *aeaeae artes*, the magic arts. The only all-vowel six-letter word known to the author. The derivation is from Aeaeae, which was a surname of the legendary pig-fancier Circe and the name of a small island off the coast of Italy, said to have been her place of abode. Useful for unscrupulous players of parlor word-games. If taken to task for using it in such circumstances, you say: 'Well, yes, strictly speaking it is foreign, I suppose – at least in origin – but, surely, it's a word everyone *knows*, isn't it?'

AFFENPINSCHER *n.* A breed of small dog, related to the so-called Brussels griffon, and having tufts of hair on the face. A young man growing a beard for the first time could be referred to in casual conversation as being in his affenpinscher phase. ('So-called,' incidentally, is a particularly useful adjective, implying as it does *without actually saying so* that there is something not quite kosher about the noun to which it is attached. After all, the Brussels griffon *is* so-called – because it is a Brussels griffon. Can you imagine it being *not* so-called, when that's what it is? 'And now, ladies and gentlemen, let's hear it for our so-called Congressman!')

AFFLATUS *n.* A sudden rush of divine or poetic inspiration. From the Latin *afflare* – to breathe or blow on. *Inspiration* itself means a breathing in. Why the ancients should have chosen the breath of the gods or muses – rather than their touch, voice, etc. – as the means of communicating super-human knowledge or creativity is not quite clear. While dining out with your beloved, you might suddenly put down your knife and fork, gasp, strike your forehead with your hand, lean forward tensely, and say, in unconcealed agitation: 'Jennifer, I think I've just had an afflatus!'

AGITOPHASIA *n.* A hysterical condition causing extreme rapidity of speech. 'Nix on the agitophasia, Maurice; the quickness of the hand may deceive the eye, but not the voice the mind. Your excuses are pathetic. You will return to the school hall, and you will take part in the pantomime, and you will sing along with little Deirdre in the feature spot in the finale, dressed as the Fairy King, whether you like it or not. Your mother has spoken.'

AICHMOPHOBIA *n.* Extreme fear of the sight of any sharp-pointed instrument, whether a needle, a nail, a thorn, a spike, etc. James I of England suffered from this phobia, and could not endure the appearance of a drawn sword.

AILUROPHILE *n.* Someone who is abnormally fond of cats. Such a one may readily be identified by the fleas and fine hairs hovering in the air like an aura about their person. Be kind to them; they have probably just spent a small fortune on canned fishwaste.

ALGOPHOBIA *n.* The morbid dread of pain. As a warning to those who have been lulled into a false sense of security at the dentist's by the latter's more or less routine use of local anaesthetics, the author, a true algophobe, relates this cautionary tale of his encounter with a London dentist. 'It's just a little one,' said the dentist, in the most casual and reassuring tone, 'do you want to bother with an anaesthetic this time?' 'No,' I manfully replied. In an instant the drill was in my mouth, and through a curtain of unendurable pain I heard the dentist say, 'Suit yourself; it won't hurt me!' Like all algophobes, I have never been able to transcend dental medication. Hmmm . . . perhaps if you said it aloud. . . .

ALGORITHM *n.* A mathematical term derived from the name of an Arabian mathematician. Its usefulness to the Superior Person derives from its very obscurity of meaning, which permits it to be used safely in almost any context – a figure of speech, a bodily function, a musical notation, etc.

ALLIACEOUS *a.* Smelling or tasting of garlic or onion. From the bulb allium (*allium sativum*, garlic; *allium cepa*, onion). Garlic was added to food in southern Europe in the Middle Ages for the specific purpose of suppressing the unpleasant flavor of meat, fish, or poultry which had gone bad in the course of its typically slow journey from supplier to consumer; in the present ago, it is added to food by persons of cultivated habits for the purpose of suppressing, for reasons unknown to the author, the pleasant flavor of meat, fish, or poultry which has not gone bad. According to the British Pharmaceutical Codex for 1934, cases have been reported where the internal administration of garlic has proved fatal to children; and, from the same source (for those in search of the ultimate frisson), the author reports that poultices made from pulped garlic are stated to be useful in accessible tuberculous lesions.

ALLIAPHAGE *n.* A garlic-eater.

ALLOPATHY *n.* Conventional medical treatment, as opposed to so-called 'alternative' medicines such as homoeopathy, reflexology, etc. If your New Age cousin is persistently refusing to see the doctor about her condition, you could perhaps convince her to do so by secretively whispering to her: 'You know, of course, that's he's an allopath?'

ALOPECIA *n.* Baldness. The Superior Person should always be alert to the potential value of medical terms when properly used in lay conversation (see also *contraindicated*). Thus: 'My husband's alopecia is very bad this morning, Mr. Purbright; I'm afraid I may not be able to get in to the office before about eleven o'clock.'

ALPHAMERIC *a.* Made up of letters and numbers. The astute reader will at once deduce that this new word, already in use, is actually a compression of *alphanumeric*, a term encountered sooner or later by all who use personal computers. 'During this term, Robert made giant strides forward in his handwriting, which is now almost alphameric.'

ALPHITOMANCY *n.* A method of determining the guilt or innocence of a person by feeding him a barley loaf. If indigestion ensues, the person is guilty. Some may say that if indigestion ensues after eating anything at all prepared by their best beloved, they are held by the latter to be guilty.

ALTERNATE *a.* Each succeeding the other in turn (said of two things). It should not be necessary to point out the difference from *alternative* (also said of two things, but meaning 'available as a different option'); but it is. A bookshop in the capital city of Australia had a sign prominently on display advertising a collection of books on 'alternate living.' The author approached the books with interest, assuming them to be variant editions of *Dr. Jekyll and Mr. Hyde*, but found them to be a curious assortment of manuals of primitive agriculture and tracts devoted to the advocacy of atavism.

AMBIVIUM *n.* Any street or road leading *around* a place rather than to it. The route that you and I invariably take.

AMIABLE *a.* Likeable – but note that the meaning goes a little beyond this, and covers also the feeling of affection or friendliness for others. An amiable person therefore is one who not only is easily liked by others but also is of a friendly disposition, with a natural fondness for others. It is in the latter sense, presumably, that the term is used by Gibbon when he refers to rape as 'that most amiable of human weaknesses.'

AMICUS CURIAE *phr.* Literally, a friend of the court (i.e., court of law). A disinterested party whose advice assists the court. Given the high cost of justice these days, perhaps a more apposite modern meaning would be 'investment advisor'.

AMPLEXUS *n.* Sexual intercourse between amphibians such as frogs or toads, in which an embrace occurs but the eggs are fertilized externally. (An *amplex-ation* is an embrace, whether between frogs or anyone.) 'So this is your first scuba lesson, Miss Pomfrey? Well, first, we'll familiarize ourselves with the equipment, have some trial shallow water dives, and finish off the day with the amplexus.'

AMPYX *n.* A general term to denote any net made of string, bands or ribbons, forming a head-dress. Also, happily, the ornamental strips of leather that fulfill a similar purpose for a horse. Your great-aunt's hair-net could be so characterized.

ANABIOSIS *n.* Revival after apparent death; reanima-tion after a coma so deep that all the vital signs have become imperceptible. As you read the morning paper and sip your *ante-jentacular* (q.v.) coffee, you call out to your firstborn: 'Roger, just pop into the bedroom for a moment, will you, and see if anabio-sis has set in with your mother yet.'

ANACREONTIC *n.* A poem the tone of which is amatory and convivial. Interesting in that the only words which rhyme with it (pontic, odontic, gerontic, mastodontic, and quantic) are all equally or even more obscure in meaning – thus affording you the opportunity to com-pose some fairly daunting verses for the next meeting of your local poetry group. Quantic, for example, means 'the rational integral homogeneous function of two or more variables.' Need I say more?

ANADROMOUS *a.* Ascending rivers to spawn. Obviously a term from the realms of ichthyology, but nonethe-less one with its uses in other contexts – for example, to characterize those among the beautiful people who believe that a Jacuzzi is the proper place for sexual congress.

ANAESTHETIC, ANALGESIC, ANODYNE *a.* There are real differences in meaning between the three. The first, like a Henry James novel, induces insensibility; the second, like a newly broached bottle of Glenfiddich, makes you feel no pain; and the third, like the welcoming arms of your beloved, removes the cares of the world from your shoulders. Simple-minded listeners can sometimes be successfully duped by the use of *anodyne* as a *spurious* (q.v.) technical term. 'It has nine transistors, four diodes, and six anodynes.'

ANATHEMA *n.* A person or thing abominated by, and hence anathema to, someone. Less often used now in its proper sense of a formal curse pronounced by an ecclesiastical authority in the process of excommunication or denunciation. Like *plethora* (q.v.) recommended for use by lispers, in whose speech the deliberate use of the sound *th* can, properly managed, create a satisfying disorientation in the mind of the listener. *Anathematic*: a pathological gathper.

ANDROPHOBIA *n.* The morbid dread of men. The existence of the term implies that somewhere, at some time, there must be someone with a morbid dread of me. I find this distinctly empowering, and would very much like to meet this person.

ANFRACTUOUS *a.* Intricate or circuitous. 'Sit down, Wilbur. I realize that you are wondering why we have decided to fire you, and I want you to know that I intend to give you the most anfractuous explanation possible.'

ANGLICIZATION *n.* Converting into English. Formerly used principally in relation to form, custom, or character. Now that there are no benefits to be derived from anglicization in that sense, its use is confined largely to the linguistic meaning, i.e., the translating into English of names, titles, etc. Thus: 'This is the BBC. Tonight we will hear a performance of the Complaining Songs, by Gus Crusher, sung by Elizabeth Blackhead.'

ANGLOPHONE *n.* A speaker of English. No – not a communication device for fishermen. It probably says something Toynbeeesque about the life cycle of civilizations that most anglophones are now anglophobes, whereas most francophones are still francophiles. (Besides, how many words can *you* think of with three successive 'e's?)

ANIMADVERT *v.* To pass a critical comment, or animadversion, upon something or someone. The term was more neutral in its original sense of a judicial recognition or reference. Thus, having said 'If you will allow me to animadvert upon your recent conduct, Richard,' and after a suitably foreboding pause, you could, strictly speaking, come out with a pontification that was perfectly bland.

ANIMUS *n.* Commonly used these days to mean animosity, i.e., hostility; but more properly animating spirit, mind, soul, or life force. 'I have listened to the last speaker's animadversions with great equanimity,

15

since I am fully aware, as I think all of us are, that underlying his criticisms there is no animus whatever.'

ANTABUSE *n.* Not, as you might be forgiven for thinking, the molestation of the formicidae, but the instrument of a form of obliquity which, if less bizarre, would appear equally deserving of *obloquy* (q.v.) – namely, the redemption of alcoholics by the administration of a drug, with the above trade name, which associates the consumption of alcohol with the most unpleasant consequences.

ANTANAGOGE *n.* A countercharge made in retort to an adversary's accusation. 'It ill becomes you, Penelope, to cavil at another's alleged action in eating the rest of the chocolate turtles when, if you will permit me to lodge an antanagoge, you yourself were the only person present last Wednesday when an entire packet of sherbet and marshmallow cones disappeared overnight.'

ANTEDILUVIAN *a.* Literally, before the flood; but commonly used to mean incredibly old-fashioned. As a reader of this book, you are more than likely to be regarded by your children as antediluvian – but you may take comfort from the fact that, until they buy their own copy, they will be unable to tell you so.

ANTE-JENTACULAR *a.* Pre-breakfast (see *anabiosis*). Goes nicely with *post-prandial* (after dinner).

ANTHROPOMORPHISM *n.* Attribution of human characteristics to what is not human. 'Are you serious?

Cousin Henry on the electoral roll? My God! How far can anthropomorphism go?'

ANTIMONY *n.* A poisonous metal. So called, according to tradition, because of its use in a famous case of mass poisoning of monks in the fifteenth century by an alchemist named, rather delightfully, Basil Valentine. Hence, *anti-moine*, or 'hostile to monks.' Its appropriate usage in the present century (i.e., the substance, not the word) would lie in its administration to people who smoke pipes in elevators.

ANTINOMY *n.* Contradiction between two authorities. Note that the accent is here on the second syllable instead of the first.

ANTIPODES *n.* Diametrical opposite. The term has hitherto been used quite incorrectly to mean Australia. The author is glad of this opportunity to set the record straight by explaining that the antipodes are in fact the British Isles – a place on the very underside of the earth where wiry little pale-faced men and large plump rubicund men hang upside-down, wearing cloth caps and bowler hats respectively. The preference for tight-fitting headgear derives from an obvious necessity.

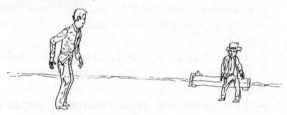

antipodes

APATETIC *a.* Imitative in color or shape. A term from the world of zoology but obviously adaptable to that of human fashion. Or, for that matter, to that of *psephology* (q.v.). 'Splendid idea to run for Congress, Simeon; who more than you to appeal to the apatetic vote?'

APOPHTHEGM *n.* *Highfalutin* (q.v.) word for an epigram. Much preferred to the latter, but easier to write than to say, in view of the problems presented by the central *ph*. Although the standard authorities permit the word to be pronounced *ph*-less, such a pronunciation would be extremely *infra dig* for a Superior Person, and should be eschewed in favor of the full version. Practice it, preferably in front of a mirror with your mouth full of salted peanuts. Become proficient in a few key sentences, such as: 'Now, Herr Doktor, is it not time for you to give us one of your little apophthegms?'

APORIA *n.* Patently insincere professings, e.g., by a public speaker, of an inability to know how to begin, what to say, etc. This is a very high-class word indeed, and should be used only in conversation with Samuel Beckett or Patrick White. Anyone else will assume you are referring to an unpleasant form of skin disease.

APOSIOPESIS *n.* Breaking off in the middle of a story. A rhetorical device. (See *oxymoron.*)

APOSTATE *a.* Guilty of abandoning one's faith or principles. The possibilities for juvenile *paronomasia* (q.v.) with this one ('I hear he's having trouble with his apostate,' etc., etc.) are too obvious for me to refrain from mentioning them.

APROSEXIA *n.* Inability to concentrate. *Not*, as might incautiously be assumed, après-sex activities. Useful when completing the 'nature of illness' section on your sick-leave application form.

ARCANE *a.* Secret, hidden. An excellent example of a Superior Word of the first order, i.e., one that is on the margin of recognition for most people, is known to many, but used by few. Suggestive of strange and wonderful mysteries and powerful knowledge. The arcane lore of the tarot cards, etc.

ARCIPLUVIAN *a.* Many-colored (literally, like a rainbow). Perhaps the right adjective for today's commuter cyclists – the ones who dress themselves up for their diurnal velocipedal progressions to and from the office in the multi-hued, iridescent, skintight Spandex uniform of the Tour de France rider. Most of these luminous apparitions are not hypnagogic hallucinations, but account clerks.

ARIGHT *adv.* Correctly. The Superior Person should be equipped with a modest range of archaisms. Their use, in moderation, will add character to his discourse, endear him to at least one elderly female relative, and go some way toward retrieving for him the forbearance of his ever-dwindling coterie of friends. Never say, 'If I hear you correctly . . .'; say, 'If I read you aright . . .' Also recommended are *goodly*, as in 'a goodly number'; *gramercy* (q.v.); *peradventure* (q.v.); and, *'sit you down'* instead of 'sit down.' The phrase '*sit you down*' should always be accompanied by an Expansive Gesture.

ARRESTING GEAR *phr.* The device on an aircraft carrier which abrupty stops the forward movement of a landing aeroplane. The Superior Person's term for the handbrake of a car.

ASPIC *n.* (i) A meat jelly in which pieces of meat, poultry, egg, etc. are set, to be served as savories. (ii) A glistening, slightly sweet-tasting slime used by airline companies to coat pieces of pork fritz, chicken-and-devon roll, etc., before serving them to entrapped passengers under the name of a light snack, or cold collation. In the latter regard, it is of course *decollation* (q.v.) that is in order for the caterer concerned.

ASPIRATOR *n.* Instrument for drawing pus from abscesses. Its natural usage is in the contemplative remark, made at the quiet fireside after the children have gone to bed. 'You know, dear, I've been thinking that it would be a nice gesture if we gave your uncle an aspirator for Christmas.'

ASRAH ILLUSION *n.* Name of a well-known stage illusion in which a woman is levitated while reclining under a large cloth, which is suddenly whisked away to show that she has vanished. 'Desirée, if you really want to appear in my Asrah Illusion, you realize, don't you, that we will need to practice down in the basement for quite a few weeks? In absolute secrecy? Oh, did I mention that it's vital to the levitation effect that you be naked? But don't worry, you'll be entirely covered with a cloth for virtually the entire act.'

ASTASIA-ABASIA *n.* A functional inability to stand or walk despite the fact that the patient retains good muscular co-ordination while lying in bed, especially in the handling of the drinks tray and the TV remote. See also *basophobia*.

astasia-abasia

ASTEISM *n.* An ingeniously polite insult. In some regards, this book may be regarded as an asteisticon.

ASTROLOGY *n.* Pathetic body of so-called learning which professes to predict the future and reveal the influence of the heavenly bodies on the affairs of men. If men want to influence the affairs of heavenly bodies, the recommended procedure is to buy *two* copies of the coming year's astrology guide, give one to the lady whose heavenly body you aspire to, *and secretly keep the other copy yourself*. In this way, you will know in advance what your lady expects or hopes for from day to day, and will be ideally placed to take due advantage of this knowledge. You don't get this sort of information in other dictionaries.

ASTROPHOBIA, OR ASTROPAPHOBIA *n.* The morbid dread of being struck by lightning, and hence the fear of thunder and storms generally. The Emperors Augustus and Caligula were sufferers from this phobia. 'Open the windows wide, my children, and let your mother rejoice in the storm in all its fury! Give her astrophobia free rein!'

ATARAXIA *n.* Absolute calm and tranquility; imperturbability; complete freedom from anxiety or strain. The condition of a lexicographer on reaching the word *zythum*, which, appropriately enough, means a kind of malt beer. A *zythepsary* is a brewery.

ATAXY *n.* Disturbance of bodily functions, especially that of motion. The interest of this word lies largely in the fact that it is pronounced exactly the same as 'a taxi.' The serious lexicologist should have at his command as many as possible such words, which permit the quiet enjoyment of many a deliberate ambiguity, in friendly or unfriendly discourse.

ATTORNMENT *n.* A formal procedure from the feudal age in which a tenant acknowledges the authority of a new lord. 'Here is the engagement ring, oh my dearest; and here the affidavit of attornment for your signature. . . .'

AUTOCHTHON *n.* Original inhabitant. A *highfalutin* (q.v.) synonym for *aboriginal*. Incidentally, there is no such word as *aborigine*; but *aborigines* is an acceptable plural for *aboriginal*.

AUTO-DA-FÉ *n.* The burning of a heretic, under the Inquisition. Literally 'act of faith.' Originally the term applied to the ceremony accompanying the pronouncement of judgment by the ecclesiastical authorities, after which the victim was handed over to the secular authorities for actual ignition; but gradually the latter came to be referred to as the auto-da-fé itself. The plural, incidentally, is *autos-da-fé*. Now that the auto-da-fé has been replaced, as an instrument for maintaining the True Church, by the Catholic Radio and Television Bureau, the nearest thing to the former is probably the author's backyard barbecues. Here the author performs the act of immolation, and the act of faith is on the part of his guests.

AUTODEFENESTRATION *n.* The act of throwing oneself out of a window. Illustrated by the true case of Mrs. Vera Czermak, who discovered that her husband was being unfaithful to her and attempted to end her life by jumping out of the window of her third-floor flat in Prague. At the moment she jumped, her husband happened to walk by beneath the window. She landed on top of him, and survived. He died.

AUTOPHOBIA *n.* Not, as might be imagined, the fear of automobiles, but the morbid dread of oneself, or of being alone. Do vampires, perhaps, have autophobia? They ought to. Politicians, perhaps?

autophobia

AUTOTOMY *n.* The spontaneous shedding by a living organism of part of itself, as for example in the case of crabs and salamanders. 'I don't mind cleaning the house, mother, but I will *not* clean Justin's room! It's autotomy hell in there! There are so many of his hairs and skin cells all over the carpet that the slightest movement creates an organic dust storm!'

AVERRING *n.* Begging by a boy in the nude to arouse sympathy. 'Er – I wonder, Mrs. Armitage, if tonight, while Mr. Armitage is out, I might try out my averring, if you wouldn't mind being my audience?'

AVICULARIUM *n.* A prehensile organ, not unlike a beak, in certain small aquatic creatures. 'If you're going to stay out in the sun, Lachlan, wear something on your avicularium!'

AVIGATION *n.* Absolutely brilliant neologism for aerial navigation.

AVUNCULAR *a.* In the manner of an uncle. An interestingly ambiguous indeed multiguous – word, since there is no fixed or universal pattern of behavior for uncles. An experimental canvassing of the author's acquaintances revealed a widespread assumption that avuncular behavior was benevolent, mildly paternal, gently jocular, mature and dignified. However, one respondent admitted to having an Uncle Morris who was twenty-three years old, wore a gold earring in his nose, played viola da gamba with an innovative rock group, and had recently been expelled from the Hare Krishna movement for tattooing indelicate mandalas on the soles of his feet.

AXILLA *n.* The armpit. References to axillary emanations would seem to be the go with this one.

AXIOPISTY *n.* The quality that makes something believable. 'The trouble with Alvin is that he has no axiopisty.'

AZOIC *a.* Lifeless. Technically, this is a geo-historical term referring to the era before life first appeared on earth; but there is no reason why you should not apply it in a metaphorical sense to the condition of your teenage daughter's bedroom on Sunday morning before the noontide *expergefaction* (q.v.).

azoic

AZOTH *n.* Mercury; the name given by alchemists to the universal remedy of Paracelsus. 'How stands the azoth this day?' you robustly inquire, on seeing a colleague peering at the wall thermometer.

B

BAKLAVA, BALACLAVA *n.* The justification for including these words in this book is to warn the reader against confusing them with each other. The former is an exceedingly rich and sweet pastry, made in layers interspersed with, and permeated by, honey; the latter is a tight-fitting woollen head-covering. Any attempt to use a baklava as a head-covering, or to eat a balaclava, could lead only to the most dispiriting consequences.

BALLADROMIC *a.* Maintaining a course toward an ultimate target. 'Look out the window. See – there at the end of the street? That's young Jimmie coming home from school. Now see the container on the kitchen table here? That's the frosted caramel slices. Now watch the path he follows. See? Turns right and crosses the road diagonally; passes the oleanders on the left but swerves to pass the power pole on the right. Pure economy in movement. Balladromic from start to finish.'

BANDOLINE *n.* A strong-smelling unguent for the hair, said by my sources to be made from boiled quince pips. This seems intrinsically implausible, but it is the function of the lexicographer to record the form of his subject matter, not examine its substance. Still . . . quince pips? *Why* quince pips?

BARBERMONGER *n.* A term used by Shakespeare in *King Lear* and defined by Johnson as 'a fop decked out by his barber.' In these days of unisex hairdressing salons and individual hairstyles for men, some reader even crustier and more conservative than the author may wish to revive this old term as a last defense against the inroads of male coiffurism. Repeatedly characterizing your dashing young coworker – the one with the Antonio Special No. 2 – as a barbermonger may at least irritate him, if nothing else, especially in view of the rather *infra-dig* (for him) connotations of the word *barber.*

BARBITURATE *n.* A well-known class of narcotic pharmaceutical, as you well know. But did you know that it is named after a Munich waitress named Barbara, who helped its discoverer, Nobel Prize winner Johann Bäyer (1835–1917), in his work by supplying him with her entire urinary output, nicely bottled, over an extended period of time, so that he would have the necessary large quantities of urea needed for his work? For that matter, did you *want* to know that?

BARMECIDE *n.* Insincere benefactor; one who holds out illusory offers, or who promises but does not deliver. One degree worse than an Indian Giver, since the latter at least delivers the goods, even if he does expect to get them back again, with interest. The original Barmecide is to be found in *The Arabian Nights*. A member of a wealthy Persian family, he decided to amuse himself one night by inviting one Schacabac, a wretched, starving beggar, to a sumptuous meal. Barmecide's little jape consisted of presenting Schacabac with a succession of grandly served courses, amid all the trappings of luxury – ornate bowls and dishes, magnificent table-settings, and so on – the catch being that there was no actual food in any of the receptacles placed before the hapless guest. The story ends with Schacabac taking it all in good humor and being rewarded for good sportsmanship with a real meal. The unsavory Barmecide was dealt with appropriately by Fate: his family became so magnificent that they aroused the enmity of the Caliph, who imprisoned or executed them; and the name of Barmecide himself has become synonymous with deceit, illusion, hypocrisy, and the proffering of bounty only to withhold it until the profferer's terms are met.

BASOPHOBIA *n.* A hysterical fear of falling which is so overwhelming that it effectively prevents the sufferer from even attempting to stand or walk. In *ananastasia*, the sufferer is unable to raise himself from a recumbent to a sitting position; and *acathisia* prevents the sufferer from remaining in a sitting position. Then there's also *astasia-abasia* (q.v.). All of these are good for deferments of exams on medical grounds, exemption from military service, excusal from jury duty, etc.

BASTINADO *n.* A punishment, of oriental origin, in which the soles of the feet are beaten. The term is useful for waiters who wish to preserve their dignity in dealing with the female American tourist. When she palpates and rejects the third avocado you have offered her and in so doing casts hyperaudible aspersions upon your integrity, you smile imperturbably and say: 'Would Madam perhaps prefer the Bastinado?' Alternatively, you might invoke the *strappado* – a torture inflicted by hoisting the victim by his tied hands and then dropping him so that his fall is cut short by the taut rope before he reaches the ground.

BATHOPHOBIA *n.* The morbid dread, not of baths, as one might expect, but of depth. Use the term in a metaphorical sense: 'Jeremy's not enrolling in Differential Calculus I after all, this year. Typical! He always was a bathophobe.'

BATHYBIUS *n.* A gelatinous deposit, dredged up in mud from the lower depths of the ocean. At first thought to be organic, but now known not to be. If unlucky enough to take your bath *after* your younger brother, you could use this term to describe the ring of waste-matter left on the sides of the bath for you to scrape off.

BATHYCOLPIAN *a.* Deep-bosomed. 'So you're both Baptists, eh, Ernest? Well, I guess I'm a lapsed Catholic – but my wife is bathycolpian.'

BATTOLOGY *n.* The continual reiteration of the same words or phrases in speech or writing. A battologer is one who battologizes. One of those words whose lack of wider currency seems undeserved and puzzling in the light of its wide potential for application to television commercials, sales pitches by car and encyclopaedia vendors, spouse's homilies, etc.

BAVARDAGE *n.* Foolish or empty chatter. Attracts the adjective *mere*, in contradistinction to words such as *balderdash* or *poppycock*, which attract the adjective *absolute*.

BAYADERE *n.* Two distinct meanings. A dancing girl; and a fabric with crosswise stripes (the kind fat people are not supposed to wear). 'It's kind of you to be so hospitable, Madgwick! Delighted to accept your suggestion that you show me what the town has to offer. Since you ask my preferences, I wonder what the chances would be of a little bayadere for the night?'

BEDIZEN *v.* To trick out; to decorate, ornament, or dress up with more ostentation than taste. When Lady Festering makes her ceremonial entry at the charity ball, wearing her Christmas Tree Dress, you whisper to your companion: 'I'm told she goes to a professional bedizener.'

BELESPRIT *n.* A finer spirit, an intellectually gifted person. The purchaser of this book. The plural is *beauxesprits*.

BELLIBONE *n.* Believe it or not, 'a woman excelling both in beauty and goodness' (Dr. Johnson's Dictionary). One of a few words that the author has taken the liberty of disinterring from the past (even Johnson refers to it as 'not in present use') because of their obvious potentialities in polite discourse.

BELLWETHER *n.* A male sheep which leads the flock, with a bell tied around its neck. Hence, anyone who assumes a leading role or takes the initiative – more appropriately, among a group of less than dynamic or purposeful colleagues. As, for example, the president of a Parents and Citizens Association.

BELOMANCY *n.* Predicting the future by the use of arrows. The future of the then reigning British royalty was accurately foretold in this fashion at the Battle of Hastings.

belomancy

BESHREW *v.* Another of those quaint archaisms which the Superior Person delights in using for their intensely irritating effect on the listener. 'Beshrew me, if it isn't old Arthur!' Literally, beshrew means 'curse,' but the general effect of 'beshrew me' is 'the Devil take me' – or perhaps, in more vulgar parlance, 'bugger me,' or its stronger variant 'bugger me dead.' In all these instances, of course, the speaker's utterance is metaphorical, not literal, in intent.

BETAKE *v.* An archaic verb, entirely appropriate for Superior Person use. To take (yourself) to something or somewhere. To go. Like 'hie', used reflexively. 'Given the weather, I betook myself to the cinema today; after which I did hie me to the pizza palace.'

BEZONIAN *n.* A rascal, scoundrel, or beggar. 'Of course I'll take a couple of your raffle tickets, Mrs. Oliphant. Heavens, I don't know what the school would do without you; you are a true bezonian!'

BICRURAL *a.* Having two legs. 'I am sorry to have to say this in front of the boys, headmaster, but I have come to regard you as bicrural, and I cannot be persuaded otherwise.'

BIGGIN *n.* A silver coffee pot with a separate container which holds the coffee as it is heated. Always make a point of asking your hostess at least once during the evening if she has a biggin.

BILOCATION *n.* Being in two places simultaneously. A difficult achievement, one would think, except in the case of the *consubstantial* (q.v.), and the fourteen-year-old human male, who has been reliably reported as having one hand in the fridge and one in the pantry in real time.

BIODEGRADABLE *a.* Capable of being easily broken down by natural decomposition, and hence not causing permanent pollution of the environment. A technical term that has in recent years been taken up by nontechnical environmentalists as part of their cant. Environmentalists are people, such as the author's children, who believe that to throw a Popsicle stick out of the car window is to pollute the environment, in contrast to the author, who thinks that a Popsicle stick *inside* the car pollutes the environment.

BIOLUMINESCENCE *n.* The generation of light by living organisms. Metaphorically speaking, one of the functions of the lexicographer.

BIRL *v.* To revolve a log in the water while standing on it. I knew it – there just had to be a word for it. We've all seen it done at the movies or on television – and now you and I know what it's called. This is powerful information. Chances are you will never meet *anyone* else who knows what this word means. Use this knowledge wisely.

BISTABLE *a.* Having two stable states. 'My husband is bistable – when he's asleep and when he's unconscious. Unfortunately he's unconscious only on Friday nights.'

BISULCATE *a.* Cloven-hoofed. 'I don't know about Bastian being the Devil, but given those shoes he wears I wouldn't be at all surprised to find that he was bisulcate.'

BIVALENCE *n.* The principle that every sentence is either true or false. Including that one. 'But, darling, I swear that every single thing I say is absolutely bivalent.'

BLABAGOGY *n.* Criminal environment. 'Taking 3B again for Personal Development Studies, Carruthers? How is it affecting you – working in a blabagogy every day?'

BLENNOPHOBIA *n.* A morbid dread of slime. 'I'm so sorry, Clifford, I know Mother told you that she thought I'd love to go out with you, but the fact is I have this medical thing at the moment, this blenno-phobia, and I'm afraid that rules out a date with you for the foreseeable future.'

BLUNGER *n.* A wooden implement rather like an oversize spatula, used in the manufacture of ceramics when mixing clay and water. Used in this sense, a boring word. But as a term of meaningless abuse . . . much more satisfying. The *g*, by the way, is pronounced as a *j*. (See *bogtrotter*.)

BLUNTIE *n.* A Scottish term for a dunce or dunderhead. For reasons unknown to the author, there are many other Scottish terms with a similar significance.

BOGTROTTER *n.* One who trots across, and by implica-tion lives among, bogs. 'Sir, you are nothing but a blunger and a bogtrotter!'

BOHORDAMENTUM *n.* In medieval times, a jousting match with mock lances. The modern equivalent is your children's play with toy *Star Wars* light sabres. 'If you kids must career all round the back yard with those sabre things, just remember we don't have bohordamentum insurance!'

BOMBILATE *v.* To make a humming, buzzing, or droning sound. **BOMBILATION**: the sound made by a well-meaning father trying to show he is 'with it' by singing along with your Led Zeppelin tapes in the car.

BOOBOISIE *n.* The slower classes; the stupid masses. A term coined by H. L. Mencken. The more savage American writers – Ambrose Bierce, Philip Wylie, Mencken, and the like – seem to have a gift for what one might term neoinvectivism, another example of which is Wylie's MICROPOOPS, for pinheaded paperpushers.

BOONDOGGLE *v.* or *n.* To carry out valueless or extremely trivial work in order to convey the impression that one is busy. Work so carried out. A necessary technique for military circles, where the classic form is the day-long carrying around of a rubbish bin while the remainder of your platoon are out on maneuvers. On being questioned by an officer, a smart 'Rubbish detail, sir!' satisfies the inquirer.

BORBORYGM *n.* The noise made by gas in the bowels. Yes, a fart. 'Mom, Quentin's doing Work Experience in Social Welfare Studies this term. He goes round a different suburb every Thursday afternoon leaving borborygms in phone booths.'

BOTHAN *n.* A booth or hut, more especially one that is used as an illegal drinking den. 'Do you have to turn the toilet into your personal bothan, Miles?'

BOTTOMRY *n.* A type of mortgage under which a ship is put up as security for a loan to finance its use in a freight-carrying venture. Sometimes also referred to as 'bummery.' I swear I am not making this up. 'I know you've always wanted to join the merchant marine, son – but swear to me that you'll never, never resort to bottomry.'

BOVARISM *n.* A magnified opinion of one's own abilities. An affliction manfully borne by most of us (including the author, whose abilities have nonetheless patently fallen short of coming up with a non-sexist alternative for 'manful').

BOVID *n.* A member of the Bovidae family, i.e., ruminant animals such as sheep, cattle, and goats with a pair of non-deciduous, non-branching horns. In the unlikely event of your being approached by a gum-chewing Mephistopheles offering a deal of some kind, you could begin by adopting a superior attitude with a remark along the lines of your not doing business with a mere bovid. (You might as well score at least one point off him; we both know he's going to win you over in the end.)

BOWDLERIZE *v.* To edit a text with prudish intent, expurgating unseemly passages. After Dr. Thomas Bowdler's 1818 *Family Edition of the Works of Shakespeare*. In fact, history has been quite unfair in branding Bowdler as a puritanical wowser, since a reading of his edition by your intrepid author revealed that his 'bowdlerization' consisted almost exclusively of the replacement of a few select words such as 'whore' while retaining all the lovely violence and sex. See for example his *Titus Andronicus*, in which, I assure you, none of the rape and dismemberment is left to the imagination. A better example of what most of us wrongly think of as Bowdlerization is the editorial work of the Reverend James Plumptre, a contemporary of Bowdler who *did* amend famous poetry from a strictly moralistic standpoint, often adding whole lines and stanzas of his own. In 'Hark! hark! the lark' from *Cymbeline*, he takes Shakespeare's lines 'With everything that pretty is / My lady sweet, arise' and changes them to 'With everything that pretty is / For shame, thou sluggard, rise'. It is not widely known, by the way, that A. W. Verity, an editor of school editions of Shakespeare recent enough to have been used in my own time, cut out passages which he thought indecent.

BOWLER *n.* In cricket, one who, on blundering badly, gets another chance – in contradistinction to a batsman, who does not. Natural blunderers should therefore always be bowlers. *Slow bowler:* one who opens the bowling for an English cricket team. *Fast bowler:* one who bowls to an Australian opening batsman. It will at once be apparent from the preceding definitions that one man may be both a slow and a fast bowler at the same time. Do not allow this to puzzle you – the game has its own metaphysics as well as its ritual and its regalia. (See *fallacy.*)

BRACHIATE *v.* To swing through the air as certain species of primitive ape do, using the hands to grasp, for example, tree branches as successive launching pads. 'How many times do I have to tell you? No brachiation at Sunday School until after the last hymn, Roderick!'

BRACHYDROMIC *a.* Following a deflected path in relation to the target. Said of missiles that miss or fall short. 'Brandon, must you be ever brachydromic? The way to the car is straight across the road, not via the ice-creamery down the street.'

BRADYKINETIC *a.* Moving very slowly. Alternative sense: one who jumps up dynamically to switch off the TV when *The Brady Bunch* comes on.

BRASH *n.* As a noun, this has nothing to do with rude self-assertiveness but means, as the Concise Oxford coyly puts it, 'an eruption of fluid from the stomach.' Yes, folks, this is yet another euphemism for 'vomit.' 'Set up the next round of drinks, fellers! *Beshrew* (q.v.) me if I'm not just going outside for a brash; and then I'll be with you.'

BRATTICING *n.* A board fence around something dangerous. 'There we are, Mrs. Lebowitz; a little work on the hemline, a tuck or two around the waist, a little bratticing around the bodice, and you'll be ready to roll.'

BREASTSUMMER *n.* Believe it or not, this beautiful word denotes the beam supporting the upper front part of a building, over its main door or portico. 'Ah, Mrs. Sandalbath, as I came in I admired your breastsummer so much. What a superstructure!'

BRIGANDINE *n.* A medieval coat of mail, made of metal rings, studs and strips sewn onto a leather jacket. In today's world, the perfect term for a bikie's jacket. Not to be confused with *brigantine*, a two-masted vessel which is square-rigged on the foremast and fore-and-aft rigged on the mainmast, and which is hardly ever worn by bikies.

BRIMBORION *n.* Something useless or nonsensical. 'I thought you'd really appreciate a little brimborion,' you can shyly say to your friends and relatives when you give them their Christmas present – a copy of this book.

BROMIDROSIS *n.* Smelly perspiration. Osmidrosis means the same thing. 'Do I *have* to sit with one of the Connolly brothers, Mom? What a dilemma – it's like being caught between Osmi and Bromi . . . what's that, Mom? . . . oh, just a classical allusion.'

BRUXISM *n.* Abnormal grinding of teeth. 'Okay, it's agreed then! Ten dollars from each of us to whoever manages to provoke Daddy to bruxism stage?'

BUCENTAUR *n.* State barge of Venice, formerly used during the annual ceremony of the Marriage of Venice with the Adriatic. This ceremony was intended to establish and maintain the true and perpetual dominion of Venice over the Adriatic, which in its turn was to be subject to Venice as a bride is to her husband. The male chauvinist piggery implicit in this is reaping its just deserts as the Adriatic comes closer and closer to submerging Venice once and for all; and the Fathers of the State are now understood to be searching for a suitable barge with which to obtain a divorce.

BULLARIUM *n.* A collection of Papal Bulls, i.e., authoritative edicts sealed with a *bulla*, or lead seal, by the Pope. 'Children, this is our first family conference for the year, and in your father's absence I'd like to suggest that it would be a nice surprise for him if we put together a bullarium of his collected statements on domestic management, child behavior, and the weather, and affixed them to the door of his beer fridge in the garage.'

BULLY FOR YOU! Nicely derisory congratulative. Thus, *A*: 'We made the trip down in just three and a half hours, and I pride myself on the fact that I didn't once exceed the speed limit.' *B*: 'Bully for you!' (See also *stout fellow!*)

BUMBLEPUPPY *n.* A nice, old-fashioned word which, according to the Concise Oxford Dictionary, means a game played with a tennis ball slung to a post. In other words, it is a perfectly correct if somewhat archaic term for any or all of those modern, glossily packaged and energetically promoted games with carefully invented, vigorous, clean-cut names such as Dyna-ball or Pole-a-Play. The connotations in *bumblepuppy* of bumbling and puppydogs give it a suitably condescending flavor for use when you arrive at your physical-fitness-fanatic sister's home and find her bounding around the back yard with her disgustingly athletic husband. 'Ah,' you say, 'I don't believe I've had a game of bumblepuppy since I was in kindergarten. You've bought it for the kiddies, have you?'

BUNDOBUST *n.* Arrangements, organization. (From the Hindi *band-o-bast*, meaning 'tying and binding.') Surely a good trading name: The Bundobust Moving and Storage Company.

BUNKUM *n.* Claptrap. Both words seem to have acquired in modern parlance the meaning of nonsense, or balderdash; but the original meaning of the former is much more specific, and ought, in the view of the author, to be revived, especially for the purposes of political journalism. *Bunkum* in the original sense is a showy but insincere political speech made for the purpose of impressing one's constituents. One might say, therefore, that it is any political speech. The original spelling was *Buncombe*, and the original bunkum was spoken by Felix Walker, a backwoodsman from Buncombe, North Carolina, who insisted on dragging out the debate on the Missouri Question in the Sixteenth Congress, on the grounds that the people of Buncombe expected a speech from him.

BUTYRACEOUS *a.* Looking or acting like butter; buttery. 'Who was that oily young man who took Sabrina out last week? The one who complimented you on your hairdo?' 'Oh, the butyraceous one! That was . . .'

BYSSUS *n.* A high-quality fabric used for wrapping mummies. Oh, all right then – your mother's beach towel.

41

C

CABALA *n.* Hebrew mystical theology. Hence, any secret, arcane, or occult system. Your husband's filing cabinet.

CABALLINE *a.* Horselike. 'Just turn your head to the right a little, Miss Montmorency, while I set the focus and shutter speed. I want to have the light falling on you in half-profile, to bring out that . . . how shall I describe it? . . . caballine quality in your facial structure . . .'

CACHINNATE *v.* To laugh loudly or immoderately. 'It's not that I don't like bridge, dear, or that I object to your friends occupying the den all afternoon. It's the cachinnation that I find a little hard to take.'

CACODAEMON *n.* A malignant spirit. (Alternatively, *cacodemon*, but the diphthong is always to be preferred – orally as well as in written form.) 'And now . . . it is my privilege, as Student Council President, to introduce to this Speech Night audience someone who for many years has been the school's veritable cacodaemon – our Vice Principal!'

CACOPHEMISM *n.* The opposite of *euphemism*; a harsh or pejorative expression used in place of a milder one. *Quack* instead of *doctor*, for instance. A *euphemism* is generally no more than the triumph of squeamishness over reality: *little person* for *dwarf, senior citizen* for *old man, disturbed* for *crazy*, etc. It is characterized by a lack of humor. Cacophemisms, on the other hand, tend to reflect an attitude of rough-and-ready good humor toward the person or object in question: *egghead, grease monkey, quack*, etc. A further difference between the two 'isms' is that cacophemisms are more readily recognized for what they are; euphemisms tend to have acquired a wider currency in normal parlance and hence to be accepted more unthinkingly by the listener. On the other hand, cacophemisms are more likely to have second meanings of their own, and this in itself can lead to confusion. If an Australian given to cacophemisms were to speak of a frog in a bog, he might be speaking of a marsh-dwelling amphibian; but he might also be speaking of a Frenchman in a toilet. The Superior Person would avoid such an ambiguity (unless, of course, it were deliberately sought after) by speaking not of a frog in a bog but a wog in a bog. Cacophemisms are not, however, the natural vehicle for the Superior Person's thoughts; he much prefers *charientisms* (q.v.).

CACOSMIA *n.* A condition in which the sufferer experiences awful tastes and smells without any external physical cause. (In the later stages of his brain tumor, George Gershwin constantly experienced the smell of burning rubber.) 'Yes, I know it's an awful smell, dear, but don't worry, it's not cacosmia, it's just that you-know-who has just passed this way.'

CADUCEUS *n.* Everyone knows what a cornucopia is, but who knows what the deuce a caduceus is? It is in fact an object as familiar as the cornucopia. It is the serpent-entwined rod traditionally carried by Hermes, regarded until recently as a symbol of commerce, and now regarded as a symbol of the medical profession. The reason for the apparent linking of commerce and the medical profession is not clear to the author. Hermes was the herald and messenger of the gods, and supposedly the caduceus enabled him both to fly and to lull to sleep the souls of the dead before carrying them to the underworld. It might thus in modern times be more appropriately the symbol of air transportation, or of late-night television talk shows. The nonmagical caduceus was carried in ancient times by envoys when they were suing for peace. This is said to reflect the fact that the two serpents twined around it are kissing, or that they have just been separated by the rod from their previous combat.

CADUCITY *n.* (i) The dropping or shedding of a disposable part of an animal or plant when its function has been performed and it is no longer needed; (ii) hence, fleetingness, perishableness, or impermanence; (iii) hence, senility, proximity to dissolution. 'Oh, all right then, Aunt Maud, I'll go to Sunday School – but only out of respect for your caducity.'

In the first sense mentioned above – the dropping of a disposable appendage – the term might apply to the author's toothbrushes, or his *zori* (q.v.).

CADUCOUS *a.* (In botany and zoology) dropping away, falling off, or perishing at an early stage of development. 'So this is the latest in your succession of caducous boyfriends, Miranda?'

CALEFACIENT *a.* A medicinal agent producing a feeling of warmth. 'Calefacient, anyone?' you inquire as you pass around the cognac.

CAMBIST *n.* One who is skilled in the science of financial exchange. A teenager on weekly-allowance day. 'But I mowed the lawn *and* bagged the grass clippings, and you owed me that other two dollars from the week before last, and you said three weeks ago that you'd give me three dollars for munchies at the movies, and although I didn't go then I will be going next week, and remember I paid the bus fare last Wednesday out of my own pocket, and I needed to get that magazine to read at the dentist's, and a month ago when I went to the store to get milk and you said I could keep the change and I forgot and left it on the kitchen table, and . . .'

CANARD *n.* A fabricated anecdote or sensational report; a phony yarn; a hoax. A word that is familiar enough, no doubt, to most readers; but how many know the derivation? It is, of course, the French word for duck, and this particular application springs from a hoax perpetrated on the public by one Cornelissen, who spread it abroad that he had killed one of twenty ducks and fed it to the other nineteen, who ate it; then similarly fed one of the nineteen to the remaining eighteen; and so on, until there remained only one duck – which had thus eaten nineteen other ducks. The story was widely covered in the papers of the time.

CANESCENT *a.* Tending to white, hoary. One of that useful class of words which permits honesty without discourtesy when treating the subject of another's personal appearance. To the hearer, ignorance is bliss.

CANONICAL AGE *phr.* The minimum age, as laid down in canonical law (i.e., church law) for ordination or for the performance of a specified function in the Church. 'So Damon wants the car keys again, eh? Tell him my answer's the same – when he reaches canonical age, and not before!'

CAPARISON *n.* or *v.* Commonly used these days (well, of course it's *not* commonly used, but you know what I mean) in the sense of a rather grand form of attire, or to dress someone in rich attire. The interesting thing is that the original meaning was simply the covering for a horse – a piece of information that may afford you some quiet satisfaction at an appropriate time. 'You are indeed magnificently caparisoned tonight, Lady Smoothe-Lewis.'

CAPRICIOUS *a.* Fickle, whimsical. As you well know. But were you aware that the derivation is from the Latin *caper* – a goat? 'When I say that our distinguished guest tonight is capricious, I hope he will realize that I am not using the term in its modern sense, but in the original sense, which of course is quite different. This is borne out by his whole career, in the union movement, in the courts of the land, and in Congress . . .'

CARAVANSERAI *n.* The Superior Person's word for a motel. Strictly speaking, a Middle Eastern caravan park, consisting of what Webster calls a 'large, rude unfurnished building' surrounding an open courtyard.

CARBUNCLE *n.* The usage to be preferred is not the common pre-penicillin-era meaning of a larger-than-life abscess, but the even earlier one of a red, precious stone. As in Conan Doyle's *The Blue Carbuncle*, in which Sherlock Holmes traces the train of events which led to the Countess of Morcar's famous blue carbuncle being found in the crop of a dead goose. But why, in that context, a *blue* carbuncle? How can a gem which is by definition red be blue? Can the great detective have been guilty of an appalling aberration? He refers to the stone in question as being 'remarkable in having every characteristic of the carbuncle, save that it is blue in shade, instead of ruby red' – but this is on a par with saying that a mountain has every characteristic of a mountain save that it is flat! It is perhaps significant that Holmes places the supposed carbuncle in his strongbox with a casual remark to the effect that he will drop a line to the Countess of Morcar to tell her of its whereabouts – *but he never does, and the Countess herself never appears in person to claim her possession.* These are deep waters indeed. Can the

Countess's carbuncle really have been an abscess instead of a gem, and if so how did it find its way into a goose's crop? Perhaps there is, behind all this, an even deeper and more chilling mystery than the great detective was prepared to reveal even to the good Dr. Watson. Be that as it may, the potential of the word itself in modern parlance is obvious. 'Ah, Lady Marbles, when I see you in that dress I have a vision of you with a great carbuncle resting upon your bosom.'

CARDIALGIA *n.* Heartburn, i.e., mild indigestion. To the uninitiated, however, *cardialgia* sounds like a serious disorder of the heart; hence suitable for excuses, sympathy-seeking ploys, etc.

CARPENTUM *n.* A two-wheeled carriage of ancient times, often covered with an awning. Perhaps a useful term now for one of those electrically driven wheelchairs for the crippled elderly. Or, even better, for your hobby-farmer neighbour's dinky little tractor: 'Ah, taking the carpentum out for a run, Frank? Oh – wait a moment – I didn't notice those two little wheels at the back! What are they – some kind of, like, trainer wheels?'

CARRACK *n.* A large ship of burden, which was also fitted for fighting. This may, but only may, be a good description of some readers' mothers, mistresses, or spouses.

CARUNCLE *n.* A small, fleshy excrescence. When you are *really* annoyed by a short person: 'Sir, you are nothing but a caruncle!'

CASTROPHENIA *n.* The belief that one's thoughts are being stolen by enemies. A condition much to be preferred over *nastrophenia*, the belief that one's thoughts are not worth being stolen by enemies.

CATACHRESIS *n.* Misapplication of a word. In using the lore and learning contained in this book, you will undoubtedly be found guilty of this. In your defense, you can at least say *(a)* that you are aware of your lapse, and *(b)* that you know what it is called.

CAVITATION *n.* The forming of cavities within an otherwise continuous material, as for example behind a solid object that is moving through a fluid, or within a solid object as a result of bombardment with sound waves. 'Don't expect too much of Jamie, Mother. All those rock concerts . . . first his hearing, now the cavitation in his brain . . . I warned him this would happen . . .'

CEPACEOUS *a.* Like an onion. 'So this is your new boyfriend, Imelda! I can tell just by looking at him that he's your type – same eyes, same cepaceous head . . .'

CERATE *n.* A medicated waxy *unguent* (q.v.). 'Warning! Warning! Your father is preparing to dice the vegetables with the new super-sharp knife! Bring the cerates and the unguents!'

CEROSCOPY *n.* Divination by means of melted wax. The wax is poured into cold water, and the diviner predicts the future on the basis of the shapes taken by the congealed wax. If you are nervous about the

outcome of the experiment, you could of course perform ceroscopy to find out what the result of the
ceroscopy would be. Are you with me here?

CHAETIFEROUS *a.* Bearing bristles. Also **CHAETIGEROUS**
and **CHAETOPHEROUS**. If your boyfriend *must*
start growing a beard, at least you ought to know
what to call him.

CHALYBEATE WATER *n.* A mineral water, supposedly
impregnated with iron, for consumption as a pleasant and restorative tonic. One of those gorgeous late
Victorian terms like 'mucilage.' You took the air at
Brighton and you had your chalybeate water afterward. Do what you can to revive this word. Ask the
checkout girl at the local supermarket where you can
find their chalybeate waters.

CHARIENTISM *n.* An elegantly veiled insult. One of the
various worthy ends to which this book is a means.

CHASMUS HYSTERICUS *phr.* Hysterical yawning. 'I'm
not bored, really I'm not – It's my chasmus, gets me
every time when I get too excited.'

CHEIROPOMPHOLYX *n.* A disease in which blisters filled
with fluid suddenly appear on the patient's skin. 'Of
course I hold no grudges, Helen; in fact I wish you
the greatest cheiropompholyx for as long as you
live.'

CHIMERA *n.* An interesting example of a word whose
metaphorical usage has gradually moved away from
the original sense. The currently accepted meaning is

a fanciful conception or scheme, an unreal ambition, or even a castle in the air. But the original meaning was an imaginary monster, an unjustified fear, a bogy. The original Chimera was a fire-breathing female monster with the head of a lion, the body of a goat, and the tail of a dragon. She was said to have laid waste a district in Asia Minor before being killed by Bellerophon. So when your hoped-for liaison with the flighty Esmeralda fails to take place, and she admits to you that your place in her affections has been taken by the *saponaceous* (q.v.) Nigel, you sigh and say to her: 'Ah, well . . . to me, Esmeralda, you must always remain a chimera, I suppose.'

CHREMATOPHOBIA *n.* Fear of money. The rarest complaint known to man. Sufferers from this condition, rejoice! Help is now at hand! Send all your money to the author, in a plain wrapper, and you need never know fear again!

CICURATE *v.* To tame, or reclaim from a state of wildness. 'Belinda, I'm not having that young man of yours in the house until he's been thoroughly cicurated.'

CIRCUMAMBAGIOUS *a.* A roundabout or indirect manner of speech. Not as effective, perhaps, on the whole, as an aid to obfuscation, as the sesquipedalianism fostered by this book, always assuming, if you will forgive a somewhat Jamesian digression (Henry, that is to say, in contradistinction to P. D.) that obfuscation is in fact the objective, and having in mind also that, setting aside the relative merits of the two different approaches toward that end, vis-à-vis each other, it can hardly be doubted that the employment of both together, as distinct from one or the other, must have a still greater obfuscatory, or perhaps more precisely, obscurantist, impact, a point well evidenced by the fact that this particular instance of circumambagiousness, aided by only the merest hint of sesquipedalianism, has, as I believe you will discover, successfully diverted your attention from the fact that nowhere in this admittedly now somewhat overlong sentence is there, despite its superabundance of subsidiary clauses, a principal subject or verb.

CIRCUMFORANEOUS *a.* Wandering from house to house. A Mormon, a Jehovah's Witness, an Avon Lady, a hungry cat, or a teenager.

CIRCUMFUSE *v.* To pour, spread, or diffuse around. 'Well, I've dug up the ground, I've fertilized it, and I've raked it level – but some other lout can circumfuse the bloody lawn seed.' Always a good idea to juxtapose the vernacular with the *sesquipedalian* (q.v.) whenever possible.

CIRRIPED *n.* A member of an order of crustaceans which in their adult stage attach themselves in a parasitic way to other creatures or objects. As, for example, barnacles. 'Dearest, do you think Kimberley might leave home this year and get her own little flat – or is she to be our permanent cirriped?'

CLAIRAUDIENCE *n.* The aural equivalent of clairvoyance. In other words, the hearing of sounds that are too far removed in time or space to be perceived by the physical mechanisms of hearing. 'So this is the club auditorium? Oh my God, I feel . . . there are terrible emanations from the past, all about us here . . . I hear line-dancing music! I hear Scottish country dance music! I hear . . . dear God, this is too much to bear . . . I hear junior elocution competitions! I hear the sound of a Little Miss Beauty prizegiving! For God's sake, get me out of here! Curse this damned clairaudience of mine!'

CLEDONISM *n*. The use of euphemistic language to avoid the untoward magical effects that might be caused by the use of plain language. Referring to the Devil, for example, as 'Monsieur,' in the belief that the simple fellow will not realize he is being spoken about and therefore will have no occasion to join the group. A reference to a spouse as 'His Lordship' or 'Her Ladyship' could be regarded as cledonism.

CLERICAL *a*. (i) Of clergy, (ii) of clerks. There are very few words with as perfectly balanced an alternativity of meaning. And yet note how readily the meaning becomes polarized once the word is set in the context of a sentence ('Putting on his clerical garb, he . . .'), of another single word ('clerical error'), or even of a prefix ('anticlerical'). Consider the phrases 'clerical gentlemen' and 'clerical officer.' There is no doubt about the meaning of the adjective in each case, even though an officer and a gentleman are traditionally supposed in some quarters to be one and the same thing.

clinomania

CLINOMANIA *n.* Excessive desire to stay in bed. Not a bad mania, as manias go; and a reasonably plausible excuse for taking Monday off.

CLISHNACLAVER *n.* Silly gossip. Another of those Scottish words. Why are they all so pejorative?

CLYSTER *n.* An enema, or other form of intestinal injection. 'No, I cannot offer you a donation at this time,' you inform the telemarketer who has phoned you at your home during dinner on behalf of an imperfectly identified charity; 'but if you were to send your representative around I would be glad to give him a substantial clyster.'

COCCYX *n.* What you fall on when your feet slip forward from under you, as when wearing thongs on moss-covered mud. The small triangular bone at the bottom of the spinal column, called 'coccyx' because it is shaped like the bill of a *kokkux*, or cuckoo. 'Please, Miss, I've hurt my coccyx – will you have a look at it for me?'

COCKALORUM *n.* A self-important little man. (From 'High Cockalorum,' a game said to be not unlike leapfrog. The exact nature of this game is unknown to the present author, but it could conceivably be that known to the present age as 'Politics.')

clishnaclaver

COCKLE *n.* A word with even more different meanings than *gammon* or *gudgeon* (q.v.). Everyone knows about the shellfish, but you should be able to disorient your friends completely with one or more of the other meanings set out as follows:

- A mineral occurring in dark, long crystals.

- A grasslike plant with black seeds growing among grain.

- A shallow boat.

- A stove, kiln, or furnace.

- A wrinkle or ripple. (Also, used as a verb, to wrinkle or to cause to wrinkle.)

- Whimsical.

55

- A cut or ringlet.

- To wobble.

- The inmost depths (as in 'the cockles of my heart' – possibly derived from the 'wrinkle' sense of the term).

- Perhaps most bizarre of all is the phrase 'to cry cockles' – eighteenth-century slang for 'to be hanged,' apparently derived from the distinctive gurglings emitted during strangulation.

CODGER *n.* Mean old fellow. The typical phrase is 'old codger,' even though the notion of age is already present in the word itself. (See also *whippersnapper*.)

COMICONOMENCLATURIST *n.* A specialist in funny names. The serious collector of funny names accepts only those of real people, and abides by certain rules of the game, just as do those who shoot quail or those who fish for trout. Chinese names are not fair game, and no self-respecting comiconomenclaturist would include in his collection a Ho Hum, a T. Hee, or a Jim Shoo. An interesting sidelight of the comiconomenclaturist's pursuit is the realization that names cease to be funny as they become famous, or even familiar – consider the case of Dingle Foot, Preserved Fish, or Mollie Panter-Downes.

COMMENSAL *a.* or *n.* Eating together; one who eats with another. Normally used in a technical sense, referring to the habits of animals and plants, but, figuratively, a nice term for a dinner companion. 'I say, waiter – would you mind sponging down the curry spillage on my commensal?'

COMPLORATION *n.* Wailing and weeping together. 'Your mother coming over this Christmas, darling, for the usual comploration?'

COMPOTATION *n.* A drinking party. 'Wayne's just in his first week at university, and they're having all these traditional ceremonies – matriculation and orientation, and he says that every night they have what they call compotation. . .'

COMPURGATION *n.* The exoneration of an accused party purely on the basis of oaths sworn by a number of other persons (presumably his friends). An ancient practice that could well be revived in the next World Cup soccer competition. 'We claim compurgation!' could be the cry of the team when one of their number is about to be dismissed from the field for illegal play.

CONCINNITY *n.* Elegance and appropriateness of style. See, for example, any volume published by David R. Godine, Publisher, Incorporated.

CONSTABLE *n.* Originally 'count of the stable'; now the Australian police force's equivalent of an army private. The recommended form of address when speaking to any Australian police officer who is wearing badges of senior rank. When speaking to a constable, the recommended form of address is *Superintendent*.

CONSUBSTANTIAL *a.* One of those words from the wonderful world of magic and myth (see *obsolagnium*) which describe entities or states that are supposed to exist even though there is no hard empirical evidence for their existence. In this case, consubstantial means 'having the same substance or essence'; yet it is said of *different* beings, i.e., beings that are not the same. So the use of the term implies a belief that things that are different are in fact the same. The classic use of the term is in Christian theology, to describe the Trinity. There may be other uses. 'Now listen closely, children. Two weeks after buying himself a state-of-the-art compact disc player, with amplifier and speakers, valued conservatively at \$1,250, your father has bought your mother, for her birthday, an ovenproof casserole dish. Imagine that! Liberality and lousiness combined in the one being! Your father is the living proof of consubstantiality!'

CONTRADISTINCTION *n.* Why say 'in contrast with' when you can say 'in contradistinction to'?

CONTRAINDICATED *a.* Inadvisable. A technical term from the realms of medical/pharmaceutical jargon. 'For the treatment of headache, amputation is contraindicated.' A word that is surprisingly useful in nonmedical discussion. 'I think, darling, a visit by your mother at this particular time is contraindicated.' Familiarity with its use is also essential to reduce the natural sense of inferiority besetting the

contraindicated

lay person who finds himself in the company of two or more doctors at any one time, e.g., at polo matches, afghan hound meets, antique auctions, or vintage-car rallies.

CONTRECTATION *n.* The act of caressing someone furtively or against their will. 'So that's agreed. We'll begin by asking each candidate about their educational qualifications and their skills in relation to the selection criteria – communication, management, finance, contrectation, and so on – then we'll. . .'

CONTRUDE *v.* To push, thrust, or crowd together. At the line at the post office, ask permission to contrude before making your forward move; there's always the chance that someone who doesn't know what it means will concur.

COPIOPIA *n.* Hysterical eye-strain. Condition of a lexicographer. But a lovely word to say aloud. Try it.

COPULATIVE CONJUNCTION *phr.* Not, not what you think at all. In grammar, this is the correct name for the co-ordinative conjunction. Still in the dark? Our old friend, the word 'and'. 'And what's more, you children, not only the way you behave but especially the way you talk needs a lot of improvement. For a start, I expect more copulative conjunctions from both of you!'

CORUSCATE *v.* Sparkle, twinkle, flash, glitter. Used in particular with regard to flashes of wit or intellectual illumination. Thus, Taylor's 'He might have illuminated his times with the incessant coruscations of his genius.' *Coruscating* may be used to good effect in place of *rapierlike*, even though the sense is quite different, in the example given under *remarks, exasperating* (q.v.).

CORVÉE *n.* A feudal duty to serve one's master; hence, any system of forced labour. 'Kitchen duty for you tonight, Kristen! No, it's no use pouting and sulking. You know the terms of your corvée!'

COUNTERPANE *n.* Coverlet for a bed, e.g., a quilt or bedspread. *Not* a window, or table-top of some kind. A nice, nineteenth-century word. People who had counterpanes on their beds used *mucilage* (q.v.) instead of glue, took portmanteaus with them when traveling, used gazogenes instead of soda syphons, wore plimsolls instead of sandshoes, and served their children's cereal in porringers instead of bowls. Oddly enough, the word is a distortion of *counterpoint*, one of the meanings of which was a stitched quilt, from the Latin *culcita puncta*, or pricked mattress or cushion.

COXCOMB *n.* Conceited fool. Similar to *popinjay* (q.v.) in meaning, but with the emphasis perhaps more on the foolishness and less on the conceit, so the two terms can be used in the one vilification without redundancy. The derivation is from *cock's combe* – the cap originally worn by the professional jester, or fool. Faintly archaic maledictories of this kind are much to be preferred even to the more dramatic modern ones – especially when the person being denounced is younger than the speaker. (See also *whippersnapper*.)

CRIME PASSIONEL *phr.* (From the French.) A crime motivated by the passions – such as the murder of a treacherous lover. As with other foreign or classical terms (see *pinus radiata*), the Superior Person always uses the original pronunciation – in this case, for example, 'crime' is pronounced as 'cream.' At the average dinner party, there is always at least one guest who is not familiar with the phrase and can be persuaded, while the hostess is out of the room, that crime passionel is in fact the name of the passionfruit cream dessert that has just been served. This can lead to some entertaining after-dinner conversation.

CRYPTOCLIMATE *n.* The climate found within a small enclosed structure, as distinct from the local climate generally (microclimate) and the wider regional climate (macroclimate). 'You seriously expect me to go into Shane's room? Have you any idea what the cryptoclimate in there is like?'

CRYPTOMNESIA *n.* The spontaneous revival of former memories, experiences, facts, and items of knowledge, without any ability to recall the circumstances which originally attended them. 'I'm sure I know her, but who is she? And how big a fool did I make of myself in her presence? Introduce me if you must, but I may have to plead cryptomnesia.'

CUCKING STOOL *n.* A chair in which disorderly women were, in olden times, ducked in the water as a form of punishment. In even more olden times, a cucking stool was something like a commode, since to cuck was to defecate. The word is ugly enough to be revived for use in American films and other vehicles for the *rebarbative* (q.v.).

CURMUDGEON *n.* Cantankerous codger. Both *curmudgeon* and *codger* (q.v.) apply to men only, and there appears to be no female equivalent. Perhaps *grimalkin*, an old she-cat or nasty old woman, comes closest to it; but it is not really synonymous.

CURSORIAL *a.* Suited to walking or running as a method of locomotion, as distinct from other methods such as swimming, flying, slithering, etc. 'What can be said in favour of Luke? Let us think for a moment. Well, for a start, he is cursorial, definitely cursorial. And then there's . . . now let me think . . . just give me a moment here . . .'

cursorial

CYMLIN *n.* A kind of squash, i.e., an edible gourd, giving rise to the obvious possibilities for its use in relation to that other squash, the tennis-like game played indoors with a small, painful rubber ball. 'Cyril and I are just going off by ourselves for a few hours to cymlinate.'

CYNOPHOBIA *n.* The morbid dread of dogs. Condition of cats and postmen.

cynophobia

CYPRINOID *a.* Carp-like. 'Entertaining another of your cyprinoid friends with your DVD equipment, Desmond? Wouldn't he be more interested in spending some time with our goldfish?'

DACTYLOGRAM *n.* Fingerprint. A casual reference to your having been invited by the authorities to let them have your dactylograms may give the listener the impression that you are a distinguished applied mathematician who is called in by the government from time to time in a consultative capacity.

DAFFODOWNDILLY *n.* The Superior Person's word for a daffodil.

DANDIPRAT *n.* A silly little fellow or urchin. Nothing to do with 'dandy,' but from the French 'dandin,' i.e., a ninny or simpleton. Your young nephews and grand-children will *hate* being jovially addressed thus, even if they haven't the faintest idea what it means – especially if you can manage to pat them on the head at the same time.

DAPATICAL *a.* Sumptuous (as of a feast). 'I hope you'll be patient with me tonight, Samantha; I find that since I got underway with my low-cholesterol diet, I can't properly enjoy a meal unless it's dapatical.'

DARK LANTERN *n.* A lantern with a shutter device enabling its light to be hidden. This apparently oxymoronic term must have puzzled many a twentieth-century reader of nineteenth-century fiction. The modern flashlight is, in effect, a dark lantern, the switch replacing the shutter.

DASYPHYLLOUS *a.* Having crowded, thick, or woolly leaves. Applying a little *anthropomorphism* (q.v.) to this, one could so characterize your typical skiers, geared and kitted out like multi-hued astronauts for their day in the snow.

DEBLATERATE *v.* To babble. 'Right – no more apologies, and the minutes of the previous meeting confirmed? Okay then, on to Agenda Item One, and let the deblateration commence!'

DECALCOMANIA *n.* A transfer – i.e., a picture or design of some kind imprinted on a paper in such a way as to permit its being transferred, after wetting, to another surface. Nowadays what used to be called simply *transfers* are coming to be called *decals* – which is simply an abbreviation of the above word. The Superior Person will always use the full word (the 'c's are hard and the stress is on the 'cal'): 'I like your son's room, Mrs. Afterbath, but I was rather staggered by his decalcomania.'

DECANAL *a.* Pertaining to a dean. Originally an ecclesiastical term, but there is no reason why it should not find currency in the groves of academe. Thus, when the Dean of Intercultural Studies observes a student sit-in team approaching his office, the sedative for which he reaches might be referred to as the decanal seconal.

DECAPSULATION *n.* The removal of the enveloping membrane of an organ. No, not the unpacking of a Korean musical instrument from its polythene wrapping, but one of those unspeakable things that surgeons and pathologists do. 'And another thing, young lady! Before you set foot outside that door, I'd like to see a little decapsulation brought to bear on that thickly made-up face of yours!'

DECARCERATION *n.* The freeing of criminals and the mentally ill from confinement in gaols and asylums, and their reinstatement in society at large, thereby making it harder for the rest of us to tell who are the politicians.

DECOCTION *n.* The Superior word for soup. Actually, anything prepared by boiling something in water to extract its essence. Note that soup can also be a concoction – provided it contains more than one ingredient, since a concoction is something prepared by cooking things in combination, or by combining things for some other purpose. This book is a concoction.

DECOLLATION *n.* Decapitation, beheading. See also *defenestration* and *jugulation*. 'And finally, ladies and gentlemen, girls and boys, I cannot let this speech night come to an end without a special mention for our Assistant Principal. We all know just how much he has contributed to the school over many years and what he means to us all – and I know you'll agree with me that, for everything he has done, for being what he is, he fully deserves a thoroughgoing decollation.'

DECONSTRUCTION *n.* An approach to the analysis of text, popular in the 1970s and associated in particular with one Jacques Derrida, who asserted that the text means something very different from what it appears to mean, whether to the reader *or the author* (my italics). No-one said out loud that this emperor had no clothes, but if the technique of deconstruction were applied to Derrida's own writings about deconstruction then it would presumably become apparent that deconstruction must be something completely different from what it is said to be.

DECORTICATE *v.* To strip or otherwise remove the bark, or husk, from; in other words, to peel. 'Would you care to decorticate a grape for me, O my beloved?'

DEFEASIBILITY *n.* In philosophy, said of a belief or statement which is open to being refuted by evidence that may be forthcoming in the future. As for example, 'I am going to enjoy myself today.' In contradistinction to *incorrigibility*, which is said of a belief or statement which events cannot possibly show to have been wrong. As for example, 'Peter Bowler is the supreme lexicographer of our time.' (An earlier example of incorrigibility was thought to be Descartes' 'I exist'; but the passage of time has proved him to be wrong.)

DEFENESTRATION *n.* The act of throwing someone or something out of a window. A word that is neologism's paradigm and justification. If the word were not needed to describe the act, the act would need to be performed to justify the word.

DEFICIT FINANCING *n.* A method of disproving the Micawber theory of budgetary financing, by achieving an annual expenditure higher than annual income. The technique seems to be restricted, for no apparent reason, to national governments.

DEGLUTITION *n.* Swallowing. 'If you're really serious about losing weight, Mrs. Hallibutt, we'll have to do something to reduce your deglutition count.'

DEIPNOSOPHIST *n.* A wise conversationalist at the dinner table. Unfortunately, the two elements of the definition rarely go together. The author, for example, claims to meet one of the two criteria (he refuses to say which) but not the other.

DELTIOLOGY *n.* The collecting of postcards as a hobby. 'In support of my application for the position of Executive Director, I should mention my skills in human resource management, deltiology, communication. . .'

DEMERSAL *a.* Sinking to the bottom, as for example certain fish eggs, or babies whose New Age mothers think it would be lovely to teach them to swim at the age of three months.

DEMOPHOBIA *n.* The morbid dread of crowds. One of the most common of phobias; if all the sufferers were put together in one place, they wouldn't like it one bit. Condition of most of us during the pre-Christmas shopping period. Pity those who are also *autophobes* (q.v.).

DENDROCHRONOLOGY *n.* The process of dating a tree by counting its annual growth rings as shown in a cross-section. 'How old, you ask, do I think Isabella is? No problem – dendrochronology will give us the answer! Just give me a cross-section of her, will you, and I'll get to work.'

DENDROPHILOUS *a.* Attracted to or living in trees. The correct epithet for militant save-the-forest conservationists, especially those who chain themselves to trees or pole-sit in the branches overhead.

DENTILOQUY *n.* The act or practice of talking through clenched teeth. Ventriloquists are almost, though not completely, dentiloquists. 'Really, dear, do we *have* to have the dentiloquy bit again? Just because of a *tiny* scratch or two on the hood – which wasn't all my fault anyway? I mean I was concentrating on reversing – how was I to know that you'd left the toolbox on the car roof?'

DERODIDYMUS *n.* A two-headed monster. 'My God, she's bringing the twins with her! Derodidymus alert! Warning, warning, derodidymus alert!'

DESIPIENT *a.* Silly, trifling, or foolish. 'How marvelous that you're enrolling your daughters with us, Lady

Fubwell! The school cherishes these traditional family links. And tell me – dare we hope that they will be as desipient as you were, in your day?'

DESUETUDE *n.* State of disuse. Some nouns have their inevitably accompanying adjectives ('ineffable bore,' etc.); *desuetude* has its inevitably accompanying verb – 'fall into.' Desuetude is never arrived at, achieved, experienced, or enjoyed; it is invariably fallen into. How nice to be able to say to your visiting sister Agatha, when she makes her ritual inquiry into the piano-playing of your ten-year-old son, Roger, that it has recently fallen into desuetude. It is possible that she will assume you to be referring to an especially difficult piece by Chopin that the lad is now learning.

DESULTOR *n.* In ancient Rome, the desultor was a circus performer who rode two horses at the same time, alternately leaping from one to the other. Today an estate agent, perhaps? A politician?

DETERRATION *n.* Not the act of deterring, but the discovery of an underlying object by the removal of the earth surrounding it. From the Latin *de* and *terra*. 'Young man, you will proceed immediately to the bathroom. The time has come for the deterration of your feet.'

DEUCED *a.* or *adv.* Exceeding(ly), devilish(ly). 'This is deuced civil of you, old man' is a pleasantly deflating response to an unwanted courtesy. The derivation is as ambiguous as the term itself. Said to be from 'deuce,' the low-scoring two in a dice game, and hence the devil of a result from your throw; but some derive it from the Old French 'dieus' or 'gods.'

DEUTERAGONIST *n.* In ancient Greek drama, the second most important actor, i.e., the actor next in importance to the protagonist. 'Let me make one thing perfectly clear – in this kitchen, I am the protagonist and you are the deuteragonist.'

DHARNA *n.* In eastern civilizations, a method of claiming justice by fasting, to death if need be, before the door of the oppressor from or against whom justice is being sought. In western civilizations we have, of course, the Teenager's Sulk. 'James, the concept of dharna, which you have so ably introduced into this little disagreement with your parents, certainly covers the refusal to eat your vegetables, but it does not extend to your taking regular trips down the road to the nearest fast-food outlet.'

DIALYSIS *n.* A word with two quite different meanings. You all know about the medical one. The other is a method of analytical argument in which all the possible pros and cons are brought forward and one by one despatched by sheer logic. 'So, Shelly – the proposal is that you go out tonight to the wet T-shirt competition down at the football club. Well, let's apply the dialysis process to this one and see where we end up.'

DIAMANTIFEROUS *a.* Yielding diamonds. 'I don't care what you say – I still prefer Julian. Craig may be younger and more handsome, and unmarried for that matter; but Julian is diamantiferous.'

DIASKEUAST *n.* One who prepares material in detail. A researcher, editor, et al. Even a lexicographer.

DICK TEST *phr.* Not what you might think at all, but rather a test of one's susceptibility to, or immunity from, scarlet fever. The test, believe it or not, consists of the injection under the skin of streptococcus toxins, and is named after George and Gladys Dick, who presumably came up with the idea. I think we'll leave that one right there.

DIDAPPER *n.* One who disappears and then pops up again. From 'dive' and 'dapper' (a variant of 'dipper'). Specifically applied to the dabchick, a small freshwater diving bird. Or, perhaps, a teenager between mealtimes.

DIDYMITIS *n.* Not something you'd wish on your worst enemy. Unless, of course, he didn't know what you were talking about. Inflammation of the testicles.

DIGNITARY *n.* An important person occupying a high and exalted office. As, for instance, the Archbishop of Canterbury. (Cf. *luminary*.)

DIMEROUS *a.* Consisting of two parts. Confronted by your hostess with The Perfect Couple, you undermine her faith in their perfection by whispering, 'Ah, yes, but have you not heard – their marriage is a dimerous one.'

DIMISSORY *a.* Sending away; permitting to depart. In ecclesiastical usage, applied to the document conveying a bishop's authorization for a candidate for the ministry to be ordained somewhere else; the candidate is said to be given his dimissory letters. When midnight approaches and Brett and Margaret are *still* sitting there talking, you say to your helpmeet: 'Well, my dear, isn't it time we offered Brett and Margaret a dimissory coffee?' If Brett says brightly, 'What's that?' you explain: 'Oh, I suppose it's more or less the nonalcoholic equivalent of a doch-an-doris.' 'What on earth's a doch-an-doris?' asks Margaret. 'Oh,' says your helpmeet, 'it's more or less the same as a stirrup cup.' At this point both Brett and Margaret start making excuses to go. A doch-an-doris, or a stirrup cup, is a last drink – one for the road – offered to the departing guest more or less at the door.

DINGLE *n.* A narrow, wooded vale, dale, or dell. (Note that the last three words are synonyms for each other, and mean a small valley or ravine.) Incidentally, never confuse (unless you do so deliberately) the use of *tingle* with *tinkle*, as in the phrase 'to give someone a tinkle,' i.e., a ring on the telephone. (See also *umbriferous*.)

DIOESTRUM *n.* The time during which a female animal is not in heat. 'This is Jenny's father speaking, Craig. We expect her dioestrum to occur tomorrow afternoon about 3:00 P.M. and to last till about 3:45 P.M., so you'd be very welcome to drop in during that time if you wish.'

DIRHINOUS *a.* With paired nostrils. As, for example, the human face. Everyone is dirhinous, but few know it.

A good word, therefore, for the Insult Apparent. 'Sir, you are a dirhinous mesomorph.' Similarly useful is *poriferous* (with pores) or *bimanal* (with two hands).

DIRIGIBLE *a.* Everyone is familiar with this word as a noun meaning airship; but of course it is originally an adjective meaning 'capable of being directed, steerable.' Thus an airship was a dirigible balloon. When the party is breaking up and everyone is starting to worry about Melanie, who is upright but distinctly glassy-eyed, you ask: 'Is she still dirigible?'

DISBRANCH *v.* Superior Person's word for 'prune' (i.e., trim a tree or bush).

DISCALCED *a.* Bare-footed. 'Okay if I go to church discalced this morning, Mom? It's an old Carmelite tradition, according to Father Ryan.' From the Latin *calceus*, a shoe.

DISCISSION *n.* Sticking a needle into the eye. A surgical term, which you yourself are unlikely to have occasion to use; but as well to know the meaning, just in case your ophthalmologist nonchalantly uses the word while casually discussing your next eye test.

discontiguous

DISCONTIGUOUS *a.* Not touching, or even near. 'It is my dearest wish to be completely discontiguous to the Honorable Senator . . .'

DISEMBOGUEMENT *n.* A discharging at the mouth, as of a stream. 'No, Mrs. Davenport, the Bulgarian cold cabbage and radish soup was delicious, absolutely delicious! It's just that I need to use the bathroom for a moment. A necessary disemboguement, you understand.'

DISFELLOWSHIPPING *n.* Excommunication from those who hold certain belief systems, such as Seventh Day Adventists, Urantians, etc. 'Go to your room, young man! It's disfellowshipping for you until you've taken down those Black Sabbath posters and cleaned under the bed!'

DISSAVE *v.* Believe it or not, this delightful word means exactly what it ought to – the opposite of 'save.' To dissave is to spend more than one's income by drawing upon one's savings or capital. In a sense, it could be said that the ultimate object of all saving is dissaving; this is something that not many people realize.

DISSIGHT *n.* Unsightly object; eyesore. 'Come in, old chap, come in! You're a dissight for sore eyes!'

DISSILIENT *a.* Bursting or springing open. 'I'm returning these shorts for a refund. The zip is irredeemably dissilient.'

DITTOGRAPHY *n.* and **HAPLOGRAPHY** *n.* Mistakes in printing or writing. In the former case, part of a word is repeated when it should appear only once; in the latter, part of a word appears only once when it should be repeated. A disadvantage of the author's neologism *unundulating* (q.v.) is that the reader, when confronted with it, may never be completely sure that is is not a dittography for *undulating* – or that *undulating* is not a haplography for *unundulating*.

DIVERSIVOLENT *a.* Looking for trouble or argument; seeking out a divergence of view. 'Dearly beloved, we are gathered together here in the sight of God, and in the face of this congregation, to join together this Man and this Woman in Holy Matrimony, duly considering the causes for which Matrimony was ordained. First, it was ordained for the mutual society, help, and diversivolence that the one ought to have of the other . . .'

divulsion

DIVULSION *n.* The act of pulling or wrenching apart. 'Okay, that's the end of that video. Switch on the lights, and let's see how much divulsion we need to bring to bear on Jason and Rachel.'

DOLORIFUGE *a.* That which relieves or drives away sadness. A *viscerotonic* (q.v.) innamorata, for example.

DOXOGRAPHER *n.* A compiler of opinions of philosophers. Domestic scene: 'You know what *I* think?' 'Hold everything! Call the doxographer, children! Your father is about to express an opinion!'

DOXOLOGY *n.* Hymn of praise to the Almighty. The Greater Doxology is the *gloria in excelsis* and the Lesser Doxology the *gloria patri*. When, at close of day, you are greeted by your spouse with a statement of the Achievements of the Day, you may wish to expostulate: 'Bravo, my dear! Now – would you prefer the Greater or the Lesser Doxology?'

DOXY *n.* A prostitute; also, surprisingly, a belief or religious doctrine. See how you can use these terms for maximum confusion.

DRACOCEPHALIC *a.* With a dragon-shaped head. Choose your own uses for this word. But be careful; you are not the only person to have bought this book.

DRAGOMAN *n.* Nothing to do with dragons, but an interpreter/guide; one who, in Middle Eastern countries, in the days when the Englishman's castle was never his home, insulated the visiting Old Etonian from the milling *autochthons* (q.v.) and ensured that the former's jodhpur-filled portmanteaus reached more or less the same destinations as he did.

DRAPETOMANIA *n.* Intense desire to run away from home. Unaccountably, there doesn't appear to be a word for that much more common condition – an intense desire for someone *else* to run away from home.

DRESSAGE *n.* The training of a horse in obedience and deportment. The thought that a human being, particularly an upper-class female human being wearing jodhpurs and a bowler hat, can train a horse, of all creatures, in deportment, must be one of the more laughable conceptions ever given credence by the otherwise sober pages of a dictionary.

DROMOMANIA *n.* A pathological urge to travel. In its most serious state, leads to membership of the International Olympics Committee.

DROMOPHOBIA *n.* The morbid dread of travel, particularly when experienced in the form of a pathological fear of crossing streets. In the case of certain streets in Paris, Bangkok or Rome, an understandable condition.

DRUMBLE *v.* To move slowly, reluctantly and sluggishly. Mode of locomotion of the teenager called to the dinner table.

DUUMVIRATE *n.* The exercise of governmental power by two people acting together. 'This isn't a family! This is a duumvirate! What happened to democracy?' (Suggested parting lines for teenager storming out of the room.)

DYMAXION *n.* Name given by Buckminster Fuller, the famous American engineer, to his concept of the maximum net performance per gross energy input. 'You're asking me to relate Owen's work performance to his gross energy input, as part of his annual staff appraisal? It's his dymaxion? Listen, Buckminster Fuller may know all about buildings, but . . . "gross energy input"? . . . the term has no meaning in Owen's case.'

DYSLOGY *n.* Dispraise; uncomplimentary remarks. The opposite of 'eulogy.' 'Okay, everyone, let's hear it for the retiring President! Let's give him the dyslogy he so richly deserves!'

DYSPHORIA *n.* Depression, pathological discontent. Opposite of *euphoria*, or extreme happiness. The novelist Thomas Hardy once told a friend that he would not read *Wuthering Heights*, because he 'had been told that it was depressing.'

DYSTELEOLOGY *n.* The metaphysical doctrine that events have no pre-ordained purpose; that there is no 'final cause.' 'Let's see, who'll be my navigator for this trip? I think in view of Mummy's lifelong adherence to dysteleology, we'd better not give her the map this time, eh Kylie?'

DZIGGETAI *n.* A kind of wild ass, rather like a mule. 'And this is my young brother Jason. He's a regular little dziggetai now that he's taken up *tae kwon do*, aren't you, Jason?'

E

EBRIECTION *n.* Mental breakdown from drinking too much alcohol. 'I hope you won't have an ebriection like my previous two bosses, Mr. Palethorpe.'

ECDEMIC *a.* Originating elsewhere than where it is found. 'These children we keep finding in the kitchen now that Damien has started school . . . I've only just realized that even though their appetites are omnipresent they themselves are ecdemic.'

ECDYSIS *n.* The shedding of a snake's skin. 'Ah, the first warm days of spring! I'll have to change to short-sleeved shirts soon – and for you, dear, the time of ecdysis must be approaching.'

ECLIPSIS *n.* Omitting a grammatically necessary word or form. A whole generation of young people has, for instance, been taught in college courses laughably called 'Communication' to do without the conjunction 'that', and so we have sentences such as 'He said the end was near.' Next, the 'the' and the 'was' will go, and our language will have finally reached the 'me Tarzan, you Jane' level.

ECONOMICS *n.* An arcane language, used by its own cognoscenti for reviewing past events in the production and distribution of wealth. There are some who would define economics as a science rather than a language; but, in the absence of any evidence that future events can be predicted by economists on the basis of fixed laws, this approach can hardly be supported by the objective lexicographer.

ECPHONEMA *n.* An exclamation engendered by a sudden emotion, such as joy, wonder, or horror. 'Okay Mum, so I've passed in mathematics. This time can we do without the ecphonema?'

ECTOMORPH, ENDOMORPH, MESOMORPH *n.* Psychology's contribution to the English language. The terms simply mean tall thin person, short fat person, and middle-sized person, respectively – but they look much more impressive than those more old-fashioned terms in a thesis on behaviorism or in an appallingly expensive textbook. They are, moreover, useful for insulting or alarming the ignorant: 'Sir, you are a miserable mesomorph'; 'One more remark like that about Mrs. Carr-Willoughby, my good man, and I shall see to it that the world knows of your ectomorphic tendencies.'

EDAPHOLOGY *n.* The science of soil as a plant-growing medium. 'You don't want a carpet-cleaning firm for Rodney's room, Mum, you need an edaphologist.'

EFFENDI *n.* Turkish title used to show respect when addressing a government official. Try using it when next you call in at the IRS to plead your case; when explaining to the bus driver exactly how it was that you lost your ticket; when scrounging for school-project material for your daughter at the tourist bureau; or when registering your VW.

EFFLATION *n.* An emanation that is breathed or blown out. 'Ah my darling, I can tell that you are repelled by my alliaceous efflations! If only you too had chosen the garlic mussels as a main!'

EFFLEURAGE *n.* A gentle stroking or caressing technique used in massage. In view of the suggestion of *fleur* and *corsage* embodied in this largely unfamiliar word, you might shyly ask your beloved to let you give her an effleurage before you go to the ball. You might even claim to be an advocate of multiculturalism and invent an old *ethnic* (q.v.) custom under which both partners give each other effleurages before going to the ball. And, for that matter, afterward as well.

EFFLORESCENCE *n.* Do not for a moment consider that your having long since left school absolves you from the responsibility for remembering, and distinguishing between, the meanings of this word and its host of friends and relatives. Now concentrate. *Efflorescence*: flowering or (in chemistry) crystallization. *Effervescence*: bubbling. *Deliquescence*: liquefaction. *Inflorescence*: floral structure of a plant. *Infloration*: inflorescence. *Defloration*: dehymenization. *Defervescence*: reduction in heat or fever. *Refervescence*: resurgence of heat or fever. Sorry; there's no refloration.

EFFLUVIUM *n.* An intangible emanation or exhalation. Normally taken now to imply an unpleasant odor, but originally a hypothesized medium to account for magnetic attraction and repulsion. Or, in the elegant words of *Dr. Gregory's Portable Encyclopaedia Comprehending The Latest Improvements in Every Branch of Useful Knowledge*, published in 1826: 'a term much used by philosophers and physicians, to express the minute particles which exhale from most, if not all, terrestrial bodies in the form of insensible vapors.' Try not to be too cruel in the use of this word when commenting upon the extent to which your various acquaintances are nice or otherwise to be near.

EGREGIOUS *a.* Exceptional. An interesting example of a word that has gradually changed from complimentary to *pejorative* (q.v.) in its usage, being now most commonly found immediately preceding the word *ass*. Interestingly akin to *consummate* in the latter regard. In its Latin origin, it carries the sense of 'out of the herd' – cf. *gregarious*. It is an excellent word for insulting strangers with. 'Sir, you are an egregious rogue (ass, rascal, blunderer, etc.).' It sounds unpleasant, and it leaves the wretched object of your wrath uncertain as to just how insulting you have been. Even more effective in this way, though of course totally unjustified on lexical grounds, can be the use of the term on its own. 'Sir, you are egregious.' Needless to say, the term should be used thus only when you are quite certain that the person you are addressing is unaware of its meaning.

ELAPIDATION *n.* The clearing away of stones. A process commonly applied to the front yards of newly built homes, the kidneys and gallstones of the middle-aged, etc. But wait – there is a second, quite different, meaning here. In zoology, the elapids are the front-fanged snakes – the ones with the venom. So the elapidation of your neighbor's front yard could involve not only clearing it of stones but also strewing it with cobras.

ELDRITCH *a.* Weird or hideous. 'In concluding my report as President on the year just concluded, I want to make special mention – and I know the Committee joins with me in this – of our eldritch member, Mrs. Porringer, who . . .'

ELECTUARY *n.* A medicine that is licked up, as distinct from being eaten, drunk, inhaled, injected, or absorbed. Usually made by incorporating the medicinal ingredient in a doughy or pasty mass. 'And now, ladies and gentlemen, the speaker you have all been waiting for – our own local Congressman, whom I am sure you will welcome as befits your chosen . . . er . . . electuary.'

EMBONPOINT *n.* Plumpness. From the French *en bon point* (in good shape). Often used of women, and with just a trace of raillery implied. Commonly pronounced in the French fashion; but may be anglicized, in which event you would choose a moment when your neighbor, the *zaftig* (q.v.) Mrs. Frobisher, is displaying her new sewing machine to your wife, to tell her how much you admire her embonpoint.

EMPORIATRICS *n.* The science of travellers' health. Embraces such aspects as jet lag, exotic infections, over-exposure to heat or cold, altitude sickness, etc. Next time when you're asking for travel insurance, ask them to include full emporiatric cover; you may get away with it, even with your heart condition.

EMUNCTORY *a.* or *n.* Of nose-blowing; an organ of the body that disposes of waste products. 'Our speaker tonight is well known to all of you. His emunctory achievements are an object lesson for all of us.'

ENANTIOPATHY *n.* A disease or affliction which protects you from another. Similarly, the curing of the latter disease by inducing the former. 'We simply must divert Anthony from his fixation with that appalling Mrs. Sandalbath; why don't we try locking him – sort of accidentally, if you know what I mean – in the broom cupboard with the nice little Miriam girl from next door? She should be adequately enantio-pathic, don't you think?'

ENCEPHALALGIA *n.* Headache. But 'encephalalgia' will look better on a sick-leave application, won't it?

ENCHIRIDON *n.* Handbook. 'I admire your new car, Gregory, but I'd pay close attention to the enchiri-don if I were you.'

ENCOPRESIS *n.* Unintentional defecation. 'Hope it goes well for you at your big performance tonight, Bene-dict! When that curtain rises and the spotlight falls on you – here's wishing you lots of applause, excite-ment, and all the encopresis in the world!'

ENDOPHASIA *n.* Inaudible speech. 'You've got only two alternatives once you get into that witness box, Simon – perjury and endophasia.'

ENGASTRATION *n.* Stuffing one bird inside another. I don't explain the definitions; I only report them.

ENGASTRIMYTH *n.* Ventriloquist. Alternatively, a tall story about how many toasted bagels you ate last night during the horror film marathon. 'And what would little Susie like Mommy and Daddy to hire for her birthday party? A prestidigitator or an engastrimyth?'

ENJAMBEMENT *n.* A literary term, denoting the running on of meaning from the end of one line of a poem to the beginning of the next. 'I don't know, Raelene; I just find Metallica lyrics . . . so *ordinary* after the Stones. Where's all the enjambement?'

EPHECTIC *a.* Habitually suspending judgment; given to skepticism. Like *aporia*, an exceptionally Superior word. The fact that ephecticism generally engenders ineffectualness should enable you to develop one or two phonically pleasing sentences. Alternatively, cultivate its use in the same sentence as *eclectic* (wide-ranging in acceptance of doctrines, opinions, etc.).

EPHEMERAL *a.* Short-lived, lasting but a day. Note that this does not mean trivial – a sense in which it is sometimes used. A devastating explosion is an ephemeral event.

epicedium

EPICEDIUM *n.* A song of mourning sung over a corpse. 'And so, once again, let me express our hopes and expectations to our elected representative for the coming sittings. It is our fondest desire, sir, that by the end of your term we will be enjoying our epicedium here in our little town.'

EPICENE *a.* Androgynous; having both male and female characteristics; hermaphroditic. Derived from the ancient Greek for 'on common ground' and originally used as a grammatical term signifying a noun whose form did not change whether for masculine or feminine gender. A secondary meaning which now seems to be in the process of taking over from the primary meaning is *weak, feeble,* or *effeminate.* It is worthy of remark that a word which means feeble is so similar in structure to *epicenter*, which means the ground above the center of an earthquake. If you wish to upbraid an androgyne, *epicene* is probably the term to be preferred, if only because of its phonic similarity to *obscene*.

EPIGAMIC *a.* Attractive to the opposite sex. Presumably it is a manifestation of the divine sense of humor that so many who are homosexual are also epigamic.

EPIPHRAGM *n.* A secretion which a snail uses in dry weather to seal its shell and protect itself from drying up. The gel which your daughter's boyfriend applies to his hair on Saturday nights.

EPIPLEXIS *n.* A kind of argument that begins by insulting the other person, or by trying to bully or shame him into agreeing with you. 'If only you had the brains of a marsupial, you would surely see that . . .' May bring on a reaction involving extreme emotion; this is called apoplexy.

EPISTAXIS *n.* Superior Person's word for a nosebleed.

EPISTEMOPHILIA *n.* An abnormal preoccupation with knowledge. The curse of the lexicographer.

EPONYMOUS *a.* Giving one's name to a book, an organization, etc. David Copperfield is the eponymous protagonist of *David Copperfield* – a fact which, if only it had been realized by Dickens at the time, might have effectively deterred him from writing the book. Not to be confused with *titular* (q.v.).

EPURATION *n.* A purge, as of officials suspected of treachery. 'Another promotion for Cyprian! He's done well in the civil service, hasn't he, Maree? What will be next? A department of his own, do you think, or epuration?'

EQUANIMITY *n.* Calmness, unconcern. For maximum effect, use in a context where the reverse of this meaning is foreshadowed by the preceding words, e.g., 'I must admit, Arbuthnot, that the prospect of our losing you is one that we all face with no little equanimity.'

EQUIPOLLENT *a.* Equivalent (in size, strength, weight, effect, etc.) 'So what if your father said you could go out with that Mitch boy? You don't for a moment imagine that your father and I are equipollent in terms of household decisions, do you?'

EQUITATION *n.* The art, or the act, of horse-riding. 'Has she shown any tendency to indulge in equitation?' you tactfully whisper to your sister as your pubescent niece leaves the room.

equitation

EREMOPHILOUS *a.* Inhabiting a desert. Condition of someone who has bought a newly built house and then been confronted by the classic choice between having curtains and having a lawn.

EREPTION *n.* Snatching away. Do not confuse with *ereptation* (creeping forth). Snuggling up to your beloved at the drive-in, you say, 'I think I sense an ereption coming on,' and suddenly snatch the M&Ms from her lap. If it transpires that she has put the M&Ms somewhere else, you will be compelled to perform an ereptation.

ERGASIOPHOBIA *n.* Fear of, or aversion to, work; diffidence about tackling the job. Another good word for using on sick-leave application forms.

ERUCTATION *n.* A belching forth. Can be applied, as by Virgil, to the eruption of a volcano, or to the eruption of rashly consumed foodstuffs or gases from the human alimentary tract. See *polyphagia*.

ERUMPENT *a.* Breaking or bursting out through the skin, as do certain fungus spores. 'And when my friends come round here tonight for our pyjama party, for God's sake stay in your room, Jefferson! I don't know whether you realize it, but you're more than usually erumpent today!'

ESCHATOLOGY *n.* The study of the Four Last Things – presumably the opened packet of rice crackers, the salami end, the kiwi-fruit marmalade jar, and the sachet of no-brand dehydrated noodles at the back of the bottom shelf.

ESCHEAT *n.* or *v.* A property that returns to state ownership, e.g., for want of an heir or through confiscation. To so reacquire or confiscate property. (An *encheat*, incidentally, is the revenue from an *escheat*.) Nothing to do with cheating. Unless . . . classroom teacher to the boy in the back row, as she seizes the *Treasure Island Classics Comic* from which he has been cribbing during the exam: 'You cheat; I escheat.'

ESCHEW *v.* To abstain from. In the preceding example, the precocious pupil might reply with a plea for the escheater to eschew escheating.

ESCULENT *a.* Fit to be eaten. 'Ah – as always at your table, Lady Hyperno – nothing in any way esculent tonight, I see. How on earth do you do it?'

ESTOVERS *n.* Those necessities of life that may legally be taken by a tenant for his own use, as for example, firewood from his landlord's property. 'Mum, can we officially declare the fudge brownies in the fridge to be estovers?'

ESURIENT *a.* Of a greedy disposition. The preferred usage is metaphorical, of a person's general character, rather than literal, of his eating habits. Rhymes rather nicely with *prurient* and *luxuriant*.

ETHNIC *a.* Pertaining to race, ethnological. *Not*, as so many seem to think, 'funny little foreign (person or thing),' as in ethnic radio, ethnic knits, or even ethnics.

ETHNOCENTRIC *a.* Firmly convinced that the characteristics of one's own race or culture are superior to those of any other. As, for example, those Australians who believe that Aboriginals should be taught to acquire the traditional culture and values of Western European civilization; or, for another example, those Aboriginals who believe that they should not.

ET HOC GENUS OMNE *phr.* And all that sort of thing. Why say *etc.* when you can say *et hoc genus omne*?

ETIOLATED *a.* Pale and drawn. A fin de siècle term, much encountered in the novels of George Moore. Since the listener can be safely assumed to be unfamiliar with its meaning, it may be used on any occasion at all ('My dear, you look positively etiolated'), the meaning being left to the imagination.

EUDEMONIA *n.* A state of absolute happiness, well-being and good fortune. A purely theoretical concept.

EUGONIC *a.* Living on artificial foodstuffs. Strictly speaking, this refers to bacteria being bred in a laboratory, but clearly the term is applicable also to the male teenager with the fast-food fixation.

EUMOIROUS *a.* Lucky or happy as a result of being good. A term not commonly encountered. 'Nuff said?

EUMORPHOUS *a.* Well-formed. 'Ah, the eumorphous Miss Mullins! Come in, my dear, come in!'

EUTHENICS *n.* The science of improving the condition of humans by improving their surroundings. In contradistinction to *environmentalism*, which is the science of improving the surroundings of humans by improving the humans. Likely to be confused in the listener's mind with *euthanasia*, enabling you to suggest, with perfect innocence, that your mother-in-law ought to be subjected to euthenics; on being questioned, you explain that you had in mind that she move into a modern home unit.

EVANESCENT *a.* Fleeting, vanishing, impermanent. When your wife's weekly number is the Grand Prize-winner in the lottery but you admit to her that you omitted to buy her ticket that week, her effervescence is evanescent.

EVERRICULUM *n.* A fishing net. (From the Latin 'to sweep out.') 'Got everything, dear? Suntan cream, bucket, spade, towel, goggles, flippers, your little everriculum?'

EVITABLE *a.* That which may be avoided. 'Who, me? Accompany you to the mall for white-goods comparison shopping, darling? I think that's absolutely evitable, don't you?'

EXCITABLE DELMA *n.* At the outset, I must make it clear that this is not one of the author's childish fabrications. Excitable Delma is the name of a lizard (scientific name *delma tincta*) found in open woodland or grassland. Called excitable because of its vigorous writhing when disturbed, the Excitable Delma is a member of the Pygopodidae family, i.e., a legless lizard. Treasure this knowledge, because one day, with any luck at all, you will meet a human Delma who happens to fit the specifications.

EXFOLIATE *v.* To remove layers of skin, scales, or similar surface laminations one after the other. 'Would you care to exfoliate your Christmas presents now, Deborah?'

EXIGENT *a.* Exacting, demanding, pressing. Thus *exigency* is a sudden requirement or pressure. Important to distinguish this from *exiguous,* which means meager or scanty. Thus, when one's lifestyle is exigent of resources, but one's resources are exiguous, one shortly becomes indigent.

EXODONTIA *n.* That part of dentistry which relates to the extraction or knocking out of teeth. 'You may think, sir, that you have a prior claim on this parking space merely because you have so aggressively driven your car at high speed across the bows of my own, but I assure you that you will retain this space at the expense of immediate exodontia.'

exodontia

EXOGAMY *n.* Marriage outside of a certain group, as laid down by law or custom. As for example the prohibitions in various societies on marriage to one's close relatives, to someone of the same sex, etc. 'I think in Willoughby's case the principle of exogamy would not rule out marriage to an orangutan, don't you?'

EXOPTABLE *a.* Extremely desirable. 'The next item on the Agenda is New Members. I think we might call on Miss Perkins to stand and read out the list of candidates. Does everyone agree that Miss Perkins is exoptable?'

EXORDIUM *n.* A beginning or preamble to the written or spoken treatment of a subject. Not to be confused with 'exodium' – the conclusion of a drama or the farce following it. Or with 'ex-odium' – absolved from blame, without fault. Sermons traditionally begin with the exordium and end with the exhortium. After which comes the exodus.

EXOTERIC *a.* Intelligible to outsiders, i.e., not esoteric 'I can read you like a book, James; you are totally exoteric.'

EXPERGEFACTION *n.* An awakening. 'Action stations! Action stations! Eight forty-five A.M., and I am about to perform expergefaction upon your mother!'

EXPISCATE *v.* To examine or discover skillfully. Your purchase of this book constitutes an act of supreme expiscation.

EXPOSTULATE *v.* To reason earnestly. One of a group of words (*matriculate* is another) which can be used to some effect, in the right circumstances, as faintly suggestive of acts too indelicate to be referred to explicitly by the author of this book. 'There they were, expostulating under a tree,' etc. Useful for disconcerting Seventh Day Adventists.

EXUNGULATE *v.* To trim or cut the nails or hoofs. 'Mom, it really is too much! I wish you could do something about it; it makes me sick. Richard is in the bathroom, exungulating himself again.'

FABIFORM *a.* Bean-shaped. 'And I'd like you to meet Brett and Wanda, and their children Jamie and Cass – round here we call them the Fabiform Four.'

FABRILIA *n.* A collective term for all the various types of tools used by a craftsman. 'If you leave your fabrilia all over the basement floor, don't expect me to clean it!'

FABULIST *n.* An elegant euphemism for *liar.*

FACETIAE *n.* Facetious sayings. 'Greetings, Herr Doktor! Can I perhaps express the hope that you will tonight favor the assembled company with some of your little facetiae?'

FACINOROUS *a.* Exceedingly wicked. 'I will speak no ill of my opponent in this election campaign. All of us recognize and accept his truly facinorous nature.'

FACUNDITY *n.* Eloquence. Not to be confused with fecundity, i.e., fertility. (But, rather wonderfully, pronounced the same way.) 'Pray silence for our next speaker, Mr. Spinelli, who will give us a demonstration of his impressive facundity.'

FAFF *v.* To dither or fumble (about). This delightful word offers the genteel alternative to 'farting about' that you've all been looking for. 'Stop faffing about, for heaven's sake, and get in the car.'

FALLACY *n.* Deluded belief. The three major fallacies of our time are that green does not go with blue, that wine tastes better than lemonade, and that the most effective type of bowler on a sticky wicket is a slow left-arm spinner.

FALL-BACK *a.* Less satisfactory, but acceptable as a last resort. As in 'fall-back position.' Negotiators typically go to negotiations equipped with Demands, Ultimate Objectives, Ulterior Motives, Acceptable Compromises, and Fall-Back Positions. Not, however, the Superior Person. He is aware that there are, strictly speaking, only two possible fall-back positions – prone and supine.

FALLIBILISM *n.* The philosophical doctrine that it is not necessary for our beliefs to be established as absolutely certain beyond all possibility of doubt. 'No, I think we will take the road to the left, darling, despite all your protestations to the contrary. My fallibilism gives me strength.'

FAMULUS *n.* A medieval sorcerer's assistant. A pleasing appellation for your husband when he is helping you in the kitchen by peeling the potatoes, drying the dishes, etc. – or when you are entertaining. 'Come into the living room and make yourself comfortable while I have my famulus mix some drinks.'

FANDANGLE *n.* (i) Silly fooling around; (ii) eccentric or grotesque ornament or ornamentation. 'Simon, this is Miss Finister, who is going to baby-sit for us tonight. Now I don't want you pestering the life out of her to look at your fandangle all the time, the way you did with poor Miss Parmenter.'

FANFARONADE *n.* Arrogant bragging or boasting, particularly in introducing something. 'The next item, ladies and gentlemen, will be little Cheryl Peabody playing *The Sparrow's Parade*. But first – can we have the usual fanfaronade from Mrs. Peabody?'

FANNY ADAMS *n.* According to both Oxford and Chambers, Sweet Fanny Adams was a famous early-nineteenth-century victim of murder and dismemberment, and hence 'Sweet F. A.,' a reference to something previously existent but now nonexistent. Readers who may have long believed that the acronym 'F. A.' stood for something entirely different now have an excellent justification for its use in civil discourse.

FANTABULOUS *a.* A hybrid word meaning 'fantastic and fabulous.' A similar, more recently coined hybrid is 'humungous,' meaning 'monstrously huge or portentous.' Such coinages are generally found to be in vogue with the callower and flashier members of our society, and tend to be, mercifully, short-lived. They ordinarily reflect a tendency to hyperbolize, and hence are particularly common among public relations officers and salespeople. A printer's representative who called upon the author recently at his place of work, to lodge her firm's quote for a particular printing job, lost all hope of credibility for the said quote when she assured him as she left that it had been 'fabulous' to meet him.

FANTASMAGORIA *n.* A changing, incoherent series of apparitions or fantasms. Late-night television. The Superior Person always spells the word with a *ph*, not an *f*, thus: phantasmagoria.

FARCEUR *n.* Strictly speaking, an actor or writer of farces, but in common parlance a wag or humorist whose japes lean toward the practical. Thus the young Barry Humphries, whose Melbourne exhibition of dada art is said to have included a pair of boots filled with custard and labelled 'Pus in Boots,' could be so described.

FARRAGINOUS *a.* Having the characteristics of a farrago, i.e., a hotchpotch or disordered mixture. Normally one speaks of a farrago of lies, or of half-truths, but there is nothing intrinsically mendacious about the farraginous; nor is farraginosity necessarily a characteristic only of statements (in theory, one could speak of a farrago of dirty linen on a teenager's bedroom floor). 'A truly farraginous effort,' you could say of your Chairperson's preliminary summation of the issues.

101

FARTHINGALE *n.* A hoop skirt or dress distended by whalebone or crinoline. The term dates from as early as the sixteenth century but may still be used to pleasing effect, whether in referring to mid-fifties rock-and-roll attire, which appears to be undergoing something of a revival, or to some aspect of your sister's party dress (should you wish to ostensibly compliment but actually unsettle her). Incidentally, for the benefit of any pedants *manqué* who are wetting their pants with impatience to take me to task for the expression in the preceding parenthesis, allow me to inform you that there is no such thing as the so-called 'split infinitive.'

FARTLEK *n.* Okay, here's one for my juvenile readers. Nothing amuses a thirteen-year-old so much as the word 'fart.' But 'fartlek' has nothing to do with the evacuation of bodily gases. (Did you know, by the way, that the average adult releases one liter of gas per day? Imagine what a senior politician must do to the ozone layer!) Fartlek, for those who are still paying attention, is a method of training long distance runners, whereby the trainee runs across country, alternating speed work with slow jogging. From the Swedish, meaning, literally, 'speed play.' Why not call out from the back of the class, during a quieter moment: 'Miss Adamson, do you know what Smith does every Thursday afternoon after school? He does *fartlek!* For two hours!'

FASCIATION *n.* Bandaging; or becoming bound up. 'I find that you have an overpowering fasciation for me, Mrs. Boddington. Every second Tuesday, perhaps – say, about P.M.?'

FEBRIFUGE *n.* Something that reduces fever. A cooling drink. To be confused – as far as possible – with 'centrifuge,' a spinning machine to separate liquids. 'Excuse me a moment, Reverend Coot; I just need to pop into the laboratory and put some alcohol in my febrifuge.'

felicide

FELICIDE *n.* Killing a cat. 'Mom, do you think it's safe for Cicely to play with Rover? After all, he *is* felicidal.'

FERETORY *n.* A shrine for relics carried in procession. A good name for that small receptacle built into the dash of your spouse's car, just beneath the stereo, where repose the torn scraps of ancient shopping lists, the packet of digestive tablets with just one left, the broken pencil stub, and the crumpled ball of used tissue. 'How should *I* know where the video membership card is – have you looked in the feretory?'

FIMBRIATED *a.* Having a fringe. 'Why are Brooke's boyfriends always so damned . . . fimbriated?'

FIRKIN *n.* A small tub for butter. The author has nothing to say about this word other than to point out that the world awaits the poet who can successfully rhyme *firkin, gherkin,* and *merkin* (q.v.) in the one work.

FITCHEW *n.* A polecat, or kind of carnivorous weasel – and one described by the O.E.D. as 'fetid' (i.e., stinking) to boot. Not a nice creature. A good name perhaps for a politician who is elected on a platform which he or she proceeds to betray as soon as he or she is in office. Come to think of it, a good name for any politician.

FLABELLATION *n.* The use of a fan to cool something. Nothing to do with flab, but everything to do with flabella, a fan. 'And now, my best beloved,' you whisper to your *viscerotonic* (q.v.) innamorata, 'would you care for a little flabellation?'

FLAGELLATE *a.* Sending out long threadlike runners, as for example the strawberry. Suggestive, for obvious reasons, of *vapulation* (q.v.). 'Well, Brother Ambrose,' you say on your annual visit to the old school, 'still having as much fun as you used to with your flagellates?'

FLAGITIOUS *a.* Grossly criminal, utterly disgraceful, shamefully wicked. Perhaps the ultimate in condemnatory adjectivism. Not even a *fitchew* (q.v.) descends to the flagitious. Well . . . not on a good day, at any rate.

FLAPDOODLE *n.* Poppycock, balderdash. Three magnificent words of identical signification, i.e., rubbish, nonsense, empty and meaningless talk. The author much prefers the first, partly because it is the most ludicrous in sound, and partly because of its potential use in alliance with *fopdoodle* (q.v.).

FLOCCILLATION *n.* The action of a feverish patient in picking at the bedclothes during his or her delirium. 'I know your father has been under a lot of stress lately, Bettina, but in future will you *please* try to remember – we don't call in the men in white coats until actual floccillation sets in!'

FLOCCULENT *a.* Covered with soft woolly tufts. Condition of a male teenager's face.

FLUBDUB *n.* A glorious nineteenth-century word meaning 'bombastic language.' Use it together with 'flimflam' (humbug, idle talk). 'Did you hear the Message to the Nation last night? All flimflam and flubdub, as usual.'

FOLIE DE DOUTE *n.* Pathologically obsessive doubt about anything and everything done by the sufferer. At once the most touching and the most charming of neuroses. To quote from *Anomalies and Curiosities of Medicine*, by G. M. Gould and W. L. Pyle (1896): 'Gray mentions a case in a patient who would go out of a door, close it, and then come back, uncertain as to whether he had closed it, close it again, go off a little way, again feel uncertain as to whether he had closed it properly, go back again, and so on for many times. Hammond relates the history of a case

105

in an intelligent man who in undressing for bed would spend an hour or two determining whether he should first take off his coat or his shoes. In the morning he would sit for an hour with his stockings in his hands unable to determine which he should put on first.'

FOPDOODLE *n.* An insignificant fool. From *fop* and *doodle* (the latter meaning, in this context, a trifler or idler). Not dissimilar to *popinjay* and *coxcomb*. The author prefers *fopdoodle*, for reasons similar to those given in the definition of *flapdoodle* (q.v.).

FORFICULA *n.* Small shears or scissors. The Superior Person's word for nail scissors.

FORMICATE *v.* To swarm like ants. 'Principal, I thought you ought to know – the Seventh Grade is formicating all over the quadrangle.'

FORTUITISM *n.* The metaphysical doctrine that chance rules – that things happen according to fortune rather than in pursuance of rational design or principle. 'Well dear, considering the way the twins turned out, I think we must draw all the strength we can from our fortuitism, don't you?'

FOUMART *n.* Heavens, another name for a polecat! Though this one sounds, perhaps, a little less unpleasant than *fitchew*. Perhaps a foumart could be a politician who betrays the platform on which he or she is elected, *and then ashamedly resigns*. But wait . . . there aren't any of those, are there?

FOUR-FLUSH *n.* A poker hand consisting of four cards of the same suit, the fifth being of another suit. This hand has no value at all in poker. When your opponent lays his cards down, showing a pair, if you quickly show yours, calling out 'Four flush' and sweeping the money off the table immediately, saying simultaneously 'Who's next deal?' you just might get away with it. If you do, you will have become a four-flusher, or sneaky bluff-artist.

FRAMBOESIA *n.* A contagious tropical disease, with yellowish or reddish swellings resembling raspberries or strawberries, on the face, genitals, etc. A word of obvious utility for cursing and ill-wishing. The invoking of visitations by bizarre diseases, or by common diseases portentously named, upon those who offend you is an art in itself. Other useful words in this context are *murrain* (infectious cattle disease – metaphorically, a synonym for *plague*), *pellagra* (skin deterioration, diarrhea, and mental decay), *alopecia* (q.v.), *seborrhoea* (dandruff), *quinsy* (an abscess on the tonsil), *rhinorrhoea* (runny nose), *acariasis* (infestation by mites), *parotitis* (mumps), *rinderpest* (cattle-plague), and *malanders* (a scabby eruption behind the knee in horses).

FRIPPET *n.* A frivolous female show-off. Not to be confused (though, let's face it, most of us do during this life) with a 'poppet,' or dear little girl. And *certainly* not to be confused with a 'frisket,' which is the iron frame of a hand press.

frippet

FRONDIFEROUS *a.* Frond-bearing. Condition of the face of the pubescent male.

FROWARD *a.* Uncooperative, contrary. One who fails to agree with the present author.

FUBBERY *n.* Cheating, deception. From 'fub,' meaning 'fob' as in 'fob off' – to put someone off with a slightly dodgy story or excuse. 'Enough of your fubbery, my good man! Tell me exactly what the total price is, including *all* on-road costs!'

FUCOID *a.* Like seaweed. 'And how would madam like her hair styled today? Bouffant perhaps? Or an impish gamine effect? Or perhaps *très* fucoid, *comme maintenant*?'

FUGACITY *n.* Fleetingness, volatility; the tendency towards transience – to changing or moving on quickly. 'It's nice that Maybelle has so many boyfriends, dear, but their universal fugacity is a little worrying, don't you think? Can it be something to do with her dasypygality? I mean, having all that hair down there is not her fault; it's just one of the realities of genetics, isn't it?'

FUGLEMAN *n.* A drill-sergeant or other soldier who stands in front of a group of drilling soldiers so that they can follow his lead; hence, any front-man, spokesman or leader who cuts an imposing figure and compels the members of an organization to dance to his tune. For example, the president of your local school's Ladies' Auxiliary Group – or would this be a *fugleperson*?

FULSOME *a.* Excessive; cloying through surfeit. As, for example, the praise given by a British sports commentator to the performance of the British swimmer who has just come last in the first heat of his event in the Commonwealth Games. Derived from *full*, but applicable only, oddly enough, to praise. One does not speak of fulsome criticism, or of fulsome abuse.

FUMAROLE *n.* A small hole from which volcanic vapors issue. The potential for metaphoric use of the term is too evident to be dwelt upon here.

FUMATORIUM *n.* An airtight chamber used for fumigation. 'If you want your brother, Annabel, I believe you will find him in the fumatorium, or, as he laughably calls it, his bedroom, in a state of substance-induced euphoria.'

FUNAMBULIST *n.* A tightrope walker. 'Political candidate requires qualified funambulist for full-time public relations officer position.'

FUNGIBLE *a.* Replaceable by, or acceptable as a replacement for, a similar item. A legal term pertaining to goods supplied under contract. From the Latin *fungi* (*vice*) – to do (in place of). Your sister's latest boyfriend could be referred to as 'one of Belinda's fungibles.'

FURCULUM *n.* Wishbone. 'Come on, let's you and I do the furculum together.' Knowing your penchant for deceptive language, your dinner-table companion is, for the nonce, nonplussed.

FURUNCLE *n.* A boil or similarly inflamed sore caused by bacterial infection. 'All right then, Harrington; if your principles prevent you from donating to our charity for retired authors, that's perfectly understandable. Off you go, then – and all the very best of furuncles to you, old chap!'

FUSTIAN *n.* or *a.* Ridiculously pompous, bombastic, or inflated language. The essence of fustian is not the use of big or exotic words but the adoption of a declamatory style that is unsuited, by virtue of its high-flown and flowery imagery, or its grandiose delivery, to the purposes for which it is being employed. Thus, any actor's speech delivered at any Oscar presentation ceremony; any address to a public gathering by any union official; any television commercial for any car or laundry detergent; any tourist guide describing any tourist attraction.

FUSTIGATE *v.* To cudgel, i.e., to beat with a stick. 'Don't worry, lady – you can safely leave little Fido in our kennels for the holidays. We feed them, we exercise them, we brush their coats, and we fustigate them daily.'

FUTTOCK *n.* A particular wooden component – the exact nature of which is unknown to the author – in the structure of a ship. A ridiculous word. If you have a yachting or otherwise nautical friend, make a point of always greeting him with the cheerful inquiry: 'And how are your futtocks these days, old bean?'

FYLFOT *n.* Swastika. 'Hoist the fylfot, your father's here!' you cry out to the children as your husband enters the room during one of his more dictatorial moods.

G

GABION *n.* A bottomless basket of earth, used in fortifications and engineering. Do I hear you cry: What use is a bottomless basket of earth? One can only presume (the privilege of the lexicographer, who by definition has no actual expertise in anything at all, let alone fortifications and engineering) that today's gabion is one of those huge iron buckets which are seen dangling from the ends of cranes and disgorging their contents when a lever is pulled to open up their bottoms. Be that as it may, there are obvious alternative uses for the term on the domestic scene. The cardboard carton that you fill with garden rubbish and which then comes apart underneath as you carry it to the corner, dumping wet compost and rose clippings on your good suede shoes. The plastic shopping bag that tears open and deposits your six giant-size glass bottles of soft drink on the concrete footpath – but not until you have got *just* far enough away from the supermarket to make it unrealistic to contemplate going back there to complain. The brown paper bag containing your lunch which you inadvertently place on the one wet spot on the table and which later chooses to give way just as you step off the footpath, dropping your salad sandwiches squarely in the gutter. These are the gabions of our time.

GALACTOPHAGOUS *a.* Milk-drinking. *Galactophage* could serve as a synonym for *milksop*. 'Now listen, you sniveling galactophage . . .'

GALEANTHROPY *n.* The delusion that you have become a cat. Not a *particularly* common disorder, but its mere existence compensates, at least in part, for the fact that so many cats suffer from the delusion that they have become humans.

GALERICULATE *a.* Covered by a hat. 'Here comes Lawrence . . . and, good heavens, he's galericulate! The alopecia must really be getting to him!'

GALIMATIAS *n.* Nonsense, gibberish; confused and meaningless speech. 'And now for our final speaker. Roderick is, as you all know from the panel discussion earlier, a consultant in educational management and someone who is well versed in the theory and practice of galimatias. Tonight his subject is 'Managing Lifelong Education for Articulation Along Its Vertical or Longitudinal Dimension.''

GALLIGASKINS *n.* Trousers, pants, breeches. Originally, loose-fitting wide hose or breeches of the sixteenth and seventeenth centuries, supposedly of Gascon origin. Suitable appellation for your wife's pantyhose, your daughter's *equitation* (q.v.) costume, or your golfing partner's expensively tailored tweed casuals.

GALLIVANT *v.* To gad about, especially with members of the opposite sex. To roam in search of pleasure. A lively word for a lively activity. ('Gad,' incidentally, comes from an Old English word meaning 'good fellowship.') Prepare little cards to leave on your front door, saying 'Gone Gallivanting'; let your unwanted visitors know what kind of a person they're dealing with.

GALOOT *n.* Loutish, clumsy oaf. *Oaf*, incidentally, comes from the same root as *elf* and originally meant an elf-child, a changeling – hence a simpleton or idiot. Galoots, however, are more clumsy than stupid; and there is a suggestion of likability in the term, the impression it conveys being that of a well-meaning but dimwitted show-off who overreaches himself. Use it by itself, without its usual companion *clumsy*, to bring out to the full its rather special charm.

GAMBRINOUS *a.* Full of beer. From Gambrinus, a mythical Flemish king who was supposed to have invented beer. 'Don't worry, darling; while you're away I swear I'll be totally gambrinous.'

GAMMON *n.* Of interest because it is one of those odd words that have multiple meanings, some of which have no obvious relation to each other. (See also *gudgeon*.) *Gammon* can mean:

- A leg or thigh.

- Smoked piece of bacon.

- To talk misleadingly and deceitfully (thus, you could gammon the lady behind the delicatessen counter by telling her how much you admire her gammon).

- The words used when gammoning, in the latter sense.

- The game of backgammon.

- A particular way to win at backgammon.

- To fasten a ship's bowsprit to the stem.

GAMOPHOBIA *n.* A morbid fear of marriage. Clinical psychiatrists bear a heavy burden, knowing as they do, when treating a phobia, that the cure may be more fatal that the disease.

GARB *n.* Attire. A ridiculous word. Derived, believe it or not, from the Italian *garbo*, meaning elegance. Etymologically quite unrelated to *garbage* or *garble*.

GELASMUS *n.* Hysterical laughter. 'Hope the sermon goes well today, dear; and don't worry so much about it – I'm sure you'll get lots of gelasmus from the congregation!'

GELOGENIC *a.* Laughter-provoking. As you line up the assembled family to be photographed on the occasion of their Christmas reunion, you look through the viewfinder and exclaim: 'Ah, good, good . . . Jennifer, would you mind standing slightly in front of Arthur? You're a little more gelogenic, I think.'

GENEALOGY *n.* The tracing of descent from ancestors; alternatively, a particular account of such a tracing for a specific individual or family. In the English-speaking world, all those who take up this pursuit announce sooner or later that they can trace their descent back to Edward III. This should surprise no one with a rudimentary knowledge of mathematics; there are probably one or two well-bred basset hounds who could also trace their descent back to Edward III. What is really surprising is that Edward III seems to be regarded as some kind of ultimate antecedent beyond whom the genealogist does not venture, even though anyone descended from Edward III is also descended from his father Edward II, and so on. The author can guess only that the prudery of the late Victorian age (when genealogy became a family pastime) chose to draw a veil before the memory of Edward II in view of the sybaritic Plantagenet's bisexual reputation and appalling death (see *impalement*).

GENIAL, GENUAL *a. Genial* (pronounced geenial) means warm, cheering, sociable; but it originally meant nuptial, or to do with generation – the genial bed was the nuptial bed. *Genial* (pronounced gennial), however, means pertaining to the chin, and *genual* means pertaining to the knee. Casual references to your genial (pronounced gennial) or genual organs can be quite effective in an appropriate context.

GENOPHOBIA *n.* The morbid dread of sex. Condition of the average male teenager's girlfriend. Or so he likes to think.

GERONTOCOMIUM *n.* An institution for the care of the aged. You could at least *try* this one on Grandpa; he might think it's a new kind of condominium.

GERONTOCRACY *n.* Government by old men. As, for example, the administration of amateur athletics, tennis, swimming, etc.

GILLIVER *n.* A wanton wench. 'What is this "gilliver" you have on your Christmas gift wish list, Morris?'

GIMBAL *n.* A device used on board ship at sea, usually consisting of two moveable rings as seating for a compass or other device to keep it as stable as possible. Also a form of rod holder used in game fishing, consisting of a moveable socket in a protuberance fixed to a belt and hanging just below the waist. 'Daddy, what does Mummy mean when she says that your gimbal would be good for holding a dildo in?'

GIMMACES *n.* Chains used in hanging criminals. 'Yes, Garth, your new gold chain *does* show off your tanned chest very nicely – but somehow I feel you'd look even better in gimmaces.'

GLABROUS *a.* Having a surface free from hair or other projections. Smooth-skinned, smooth-leafed. When introducing a guest speaker who suffers from *alopecia* (q.v.), you could insert into your remarks a passing reference to his 'glabrous pinnacle' without giving offense.

GLEBOUS *a.* Full of clods. The amenities room at your office during the lunch hour.

GLOBOSE *a.* Spherical. Pronounced with the accent on the 'bose.' It seems, somehow, less hurtful to refer to an obese acquaintance as 'globose' than as 'globu-lar,' doesn't it?

GLOSSECTOMY *n.* The removal, partial or complete, of the tongue. 'You're being a little unfair to Mrs. Wambuddy, aren't you? I mean – sure, she does go on a bit – but there's nothing wrong with the way she talks that a little glossectomy wouldn't fix.'

GLYCOLIMIA *n.* A craving for sweets. 'Robert, before you leave those frosted caramels on the kitchen table, please take cognizance of the fact that you are in the presence of your younger sister, a registered glycolimiac, and that I take no responsibility for her actions after sundown.'

GNATHONIC *a.* Obsequious, toadying, parasitical, flattering, deceitful. Yes, all of these at once. From Gnatho, a character in Terence's *Eunuchus*. A good one to use in written references for Upwardly Mobile Young Managers, who certainly won't know what it means and are unlikely to be able to find out. 'Andrew has a pleasant manner, presents well, and has been responsible for the introduction of Mission Statements and Output-Related Performance Indicators in this Department. He has been consistently gnathonic, especially when under pressure, maintaining good relations with senior management and . . . etc., etc., etc.'

GNOME *n.* A word whose special interest lies in its secondary sense of aphorism, maxim, or pithy saying. Thus *gnomic* means either consisting of aphorisms, having the quality of an aphorism, or given to the use of aphorisms. When your sententious employer, a man of less than average height, returns from his holidays and greets you with a particularly pithy remark, you say brightly: 'Ah, you're just as gnomic as ever, I see, Mr. Bolingbroke!'

GNOSIS *n.* Knowledge of spiritual truth and of the deeper wisdom that is concealed from those without the necessary faith or insight. As claimed by the Gnostics. An ecclesiastical *dignitary* (q.v.) who finds himself on a television talk show, defending the faith against the earnest protestations of a pair of agnostics, could suddenly lean forward, as though he had just noticed something, and say, urgently but in a low voice: 'For heaven's sake! Whatever's happened to your gnosis?' His adversaries will spend the rest of the program rubbing their faces with studied nonchalance and worrying about their appearance.

GODWIT *n.* A marsh-wading bird with a long, upward-curving bill. One can only wonder at the derivation; but the potential of the term for the denigration of the sanctimonious is obvious.

GOMPHOSIS *n.* Technical term for the connection of two bodily elements by the firm implantation of one in a socket situated in the other. As, for example, a tooth in a jaw. The potential metaphorical uses of the term are too evident, and indeed too indelicate, for the author to specify in a work of this nature.

GONAPOPHYSES *n.* A collective term for the genital organs of insects generally. 'Welcome to our sorority dance, Dean Archworthy. The refreshments are at the end table; and over there, standing along the wall near the fire exit, those boys are our guests from the fraternities – the gonapophyses, as we call them.'

GONGOOZLER *n.* One who stares for hours at anything out of the ordinary (such as the word *gongoozler*).

GOODPASTURE'S SYNDROME *n.* Pneumonitis with haemoptysis followed by glomerulonephritis and uraemia. Thanks a bunch, Goodpasture.

GORGONIZE *v.* To petrify or paralyze, as if by the gaze of the Gorgon Medusa. 'Mormons at the door, Charlotte – up you get and gorgonize them, quick, before they get started!'

Gorgonize

GOSSOON *n.* A young lad. From the French *garçon*. Somehow the term seems to have connotations of well-intentioned brainlessness, no doubt because of the listener's subconscious awareness of other words that end in *–oon*, such as *goon* and *loon*. Useful for alienating the offspring of unwelcome relatives, etc., by using it in unwantedly avuncular remarks: 'Well, Cousin Henry – and how are your young gossoons these days?' (Also goes well with a pat on the head.)

GOZINTA BOXES *phr.* An item of magical equipment, consisting of two boxes, which though clearly the same size, will alternately fit inside each other – an apparent impossibility. The derivation? Each box gozinta the other. I am not making this up. Ask any magician.

GRACILE *a.* Slender. Not connected etymologically with *graceful*, but the obvious similarity in spelling inevitably has its effect on the impression conveyed, which is thus one of 'gracefully slender.' A beautiful word meriting revivification.

GRALLATORIAL *a.* Pertaining to long-legged wading birds. From the Latin *grallator*, or stilt-walker. A dignified way to describe the gait of your lankier acquaintances.

GRALLOCH *v.* To disembowel a deer. From the Gaelic word for intestines. The existence of the term implies the prevalence of the act, which the author assumes to be one of the pastimes of the English upper classes, along with fox-chasing, train-spotting, and bird-murdering.

GRAMERCY *int.* The Superior Person's way of saying thank you. A graceful archaism well worth reviving. From *grand merci*. Can also be used as an exclamation of surprise, meaning, more or less, 'mercy me!' Equally delightful in this sense. The ideal use is on occasions which inspire both surprise and gratitude, as for instance when there is a sudden power blackout just as your sister has put on one of her Scott Joplin records.

GRAMINIVOROUS *a.* Grass-eating. Perhaps a passable, if slightly unfair, epithet for your vegetarian acquaintances. 'And could my friend see your graminivorous menu, please?'

GRAMPUS *n.* A blowing, spouting, whalelike sea-creature with a blunt head and having teeth only in the lower jaw. The heavy-breathing fat person who sits beside you in the bus. A plausible nickname for Grandfather.

GRANDILOQUISM *n.* A grandiloquent utterance or term; a grandiose expression used in place of a more common one, just as a euphemism is a mild or delicate expression used in place of a blunt one; any word in this book – including, now that you mention it, the word *grandiloquism*.

GRAPHOLAGNIA *n.* A fascination for obscene pictures. 'Well, Reverend, I've been at art school for a year now, and it's been the making of me. I think I enjoy the grapholagnia most of all; it's not as practical as industrial design, of course, but then personal satisfaction is so important too, isn't it?'

122

GRAVISPHERE *n.* The spherical space within which a body's gravitational field is overpowering. 'Watch out! You're getting close to her gravisphere!' you cry, as your friend backs, all unawares, towards a fully-bedizened matron at the annual DAR Ball.

GREGORY-POWDER *n.* A laxative powder, containing rhubarb, magnesium, and ginger, invented by a Scottish doctor named Gregory, who died in 1822, which should surprise no one. 'Mmmm,' you murmur appreciatively as you try the herbal powder your hostess has just sprinkled on your spaghetti Bolognese, 'it's not unlike gregory-powder, isn't it?' Without noticing your triple negative, she agrees happily.

GREMIAL *a.* Pertaining to the lap or bosom. As a noun, according to Chambers, 'the cloth laid on a bishop's knees to keep the oil off his vestments during ordinations.' As usual, Chambers excites our interest and then leaves us in some uncertainty. Why *knees*, when 'gremial' refers to laps and bosoms? Do bishops not have laps or bosoms? Is oiling a bishop's bosom more acceptable than oiling a bishop's knees? And just what exactly is going on at these so-called 'ordinations,' anyway? Perhaps we should set such considerations aside, and merely note that you could quite properly refer to a table napkin as a gremial, especially given its alternative placings – upon the lap or tucked in at the neck.

GRIDE *v.* To scratch, scrape, or cut with a sound that grates upon the ears. An expressive and useful word that deserves to be better known and more often used, especially in relation to the drawing of a finger across a blackboard, or the compositions of serious musicians of the present day.

gride

GRIFFONAGE *n.* Careless handwriting; illegible scribble. When you've picked up your prescription from the doctor and you're paying the receptionist, don't forget to ask if there is a charge for the griffonage.

GROAK *n.* One who stands around while others eat, in the hope that he will be invited to join in. A good name for a female relative's boyfriend. 'How's your galactophagous groak these days, young Jennifer?' you inquire patronizingly.

GROBIANISM *n.* Rudeness, boorishness. 'Heavens, how did you manage to bring up the children to such a perfect state of grobianism? My husband's been working on ours for years but never seems to get anywhere.'

GROYNE *n.* This is the correct term for one of those little wooden fences or brick walls that run down English beaches and out into the water for some distance, as a device to check the drifting of the same. Pronounced, and sometimes spelled, *groin*. 'Shall we get together down by the groyne?'

GUBERNACULUM *n.* A rudder; originally a broad-bladed oar, one of which was placed at each side of the boat. 'Hard left on the gubernaculum! The gubernaculum, Daddy, the gubernaculum for God's sake!' is the cry as your father approaches the door jamb when backing out of the garage in his new Mercedes Benz for the first time.

GUDGEON *n.* One of those rather delightful words that sound as though they can, and in fact do, mean practically anything. A gudgeon can be:

- A pivot at the end of a rod, serving as the base for a rocker or wheel.

- A ring that fits over a hook to keep a gate closed.

- A pin connecting two blocks of stone.

- A pin holding a piston rod and a connecting rod together.

- A metal eye or socket on the stern of a boat, to receive the rudder.

- A gullible person.

- A bait.

GUGUSSE *n.* According to Mrs. Byrne's amazing dictionary, a gugusse is 'a young, effeminate man who trysts with priests.' Can such things be? And can you say 'trysts with priests' three times quickly?

GULOSITY *n.* Gluttony. (See also *guttle*.) It is astonishing just how many now-obsolete words refer to over-eating; presumably this reflects the social mores of bygone days. There are indications of a returning need for a range of terms of this kind, and the Superior Person would be well-advised to equip himself with some of the more esoteric.

GUMMA *n.* Syphilitic tumor. The plural is *gummata*. 'Where's Uncle Andrew now, for God's sake?' you can safely exclaim in the presence of the children. 'In the bedroom again, playing with his gummata?'

GUTTATE *a.* Covered in colored spots like little drops of liquid. Another unkind one for pimply people.

GUTTLE *v.* To eat gluttonously; to gourmandize; to show *gulosity* (q.v.).

GYMNOPHOBIA *n.* Fear of nudity. But – fear of *whose* nudity? One's own or someone else's? And what has this got to do with gymnastics? And why?

gymnophobia

GYNAECEUM *n.* Women's apartments in an ancient Greek or Roman house or other building. A nicely high-flown, whilst slightly deprecatory, way to refer to your sister's bedroom.

GYNECOCRACY *n.* Goverment by a woman or by women; the supremacy of the female. Well, if there's a word for it, it must exist, mustn't it? The ontological argument for the supremacy of women. I'm a believer.

GYNEPHOBIA *n.* Morbid dread of the company of women. 'Desirée, I need your help. The psychiatrist thinks that I'm cured of my gynephobia, but there are certain tests that he feels I must successfully undergo before he can finally pronounce me well again. Now, for these tests I need the assistance of someone such as yourself . . .'

GYNOTIKOLOBOMASSOPHILE *n.* Someone who likes to nibble on a woman's earlobe. Truly, there is a name for everything. This one is reported in the amazing dictionary of verbal exotica compiled by Mrs. Josefa Heifetz Byrne (the daughter of Jascha Heifetz, incidentally). One for the Personals: 'Gynotikolobomassophile wishes to meet woman with large ears.'

GYROVAGUES *n.* Monks who were accustomed to wander from place to place. In modern times, perhaps, any of the various circumforaneous proselytizers who go from door to door – Jehovah's Witnesses, Mormons, et al.

H

HABILIMENTS *n.* Superior Person's word for items of clothing.

HABROMANIA *n.* Extreme euphoria. 'Of course, after my first wife died, I went through a period of profound habromania. . .'

HAEMOPHOBIA *n.* The morbid dread of blood. Most commonly encountered, in the age of the human immunodeficiency virus, in the world of surgeons and nurses – ironically, those whose occupation renders it the most disabling.

HAGIOSCOPE *n.* An oblique opening beside the chancel-arch of a church, to provide a view of the high altar. Sometimes called a 'squint.' 'Ah, at the old hagioscope again, eh, Lachlan?' you might say, on catching your young brother peering around the edge of his bedroom curtain at the young lady who has come to live opposite. 'Be careful – too much of that and you'll have a squint.'

128

HA-HA *n.* A boundary to a park or garden, usually in the form of a fence sunk in a ditch. The nature of the term evidently derives from the consideration that a fence without a ditch, or a ditch without a fence, might ordinarily serve the purpose of a boundary, but a fence *in* a ditch would appear to be broadly comparable, in terms of actual usefulness, with a tower in a well.

HALIDOM *n.* Some readers will be familiar with this archaism through its use in the expression 'by my halidom'; but few will be aware that its meaning is 'holy thing,' so that the expression just mentioned really means 'by my holy thing.' You may care to cultivate the use of the translated version.

HALIEUTICS *n.* Fishing. 'No, I can't claim any great expertise in nonparametric statistics, and I realize their relevance to the selection criteria. On the other hand, I have some twenty years' experience in halieutics, and I'd be looking to build further on that if I were to get the job.'

HALITUS *n.* Exhalation, breath. Easily confused with 'halitosis,' or bad breath. A few of us may have halitosis but *all* of us have halitus. 'Your halitus is a little strong this morning, Reverend; you haven't been out jogging again, have you?'

HAMADRYAD *n.* One of those rather delightful words that have several totally different meanings. A hamadryad can be a tree-dwelling nymph, a venomous Indian snake, or an Abyssinian baboon. You may thus use the word, for example in the latter sense, when insulting a female, but on being taken to task you may if you wish explain that you were using the word in its nymphal sense. Alternatively, you may use the word as an apparent compliment, conveying by your manner the impression that you are invoking the nymphal sense, but at the same time revel in the private knowledge that one of the other senses is the applicable one.

HAPHALGESIA *n.* A condition in which the patient suffers torments from the mere pressure of clothing or weight of bedclothes. 'So, Craig – you are seriously intending to go out to line dancing tonight wearing your cowboy boots, your leather jacket, your trench coat, and on top of that your Russian winter headgear. Why in God's name would you want to suffer all the symptoms of haphalgesia without actually having it?'

HAPTEPHOBIA *n.* The morbid dread of being touched. Condition of . . . (see *genophobia*).

haptephobia

HAPTODYSPHORIA *n.* The shiveringly unpleasant feeling experienced by some people when they touch certain surfaces, such as peaches or wool. 'Yes, I *know* Roger plays jazz piano and earns $100,000 a year; but I can't help it, he just brings out the haptodysphoriac in me.'

HARMATIA *n.* (From the Greek word for 'error'.) A literary term referring to the fatal error, either from moral shortcoming or from ignorance, which ultimately destroys a great man, or woman, in tragic literature. Othello's jealousy, Hamlet's indecision, etc. In the words of the chorus in *Dido and Aeneas*, 'great minds against themselves conspire.' Why not propose, for your next assignment in Media Studies 111A, 'The Role of Harmatia in the Character of Tim-the-Tool-Man Taylor'?

HARMATIOLOGY *n.* That part of theology which deals with sin. 'So, little Sharon is doing Divinity this year! That must be very gratifying for you, Mrs. Mulholland – and she'll be doing her work experience in harmatiology, then?'

HARRIER *n.* A small hound used in Britain for hunting hares. In similar fashion, the good people of the old country use foxhounds to hunt foxes, ferrets to hunt rabbits, German shepherds to hunt criminals, buckhounds to hunt stags, dukes to hunt pheasants, and basset hounds to hunt badgers. A moment's reflection will reveal that, seen from the point of view of the systems analyst, all this is extremely wasteful of resources. What we have here, in essence, is a series of one-to-one relationships. Now imagine the individual components set out vertically in a single chain. We would have a self-contained and fully integrated system in which German shepherds hunted criminals, criminals hunted dukes, dukes hunted buckhounds, buckhounds hunted foxhounds, foxhounds hunted basset hounds, basset hounds hunted stags, stags hunted foxes, foxes hunted badgers, badgers hunted ferrets, ferrets hunted rabbits, and rabbits hunted pheasants. No duplication of effort, no wasted resources; another triumph for the systems approach!

HEALFANG *n.* The pillory. 'Mummy, Amanda and I have made a lovely little healfang in the back yard. Would it be all right if we put the baby in it for a while?'

HEBDOMADAL *a.* Weekly. (The Hebdomadal Council of Oxford University is a representative board that meets weekly.) Surprise the next office management group meeting by suggesting that it is not really necessary for the group to meet hebdomadally.

HEBETATE *v.* To grow dull or stupid. 'Remember,' you say sententiously to the Seventh Grade as they struggle with their arithmetic test, 'he who hebetates is last.' The verb can also be transitive, meaning to make someone else grow dull or stupid – a sense of which it is hard to conceive an example, except perhaps for the action upon the mind of prolonged exposure to radio talk shows. The noun is *hebetude*.

HEDONICS *n.* The science of active enjoyment and pleasure. There's a science of this? Where can I enroll?

HELMINTHOLOGY *n.* The study of parasitic worms. Some universities give courses in this and call it Political Science.

HENCHPERSON *n.* Close and trusty follower. This new word has been created by the author to replace its *sexist* (q.v.) and thus outdated equivalent, *henchman*, which had gradually acquired, over the years, a *pejorative* (q.v.) flavor. Villains have henchmen; heroes have right-hand men – or, more properly, right-hand people.

HENOTHEISM *n.* (i) Belief that God is a hen; (ii) belief that Henny Youngman is God; (iii) belief in one God without necessarily accepting that he or she is the only God. Of these three meanings, the author much prefers the first; the last is, however, the only one accepted by other lexicographers, despite the fact that it seems intrinsically the least convincing of the three.

HERDWICK *n.* A pasture for cattle or sheep. 'Off to the herdwick again, old chap?' you jovially inquire of your civil servant neighbor as he sets off for work in the morning. A nice effect can be obtained with this word by pronouncing it 'herrick,' which is quite inauthentic but *deuced* (q.v.) plausible.

HERMENEUTICS *n.* The art of interpreting the Scriptures or other ambiguous texts. 'Okay, we've got the new mobile phone out of its box, and here's the little fifty-page booklet with the miniaturised ideographic instructions. Charles, you're the one who's done hermeneutics at college. Get to work on it, and we'll see you in the morning.'

HESTERNOPOTHIA *n.* A pathological yearning for the good old days. You know – when World War II was in full swing, your children got diphtheria, and dentists used slow drills and no anaesthetic.

HETAERISM *n.* Promiscuous living and sleeping with women to whom one is not married. Ah, sweet dream of youth.

HETEROMORPHIC *a.* Having different forms at different stages of the life cycle. As for example the caterpillar/butterfly. Or your friend Marion, who goes to the office on Friday in her Dragon Lady With Full Make-Up form and then appears in her back yard on Saturday in her Jumpsuit And Thongs Without Make-Up form.

HETERONYM *n.* A word having the same spelling as another, but a different pronunciation and meaning. To be distinguished from a homonym, which is a word with the same pronunciation as another but a different spelling. Then of course there's a homograph, which is a word with the same spelling *and* pronunciation as another but a different meaning. Enliven the after-dinner conversation by brightly asking: 'Can a word be a homonym of its own heteronym, and if not why not a homograph?'

HETEROSEXUAL *a.* A word that has, paradoxically, come into its own along with increasing acceptance by society of the behavior described by its antonym. Its modern usage is thus essentially defensive. When in receipt of homosexual advances, the correct response is, 'Sir [or madam], I am strictly heterosexual.' n.b. Not to be confused, especially in the context just mentioned, with *bisexual.*

HEURISTIC *a.* Serving to promote discovery. Sometimes used as *highfalutin* (q.v.) jargon to describe the so-called 'discovery method' in education, through which children supposedly find things out for themselves instead of being taught. Teacher trainees – or teacher education students, as they are now called – never find out about the heuristic method by themselves; they are taught about it by their lecturers.

HIBERNACULUM *n.* A case in which to hiberate (i.e., sleep through an inactive period such as winter), put together by certain insects from found materials. 'Pyjama party tomorrow night! Everyone got sleeping bags you can bring? Oh, all right, Candice, your hibernaculum then.'

HIERODULE *n.* Temple slave. 'When I am engaged in creative cuisine, O my beloved, this kitchen is my temple and you my hierodule. So wash the dishes!'

HIGHFALUTIN *a.* High-flown, pretentious (of language). As, for instance, the words in this book. Other lexicographers give the ending *-ing* for this word as an alternative, but the properly highfalutin usage is the ending *-in* – without, be it noted, any following apostrophe. The etymology is obscure, but the author likes to think that the original derivation may lie in the verb 'to faloot,' from the vigorous patois spoken by the early settlers of the Mississippi region – even though the meaning is too indelicate, and its application to the present case too preposterous, for this possibility to be explored in depth in the present work.

HILARODY *n.* Not a misspelling of *hilarity*, but something not far removed from that. Hilarody is a form of ancient Greek mime in whch some great tragedy is made fun of. A burlesque. 'Oh, most amusing! I come home covered in mud after having to deal with two flat tyres in the rain, getting towed away, using all my remaining money for new tyres and waiting for two hours to get the job done. And all you can greet me with is hilarody.'

HINNY *n.* The offspring of a female donkey and a male horse. Less common than *mule* (the offspring of a male donkey and a female horse). The words *tigon* and *liger* have been coined to describe the outcome of an unlikely liaison between a lion and a tiger. *Catalo* means the offspring of a cow and a buffalo; *jumart* that of a cow and a donkey; *yakalo* that of yak and a catalo; and *zebrula* that of a zebra and a horse.

HIPSANOGRAPHER *n.* Someone who writes about relics. 'Well, if you really can't find anyone to ghostwrite your mother's stupid memoirs, why not look up "hipsanographers" in the phone book?'

HIRCINE *a.* Goatish, lewd. (See *abecedarian insult, an*.)

HISPID *a.* Rough with stiff hairs or bristles. 'Have you shaved, or are you still hispid? And if the latter, don't tell me that "it's a statement." That won't wash with me.'

HISTRION *n.* An actor. The adjective *histrionic* today carries implications of exaggeration in acting style, and in the eighteenth century a histrion was someone who played the buffoon. Perhaps well illustrated in the person of Robert Coates, universally known in his time as 'Romeo Coates' because he specialized in the role of Romeo, which he played in a blue silk coat covered with spangles, a Charles II wig and a top hat. In playing the death scene, he would first carefully sweep with his silk handkerchief the spot on stage where he intended to fall; then remove his hat and set it neatly beside him on the floor; then take several minutes in lying down, turning around and about until he had found the most comfortable position. Audiences hysterical with laughter would demand, and receive, numerous encores of this scene. According to Caufield, contemporary reports of his acting style describe him as having 'an inflexibility of limb, an awkwardness of gait, and an idiotic manner of standing still which evoked hysteria even before he opened his mouth to speak.'

HOCKTIDE *n.* Otherwise known as Hoke Day, an annual festival held in the English town Hungerford in the week following the second Tuesday after Easter. According to T. Sharper Knowlson's *The Origins of Popular Superstitions and Customs* (1930), on the Tuesday of the festival the women bind the men. According to my other source, the *AA Illustrated Guide to Britain*, a somewhat more recent publication, a team of 'tutti men' go around town with a posy of flowers on a stick, collecting kisses from the women. Either way, it sounds like a lot of fun. 'So, Miss Purdue, here we are alone together. Did you know that today is Hocktide? We should celebrate it in the traditional fashion, don't you think? Which will it be – the rope or the pole?'

HODIERNAL *a.* Of or pertaining to the present day. 'Do not have any doubts on this score, Arabella; my love for you is hodiernal.'

HOMEOPATH, NATUROPATH, OSTEOPATH, ETC. *n.* So called because of the pathologically gullible, and pathologically talkative, nature of their patients. *Path-* from the Greek *pathos*: suffering, affliction. If you suffer from the affliction of a close friend or colleague who devotes a considerable part of his conversation to lengthy accounts of mysterious ailments cured miraculously by a rather wonderful little *-path* of some kind whom he has discovered in a nearby suburb, the correct approach is to say: 'I'm interested to hear you say that, because only the other day I discovered a rather wonderful little psychopath who I think could do wonders for you.'

HOMUNCULUS *n.* Manikin. A wonderfully offensive word for the modern miss to use in addressing any male of less than average height, especially in the process of deterring unwelcome advances on his part. Happily, there appears to be no feminine counterpart.

HOPLITE *n.* A heavily armed foot-soldier of ancient Greece. The word 'panoply,' meaning an impressive array, derives from *pan hopla*, i.e., the full armor of a hoplite. Who are our modern hoplites? American football players, perhaps? Skateboarders? Ice hockey players? Fencers? Not at all. 'Back, cursed hoplite!'

you might well cry through your open car window at the commuter cyclist who appears beside you at the traffic lights, with his bulbous helmet, his luminous multicolored knee-length Spandex tights, his orange Day-Glo knee and elbow protectors, and his canary yellow stormproof backpack.

HORNSWOGGLED *a.* What Popeye is by the actions of Brutus. Repeatedly so. 'I's bin hornswoggled!' is the doughty little sailor's constant complaint as he is hurled into the air, the water, the nearest brick wall, etc. From the ancient maritime practice of the same name. Though why the term should be applied to the doings of characters who appear to be members of the United States Navy is not entirely clear. (It was, of course, *British* seamen who traditionally hornswoggled each other.)

HOROLOGY *n.* The study of time. Not as easy as you think: have you ever thought really hard about the International Date Line? The actor Patrick MacNee, of *Avengers* fame, told the story of the time his death was mistakenly announced on U.S. television. 'When they rang my daughter, she said that couldn't be right, because she had just been talking to me on the phone a few minutes ago in Australia. They said: "No, he's dead. It's just the time difference."'

HORRIPILATION *n.* A feeling of cold, accompanied by goose pimples and bristling hair. 'Thank you for asking me out, Brent, but I just can't. Please don't be hurt. The thought of going out with you gives me genuine horripilation, it really does; but I've got a prior engagement, I'm afraid.'

HORRISONANT *a.* Sounding terrible. Your neighbor's cornet practice; your son's rap records; almost any modern so-called 'serious' music; and the piano music of Scott Joplin.

HUGGERMUGGER *n., a., adv., v.t.* or *v.i.* This grammatically chameleonic term denotes secrecy, clandestine activity, muddle, and/or confusion – generally all at once. A useful synonym for 'Executive Management Team Meeting.' The author admits to a weakness for such double-barrelled colloquialisms: 'argle-bargle' or 'argy-bargy,' meaning a dispute or wrangle, and 'arsy-versy,' meaning topsy-turvy. Come to think of it, all these terms relate pretty well to the Executive Management Team Meeting.

HUMICUBATION *n.* The act or practice of lying on the ground – more especially in penitence or self-abasement. Some potential uses: *Bank robber*: 'Humicubate, or die!' *Advertisement in the Personals*: 'Gretel – in your home or motel – bondage and humicubation.' *Superior Person*: 'No, Roger, I am not intransigent; all I expect from you is a little humicubation.'

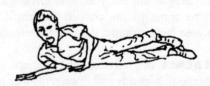

humicubation

HURLEY-HACKET *n.* Archaic and therefore Superior Person's word for a sledge or toboggan.

HYDROPHOBIA *n.* The morbid dread of water. Experienced by rabies victims because of the agony of swallowing. Also experienced by the teenage male, who, offered water to drink, will reject it in favour of any other available liquid.

HYGEIOLATRY *n.* Fanaticism about health. More useful, these days, would be a word for fanaticism about *fitness* – an increasingly prevalent condition, judging by the thousands of goggle-eyed whirling dervishes of our time bounding about in aerobics classes and jogging their way doggedly around what, but for their presence, would be scenic tracks and pathways.

HYLOTHEISM *n.* The belief that God is the whole of the material universe in which we live. An uncomfortable faith to hold, given the purposes to which we put certain objects. And, of course, the existence of cockroaches.

HYPAESTHESIA *n.* Diminished power of sensation or sensitiveness to stimuli. (Alternatively 'hypesthesia,' but no reader of this book would, I trust, ever use 'e' where they could use 'ae.') 'I don't suppose you'd want to come to the concert tonight, Simon? Not with your hypaesthesia, poor dear?'

HYPERHEDONIA *n.* A condition in which abnormally heightened pleasure is derived from participation in activities which are intrinsically tedious and uninteresting. For a case study near you, see any golfer.

HYPERPROSEXIA *n.* The concentrating and focussing of what would otherwise be normal human powers of observation to such a high degree that extraordinary achievements in perception are possible. As seen for instance in the ability of Australian Aboriginal trackers to follow trails which are imperceptible to others. 'I sometimes wish, Damien, that you would direct your powers of hyperprosexia to your schoolwork rather than to the comparative study of zombie film make-up artists.'

HYPERTHYMIC *a.* In a state of morbidly exaggerated activity of mind or body. 'Hmm, I see hyperthymia has not set in yet,' you remark as you pass by your deeply encouched teenager on your way through the TV room.

HYPERTOKENISM *n.* Appointment of a female member of a minority group to a government committee. (See *tokenism*.)

HYPETHRAL *a.* Without a roof, open to the sky; as for example a building uncompleted or partly demolished. A suitably inoffensive descriptor for your balder friends.

HYPNOPAEDIA *n.* Training or instruction during sleep. 'Good morning, class! Are we to start today with the usual half hour of hypnopaedia?'

HYPNOPHOBIA *n.* The morbid dread of falling asleep. Especially when you're sitting right across the table from the guest speaker.

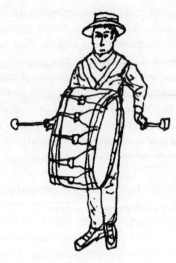

hypnopaedia

HYPOBULIA *n.* Difficulty in making decisions. The real difficulty for most of us, of course, is in making the *right* decisions; but, typically, there doesn't appear to be a word for that.

HYPOCORISM *n.* The use of nicknames and similar familiarities, as in 'honey, I'm home!' or 'good old Charlie Dickens would have written it differently.' From the Greek for 'playing the child.' 'And another thing – do you really have to ask me every evening if I'd like a "drinkie-poo"? I mean, I expect a certain amount of hypocorism from you, but this is pathetic!'

HYPOGEAL *a.* Pertaining to, or occurring in, the earth's interior. A journey by underground railway might be described as hypogeal – as might the daily parking of your car in the subbasement level of the office parking lot.

HYPOGENOUS *a.* Growing on the under side of anything, as for example a fungus on the underneath of a rock. 'Wash those bare feet of yours this instant, young man! You've already introduced enough hypogenous life forms into the carpet to keep a team of microbiologists busy for a month!'

HYPONYCHIAL *a.* Under the fingernails or toenails. 'Sorry to hear the naturopathic herbal treatment's not working, Mavis. Have you thought of trying hyponychial acupuncture?'

HYPOPLASIA *n.* Arrested development. Condition of a collector of empty beer cans, a golfer, a line dancer, etc.

HYPOTHIMIA *n.* Profound melancholy or mental prostration. State of a householder whose electricity bill and rates notice have arrived in the same week. Useful for sick-leave applications, combining as it does an element of truth about the applicant with a vague suggestion of contagious skin eruptions, thereby serving to keep one's colleagues at work at and indeed beyond arm's length.

I

ICK *sf.* The Superior Person should be alert not only to the *conversational* potential of words and word-forms but also to their potential for *written* use. A nice effect can be obtained by the addition of the archaic 'k' to otherwise uninteresting 'ic' suffixes. Thus 'comick,' not 'comic'; 'physickal' (or, better still, 'physickall'), not 'physical'; 'garlick,' not 'garlic.' Mind you, like the garlick itself, this little device should be used sparingly. Once per missive, at the most. You want to gain a reputation as a lovable eccentric, not a laughably bad speller.

IDIOGLOSSIA *n.* A secret language invented by children, or a psychological condition in which speech is so distorted as to be unintelligible. 'Ixnay on the ermonsay, Dad!; your idioglossia's more potent than ours.'

IDIOLECT *n.* A collective term for all the distinctive speech habits that are characteristic of a particular individual. 'Do you think it's really wise for Rodney to drop English? I mean, his idiolect has barely passed the *phatic* (q.v.) stage, has it not?'

IDIOTROPIC *a.* Turned in upon oneself, introspective. The same sense is apparent in *idioticon* (the private possession of someone, something peculiarly the property of its owner) and *idiotropian* (a characteristic peculiar to the individual). In all these cases the presence of the letter *t* is misleading; the meaning is not as in *idiot* but as in *idiosyncrasy*. Nonetheless, it is possible to derive a certain amount of quiet pleasure from the suggestion of ambiguity inherent in these terms.

IGNIFY *v.* To burn or set something alight. 'Yes, I have indeed studied the new draft mission statement and corporate code of ethics, Mr. Malperson; in fact I've had it put up on the section notice board, and I'll see that it's thoroughly ignified.'

IGNIS FATUUS *n.* Will-o'-the-wisp, i.e., the elusive lights generated by marsh gas at night and likely to lure incautious travelers from their path. Literally, 'fool's fire.' Observing Jason and Priscilla arrive, arm in arm, at the party, you whisper to your companion: 'Ah, the fatuous and the *ignis fatuus*.'

IGNOTUM PER IGNOTIUS *n.* An explanation which is even more obscure than the thing it purports to explain. Literally, 'the unknown by the more unknown.' There are two forms – the unintended and the intended. For an example of the former, see the printed instructions for setting up and operating your wife's sewing machine. The art of the latter should be materially advanced by the lore contained in this book, and could well be cultivated by the Superior Person along with the arts of *charientism* (q.v.) and *parisology* (q.v.).

ILK *n.* The final and perfect pejorative-in-a-nutshell.

ILLOCUTIONARY *a.* In linguistics, an act carried out as an intrinsic consequence of an utterance, as for example the performance of a baptism ceremony, or the fulfillment of a promise. 'You remember what I said I would do to you, young man, if you disobeyed your parents and failed to attend Sunday School this morning? And you remember my mention of the word "illocutionary"? You will not, then, be surprised to hear me say now that I hereby baptize you with this garden hose.

ILLUMINATI *n.* People who have, or claim to have, exceptional intellectual or spiritual awareness. Add to these the cognoscenti, the literati, the luminaries . . . why are there so many of these and so few of us?

IMAGO *n.* The final and perfect stage of an insect after it has gone through all its metamorphoses. For example, a butterfly. 'Ah,' you exclaim, as your sister at last emerges from the bathroom, fully decorated and ready to receive her latest *fungible* (q.v.), 'the ultimate imago!'

IMBRICATED *a.* The manner in which roof shingles or, say, fish scales, are laid down in an overlapping manner so that the breaks between them are at least partly covered, protecting the structure beneath. 'Is she fully imbricated and ready to go?' you ask the hairdresser when you drop in to pick up your best beloved.

IMMORIGEROUS *a.* Unyielding, inflexible. 'No way am I immorigerous!' you might shout, over and over again, hammering at the table to emphasize the point, your expression brooking no denial.

IMPALEMENT *n.* Transfixion. Commonly applied now to the transfixion of drunken drivers by steering wheels, but originally the only sedentary form of capital punishment until the electric chair, involving a pointed stake, or *pale* (the latter being the predecessor of our innocent paling fence). 'Beyond the pale' meant 'on the wrong side of the fence' in Ireland, i.e., in the part not under English rule. For an account of a particularly nasty nonsedentary impalement, read Hume's sympathetic and enlightened account of the reign of Edward II.

IMPAVID *a.* Fearless, unafraid. Condition of a Hell's Angel during a confrontation with a lexicographer

IMPECCABLE *a.* Flawless; not able to be faulted. Curiously, although the original sense was 'not susceptible to sin,' the term has come to be used less in relation to human character and morals than in relation to human aesthetics. Thus, 'her appearance was impeccable'; or 'a person of impeccable taste.' (As, for instance, the person who gave you this book for your birthday.)

IMPEDITIVE *a.* Getting in the way, causing obstruction. A little something for that difference of opinion at the traffic lights. 'You impeditive moron!'

IMPERCUSSIVELY *adv.* In a manner free from percussion. After a cursory inspection of the family car's paintwork, you jovially exclaim to your spouse: 'Ah, I see that you drove impercussively today, my beloved.'

IMPOSTHUME *n.* An abscess. Nice eighteenth-century word for a nasty pre-penicillin affliction. 'It's been wonderful having you with us, Martin; "go quickly, come back slowly," as they say in the Gaelic – a lovely saying, isn't it? – and may you have all the imposthumes in the world!'

IMPUDICITY *n.* Shamelessness, lack of modesty. 'You ask me about Briony's potential as a TV talk-show presented? Hmm, let me think. Well, she certainly has all the necessary impudicity. . . .'

IMPUTRESCIBLE *a.* Not subject to corruption. 'It is my pleasant duty to introduce to you all tonight our local candidate for the coming election. Not all of you know him as well as I do, so let me say right away that imputrescibility is totally foreign to his nature. . . .'

INCONVENANCE *n.* Impropriety. The accent is on the 'con,' which helps to avoid confusion with 'inconvenience' – always assuming, of course, that you *wish* to avoid such confusion. 'Madam, for your sake, no inconvenance would be too great.'

INDEFECTIBLE *a.* Not capable of being faulted; not liable to defect, flaw, or failure.

INDEX EXPURGATORIUS *phr.* We all know about the *Index Librorum Prohibitorum*, i.e., the list of books forbidden to Catholics, but you may not have heard of this one. It is the official Catholic list of specific passages which must be deleted from a book before it can be read by the faithful. What a wonderful idea, to have a guide to all the best naughty bits! But where can I get a copy?

INDIFFERENTISM *n.* Indifference as a basic principle or guiding spirit in religious matters. The only religious persuasion (if that is not too inappropriate a word) in whose name no one has ever been imprisoned, tortured, or killed; hence widely condemned by earnest believers. The most disarming and charming of prejudices. 'I regret to announce that the meetings of the Indifferentism Society for the remainder of the year have had to be canceled because of lack of interest among members.'

INDOCIBLE *a.* Unteachable. 'Can't understand why you should have any trouble with 3B, Cartwright. I've always found them utterly indocible.'

INEFFABLE *a.* Unutterable. Only two things are ineffable – a bore, and bliss. 'Sir, you are an ineffable bore.' Indeed, bores are seldom anything other than ineffable. Bliss, however, can alternatively be *unalloyed*.

INELUCTABLE *a.* Inescapable. Note that this is not a synonym for *unavoidable, inexorable,* or *inevitable*.

The sense of the Latin root is 'that cannot be struggled out of.' Thus the conversation of an *ineffable* (q.v.) bore may be avoidable but, if not in fact avoided, may prove ineluctable; whereas the daylong television coverage of a golf tournament may be unavoidable, without being ineluctable.

INEXPLICABLE *a.* Unexplainable. To be preferred because of the effect that can be achieved by pronouncing it, as did Olivier in *Hamlet* ('inexplicable dumb shows and noise'), with the accent not on the third syllable but on the *second*. Note, however, that this requires intensive practice.

INFRA DIGNITATEM *phr.* Always use this, the full version. Never just say 'infra dig.'

INFRASTRUCTURE *n.* A modern piece of cant, of no discernibly useful meaning, much employed by jargonizing social scientists. Respond to its use with the same technique recommended for *structure* (q.v.).

INFUNDIBULAR *a.* Why say 'funnel-shaped' when you can say 'infundibular'?

INGEMINATE *v.* To repeat or reiterate. 'At the risk of offending Mrs. Suddaby, I will now ingeminate.'

INGRAVESCENT *a.* Growing worse or more severe. A medical term used of illnesses, a patient's morbid condition or disease, etc. Suggested for use instead as a faintly *pejorative* (q.v.) descriptive for your less savory acquaintances. 'How's Isidore these days?' 'Oh, ingravescent, I'm afraid – distinctly ingravescent.'

151

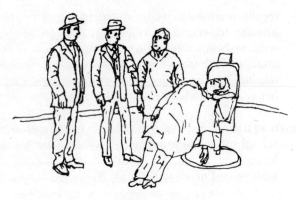

ingravescent

Wider figurative potential too, for example: 'Now that he's elected to office, we can expect him to be ingravescent, I'm afraid.'

INNASCIBLE *a.* Without a beginning. God; the circumference of a circle; and the fame and fortune of a lexicographer.

INOSCULATE *v.* To unite by mouths or ducts. (Or, one assumes, mouths and ducts.) 'Shall we inosculate, dearest? Your mouth, my duct? Or vice versa this time?'

INQUILINE *a.* Dwelling in another's place of abode, as for example an insect occupying a gall already chosen as home by another. 'I don't mind your mother coming to town occasionally to visit us, but I have to say I wish she wasn't so damned inquiline.'

INSENSATE *a.* and **INSENTIENT** *a.* The meanings are related but not identical. *Insensate* means without sensitivity or humane feeling, whereas *insentient*

152

means inanimate, i.e., *incapable* of sensitivity, humane feeling, or indeed awareness. Thus, only a sentient being can behave insensately. 'I'm sorry I attacked Pillburn with such intense rage, Headmaster, but I did so under the impression, based on his behavior over a whole term, that he was insentient.'

INSOLATION *n.* Exposure to the rays of the sun. A useful substitute for *sunbathing*. 'I'll be taking a long lunch-hour today, Mr. Fernberd, if that's all right with you – I'm overdue for my insolation treatment.'

INSPISSATE *v.* To thicken, especially a liquid, by evaporation. 'Excuse me for a moment while I inspissate the soup.'

INTERBASTATION *n.* Evoking as it does an impression of some unseemly form of sexual congress, this word could be useful for the disturbing of maiden aunts – especially since the actual meaning is 'quilting.'

INTERMINABLE *a.* Apparently incapable of being brought to an end. As, for example, a long-playing record of Scottish country dance music, or of the piano rags of Scott Joplin.

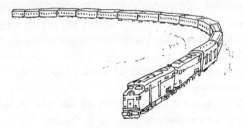

interminable

INTERMITTENT *a.* Literally, placing between; but of course in common use as meaning 'coming and going' or 'on and off' – as for example the lowest setting on your windshield wiper switch. This otherwise commonplace phrase is included here because of the inventive way in which it is used by Oliver St. John Gogarty in *Rolling Down the Lea*: 'Inarticulate sounds of inattention' [from the person to whom Gogarty was speaking] 'told me that I was talking to an intermittent mind.'

INTEROCULAR *a.* and **INTEROSCULAR** *a.* It is quite important to get these right. *Interocular* means between the eyes (as in the case of some insects' antennae) or within the eye (as in ophthalmic surgery); *interoscular*, on the other hand, means mutual kissing, a different thing entirely. *Oscular* by itself means kissing. In fact, come to think of it, what difference can there be between *oscular* and *interoscular*? If it's *oscular*, it presumably must be interoscular – unless your lips are so protuberant that you can kiss yourself. But such things are beyond the province of pure lexicography.

INTERPELLATION *n.* A formal demand made upon a member of a government to explain an official act or policy. How many of you knew you could do that? Get cracking! Lodge those interpellations right now!

INTERSILLENT *a.* Suddenly emerging in the midst of something. 'I'd ask you round to my place tonight, Rory, but my little brother Wilbur is at home, and he's so intersillent.'

INTESTACY *n.* The state of not having made a will. 'Have you heard about poor Arthur's intestacy? I suppose he won't be able to have children now.'

INTINCTION *n.* Delivering both elements of the Eucharist at once, by dipping the bread into the wine. The Superior Person's word for cookie-dunking.

INTROJECTION *n.* A term from the Magic Land of Psychoanalysis, defined as 'the incorporation into the ego of mental images of persons or objects to the extent of being emotionally affected by them.' (Or, in plain English, liking someone or something.) Or, the absorption into one's very self of beings from the outside world, so as to experience oneness with them: 'I don't mind your damned dogs in themselves, but with all those bloody fleas the possibility of introjection is something I don't want to even think about.'

INTROMITTENT *n.* Literally 'putting something into' – more technically, something which has the capacity to be put into, specifically in the context of the reproductive processes of biological organisms. Birds and bees stuff, this . . . need I say more? A reference to your 'intromittent part' could be introduced into polite conversation with your young lady without necessarily giving offense.

INTUMESCENCE *n.* Swelling. Why refer to the high tide, or to the rising tide, when you can use a phrase as glorious as 'the intumescence of the tide'?

INTUSSUSCEPTION *n.* The taking in of foreign matter by a living organism; or the inversion of one part of an intestine, or similar organic tube, into another. Useful, perhaps, to describe your adolescent children's eating habits. And a guaranteed stumper for smart-aleck know-it-alls in spelling competitions.

INURBANE *a.* Not urbane. There are both metaphorical ('uncouth') and literal ('rural') meanings here; seize every opportunity to confuse the two. 'I think it would be probably fair to say about Charlie that, whilst he's . . . inurbane, I don't think it could be said that he's . . . inurbane.'

INVULTUATION *n.* The act of sticking pins into a wax doll to cause pain and injury to a particular person whom the doll is designed to represent. 'Well, dear, let's see. You've tried naturopathy, homeopathy, and iridology, and they don't seem to help. The only option left would seem to be invultuation; would you like me to arrange a little of that for you?'

IOTA *n.* A tiny particle. From *iota*, the Greek letter corresponding to the English *i*. Received perhaps its most charming use from John Barrett, Professor of Oriental Languages at Trinity College, Dublin, in the late eighteenth century. One of his finest achievements was the discovery, hidden away in the folds of another manuscript, of an ancient Greek text of the Gospel of St. Matthew. Barrett had been glancing at a pile of papers when he noticed (in his own words) 'a dear little iota in the corner'. Barrett spoke and wrote ancient Greek and Latin with absolute fluency, but his English was appalling. He lived within the walls of the College from the age of fourteen, and had virtually no knowledge of the outside world, and, from all accounts, no common sense at all. He once had two holes, one big and one small, cut in his door to allow access for his two cats, one of which was big and one small, because it had not occurred to him that the small cat would be able to go through the big hole.

IRREDENTIST *n.* One whose faction advocates the annexation of foreign territory because of its historic links with one's own country. When your beloved's mother icily eyes your faded jeans upon your being introduced to her for the first time, and asks you what you do for a living, you could say that you are an irredentist, and that you don't actually work anymore. She will assume you to be a wealthy orthodontist, and your romance will prosper.

IRREFRAGABLE *a.* Not refragable. Or, if you are so *pernickety* (q.v.) as to require a fuller definition – unbreakable. Normally used of argument or evidence. Something that is incontestable, i.e., cannot be gainsaid. (To gainsay something is to against-say, or contradict, it.) Note that in litigation an irrefragable bank balance always wins out over an irrefragable case.

IRRESPONDENCE *n.* Lack of respondence, failure to reply. Typical irrespondents are nieces, nephews, debtors, appliance service centers, prospective employers, government offices, and literary agents. 'And to my dear relatives, in return for twenty years of irrespondence, I bequeath my pens, envelopes, embossed stationery, staplers, and rubber bands.'

ISOMORPHIC *a.* Being of the same shape and general appearance, but not of the same ancestry, as something else. As, for example, any pet dog and its owner – more especially any show-dog and its owner.

ISONOMY *n.* Equality of civil rights, status in the community, etc. 'I hate to shatter your illusions, Debbie, but this household is not a democracy, nor do you have isonomy with your parents. You will not, I repeat not, be going to the football team's end-of-season party.'

ISOPYCNIC *a.* Equally dense (said of different mediums such as a liquid or gas). 'Who wants Hayley and Harvey on their team? They're isopycnic, you know.'

ITAIITAI *n.* A bone disease caused by cadmium. Said to be derived from the Japanese equivalent for 'Ouch, ouch!' The interest of this to the lexicographer lies in the possibility of forming similar neologisms in English to provide more directly meaningful names for other diseases and conditions. Thus, 'Eek, eek!' for arachnophobia; 'Er, er' for aphasia; 'Unh, unh!' for constipation; 'Ha, ha!' for alopecia; 'Oh, no!' for impotence; and so on.

ITHYPHALLIC *a.* Obscure, impure, indecent. From the phallus carried in Bacchic festivals. The slight similarity of the prefix to *ichthyo* (to do with fish) may enable you to venture upon some little *jeu d'esprit* of your own devising with your Aunt Ethel who keeps tropical fish. In fact, some of the doings of her Egyptian Mouthbreeders, her Kissing Gouramis, or her Slippery Dicks may well deserve the above epithet.

J

JACK-A-DANDY *n.* A ridiculously foppish person. A television chef, an art critic, a society butterfly, etc.

JACKANAPES *n.* A silly, impertinent monkey of a fellow. Authorities differ on the derivation. The Concise Oxford Dictionary links the names of Jack Napes and William de la Pole, Duke of Suffolk in the fifteenth century, whose badge was a clog and chain of the kind used for a tame ape. Brewer offers two possibilities – Jack of Apes and Jack apes (the latter on the analogy of jackass). Webster suggests Jack of Naples, the word *jack* in this case meaning monkey. Goes nicely with *popinjay* and *coxcomb*. When you finally get through to the general manager of the department store with your complaint, you begin by explaining that you have already spoken to a jackanapes, a popinjay, and a coxcomb. You may use the same remark even if you have spoken only to one person.

JACTATION *n.* Boasting, bragging. A specialized – indeed highly specialized – variant is *jactitation*, as in 'jactitation of marriage': falsely putting it about that you are married to a particular person. Both words may be of use in wedding-reception speech-making, but the author leaves the specifics of this to the reader.

JACULATE *v.* To throw, especially a spear or dart. Throwing the used plastic picnic cutlery into the waste bin at the park, you call back to the car: 'Okay, Miranda, I've jaculated, and I'm ready to go.'

jaculate

JACULIFEROUS *a.* Possessing spines like darts. Suitable epithet for a punk hairdo.

JAGUARUNDI *n.* A flesh-eating weasel-like wildcat of the tropical Americas. If you know any weasel-like wildcats, this is the word for them.

JANIZARY *n.* (Sometimes spelt janissary.) In former times, a member of the Turkish Sultan's corps of bodyguards. Originally, these were young law-breakers who had been taken out of prison and trained for their duties. Perhaps a good term for the well-dressed young men with grim faces who crowd around United States Presidents at all times (except in windowless rooms at the White House).

JAPE *n.* A prank or joke. The word has overtones of English public (i.e., private) school humor and the writings of Frank Richards. Should be used in relation to the more tiresome antics of your office comedian. 'This is hardly the time for one of your junior-high japes, Plunkett.'

JARGOGLE *v.* To befuddle or mess up. 'Congratulations, dearest; I wouldn't have thought it possible, but you've found something else to jargogle.'

JAR-OWL *n.* The European goatsucker. I swear that this is the complete definition as given by my source. Goatsucker? Do not write to me or to the publisher to explain this. Neither of us wishes to know.

JAWBONING *n.* Making use of the government's authority and prestige to persuade business and labor to moderate their demands in the national interest. Comparable with an antelope's using its authority and prestige to persuade a lion and a tiger to moderate their demands in the interests of environmentalism. Hence, no doubt, the reference to the jawbone, which is all that remains of the antelope.

JEHU *n.* Everyone knows this term in the sense of a coach driver; but the primary sense is of a furiously *fast* driver. (Pronounced 'geehaw,' by the way, with the emphasis on the 'gee.') 'So, will Daddy drive or will we place our lives in Timothy's hands? What a choice – between the tardigrade and the jehu!'

162

JEJUNE *a.* Short on worthwhile content. A perfect example of the Superior Word, were it not for the inhibitions aroused even in Superior People by the prospect of having to pronounce it not only correctly but casually.

JEOFAIL *n.* A mistake made by a lawyer and acknowledged as such by her to the court. There appears to be no comparable word for a mistake made and acknowledged by a judge; but then, when a lawyer becomes a judge, as everyone knows, she ceases to make mistakes.

JIGGER *n.* One of those brilliant words with a multitude of meanings and therefore ideal for confusing, or at least vaguely unsettling, the person being spoken to. A jigger can be: one who jigs, i.e., dances; a machine for separating ores; a potter's wheel; a small sail; a small mast; a golf club; a billiards bridge; a measuring glass for liquor; a flea or mite that burrows into the skin; or any small device the proper name for which is not known. I love words like this. 'So Megan's into Irish dancing now? Ah, I bet she's a right little jigger!'

JOBATION *n.* A long, tedious scolding; a lengthy reprimand; a tirade. When you find yourself on the receiving end of yet another insultingly patronizing suggestion from Colonel Carstairs about how you could improve the appearance of your yard, you say: 'By gosh, old boy, that's awfully nice of you! Look – next time you come around I really *must* remember to get my wife to give you one of her jobations.'

163

JOCOSE *a.* Having the quality of a joke. Notice that this is not quite the same as *jocular* (joking/in joking mood) or *jocund* (in merry mood). One of Dr. Johnson's eating and drinking companions, the actor David Garrick, grew disenchanted with the good Doctor's habit of imposing heavy witticisms on the gathering, and henceforth, whenever Johnson silenced those around him with one of his pontifical witticisms, Garrick would unsmilingly remark, quietly but audibly, 'Oh, most jocose, most jocose!'

JOLLOPED *a.* Equipped with a jollop, or fowl's dewlap. A nicely jovial term for references to double chins. 'More jolloped than ever, I see, Henry – good to see!'

JUBATE *a.* Fringed with long, hanging hairs, such as a mane. 'I see that you've become even more jubate with the passing years, Willoughby – have you achieved Rastafarianism yet – or are you aiming for full equinization?'

JUGULATION *n.* (i) Interruption of the progress of a disease by dire measures; (ii) throat-cutting. The second use makes this a rather nice companion piece for *defenestration* (q.v.).

jugulation

JUGUM *n*. A yoke for cattle. Also a metaphorical expression for the yoke imposed by Roman rule over its conquered peoples. When your father enters the kitchen after his day's work and happens to ask your mother what she thinks he should wear for the evening, you pipe up: 'A jugum, I should imagine.'

JUKES, THE *n*. The pseudonym adopted by researchers for a real-life New York family who were the subject of a major psychological and sociological study in the nineteenth century. The study took the Jukes, who had an abnormally high incidence among their family members of criminal behavior, poverty, and disease, and followed them over several generations, showing that this pattern persisted through every generation studied. On meeting your new in-laws for the first time: 'Are you related to the Jukes at all, by any chance? No? Oh, it's just that I thought I saw a resemblance there for a moment.'

JUMENTOUS *a*. Pertaining to the smell of horse urine. So says the dictionary. But what could possibly *be* pertaining to the smell of horse urine? And how could it so pertain? Is this word really necessary?

JUSSIVE *a*. A grammatical concept, originating in the Semitic languages, signifying that a verb is being used in a mood (in the grammatical sense) of mild command. But listen, guys: I've used the jussive mood many times, talking to my work colleagues, to my wife, to my children, to visiting tradesmen . . . and let me tell you, it doesn't work.

JUVENESCENT *a.* Becoming youthful. An extraordinary word, when you think of it. After all, no one does this. Why should there be a word for it?

K

KAKISTOCRACY *n.* Government by the worst citizens. For reasons which can only be speculated upon, there is no word for government by the best citizens. *Aristarchy* means government by the best-qualified persons, but the latter are not necessarily the best – indeed, an aristarchy could quite conceivably be a kakistocracy.

KAKORRHAPHIOPHOBIA *n.* The morbid fear of failure. Imagine a sufferer reporting to the clinic for treatment, knowing that the first thing he will have to do, at the reception desk, is give them the name of his complaint. Think about it.

KALOKAGATHIA *n.* A condition or state in which the good and the beautiful are combined. The author's natural modesty precludes his revealing at this time the identity of the only true kalokagathical in our society; but the general absence of the condition in the community at large should not deter you from making some use of the term in polite discourse, for example in ironic references to those who most noticeably do *not* possess the condition. 'Not a very kalokagathical sight,' you might observe wearily, as a panting IRS official, naked from the waist up, jogs effortlessly past you at the lakeside during your lunch hour.

KALOPSIA *n.* A state in which things appear more beautiful than they really are. Presumably love.

KAMALA *n.* The reddish powder obtained from the fruit of an Indian tree so-named. Used as a strong purgative. 'A little kamala on your couscous?' you solicitously inquire of your pretentious *soi-disant* gourmet acquaintance over dinner at the latest preciously exotic restaurant.

KAMALAYKA *n.* A waterproof shirt made from the entrails of seals. You may think not many people would be that anxious to be waterproof. But no doubt it helps the market for entrail-proof undershirts.

KAMICHI *n.* The horned screamer (a South American bird). 'And this is my wife Kay – though her friends and I have an affectionate little Japanese nickname for her – Kamichi.'

KANOON *n.* An early instrument, being a type of dulcimer having fifty or so strings and played with the fingers. A little like a giant-size zither. Your little niece Cecily comes to visit, accompanied by her mother, who as usual insists on the child's showing off her latest party piece on the piano, the seemingly interminable Durand Waltz in E-flat major. 'Ah,' you say, vigorously ruffling the child's hair with your hand – a thing you know she hates – 'in my day we used to rattle off a tune on the old kanoon. Do you know what a kanoon is, little dearie?' Being asked a question she can't answer and being called 'little dearie' in the same breath – both also things that you know she hates – she loses her presence of mind, and forgets the repeat in the Durand.

KATABATIC *a.* In the manner of a downward-flowing wind which descends into a valley from higher ground. (See *williwaw* for a stronger manifestation of the same phenomenon.) Use, perhaps, to describe a tall person farting.

KEDOGENOUS *a.* Brought about by worry, or anxiety. Useful for excuses. 'I'm awfully sorry, darling, but I'm afraid I seem to have another of my kedogenous headaches.'

KEF *n.* A state of voluptuous dreaminess, full of languid contentment. (From the Arabic *kaif*, meaning good humour.) 'No use calling Justin to dinner, mummy; he's in one of his kefs in the toilet, drooling and giggling at his toothbrush. Which I might say he never seems to use, despite having that old tin full of toothpowder.'

KENNEBUNKER *n.* A large suitcase. 'So Meredith is coming to stay next month, eh? And how many of her kennebunkers will she be bringing this time, do you think?'

KENOGENESIS *n.* A type of biological development in which the characteristics of a particular organism are not typical of those normally possessed by the group to which it belongs. 'Most clerical support officers would be able to spell the word "receive," Barnaby, without any difficulty and without claiming stress leave because of the effort involved. But then . . . in your case I suppose a certain allowance must be made for kenogenesis.'

KENOSIS *n.* The theological term for Christ's setting aside his divinity to assume human form. 'Oh, all right, if the rest of the family really wants to go and see *Dumb and Dumber*, I suppose as *pater familias* I must accept the necessity of kenosis and join you.'

KERATIN *n.* A substance found in hair, or fingernails. The author would like to be more explicit, but none of his references identify the actual substance. He can only assume it to be sump oil, sandwich spread, or garden compost.

KERCHIEF OF PLEASANCE *phr.* An embroidered cloth worn by a medieval knight in his helmet, or round his arm, in honour of his lady (also sometimes called a favor). Today's young men could do worse than adopt a similar practice, perhaps obtaining from their girlfriend one of her small handkerchiefs, and wearing it proudly in their lapel, their fob pocket, etc.; taking, of course, every opportunity to casually refer to it as 'my kerchief of pleasance.'

KIBE *n.* A nice, short, simple word. Should be more like it. My dictionary defines this as meaning 'a chilblain, especially on a heel.' 'Medical report for Sixth Battalion, sir: ten men with chilblains – no, make that nine men with chilblains and Major Featherbed with kibes . . .' Why 'chilblain'?, I hear you ask. From 'chill' and 'blain' – the latter being a boil or blister.

KICKSHAW *n.* A gimcrack gewgaw. Three weird and wonderful words that merit a wider currency in the spoken language. *Kickshaw* derives from the French *quelque chose*; *gimcrack* possibly from *gim* (pert) and *crack* (boaster); and *gewgaw* possibly from *give-gove* (present). All mean trinket.

KILDERKIN *n.* A little barrel or cask, about half the size of a normal wine barrel, containing about nineteen gallons. 'A kilderkin for the road, before we part, Jock? Your turn to pay, I think?'

KINDERGRAPH *n.* Photograph of a child. A word which, unlike *kindergarten*, has passed into obsolescence, but which undoubtedly merits revivification in view of the widespread occurrence of the phenomenon in question.

KINEPHANTOM *n.* An interesting one this. The technical name for a phenomenon that we have all seen, have all been puzzled by, and have never known the name of. When you are watching a movie or video of a car in motion, and the wheels appear to be going *backward*, even though you know they must be going forward, you are witnessing a kinephantom.

KINETOSIS *n.* A fancy name for travel sickness.

KINKAJOU *n.* A furry, domesticatable mammal with a prehensile tail. Rather sweet as an outré term of endearment for your beloved. 'Come, my little kinkajou.'

KINK INSTABILITY *phr.* Once again, I have to say at the outset that I have not made this up. Check in any good science dictionary. The potential for metaphorical uses in home, work, and play situations are so evident as not to bear spelling out here. This is a nuclear physics term which describes the bending of plasma, one of the principal forms of instability in plasma. Plasma itself, as every schoolgirl knows, is an ionized gaseous discharge with no resultant charge, since the numbers of positive and negative ions are equal, in addition to unionized molecules or atoms. Do I hear you express doubt about the concept of unionized particles? Then spell it with the hyphen, if you must.

KINNIKINIC *n.* The leaves or bark of certain plants such as the willow when prepared for smoking. 'That? Oh, that's nothing, officer; just a little kinnikinic of my mother's.'

KIPPAGE *n.* Commotion, confusion. 'Rest assured, Mrs. Foskit, that little Jimmy will be completely safe on the school excursion. We don't just put them on a bus and cross our fingers, you know; we have teachers who are especially trained in kippage skills to go with them.'

KLIEG LIGHTS *n.* The interesting thing here is not the meaning (you all know klieg lights are those ultrabright arc lights used on movie sets etc.) but the derivation. They are named after the Kliegl brothers, who invented them. So, in the unlikely event of your ever having to mention klieg lights in casual conversation, why not use the pronunciation 'kleegle'? After the inevitable argument, that should effectively confirm your growing reputation as a scholar and a nut-case.

KNICKERBOCKERS *n.* Loose-fitting pants gathered in at the knee. For some reason as yet unfathomed by the author, the enunciation aloud of the abbreviated form of the word, *knickers*, will make any Englishman laugh uncontrollably. The reaction is invariable, and indeed can be made use of by medical men as an alternative to the patellar reflex in testing the neurological system of an Englishman whose legs have been amputated above the knee. The reflex does not occur in Americans or Australians, and appears to have deep-laid ethnic origins.

KOBOLD *n.* (From German folklore.) A goblin or gnome who lives underground in caves or mines. Your young brother who spends all his after-school hours locked in the basement with his supposedly secret collections of trading cards and magazines.

KOPOPHOBIA *n.* Fear of exhaustion. Otherwise known as Lexicographer's Curse.

KRATOGEN *n.* The dormant area of land lying next to one which is prone to earthquakes. 'And this is the main bedroom. We've had this double bed for twenty years now, ever since we were married. Oscar sleeps on that side, and I sleep here on this side, which I call the kratogen.'

KROTOSCOPE *n.* An applause-measuring instrument. Surely a two-edged sword worthy of comparison with the magic mirror on the wall in *Snow White*, in that those who have the greatest hunger for its readings are those least likely to be satisfied by them.

KURBASH *n.* A heavy hide whip used as an instrument of torture in former times by the Turks. 'Sorry to hear that crystal therapy hasn't cured your chronic fatigue syndrome, Simon; perhaps a course of the kurbash would do the trick?'

KYRIOLOGIC *a.* Presented in pictorial hieroglyphics form. 'Just essaying a little kyriology,' you proudly say to the person who looks over your shoulder at the doodling in your notebook during the management team meeting.

L

LAABA *n.* A storage platform high enough to be beyond the reach of animals. (An Alaskan word.) Also, the top shelf of the pantry, where the kids can't get at the animal-shaped gingersnaps and the packets of colored cake sprinkles.

LABEFACTION *n.* Shaking, weakening, and/or downfall. 'Not in *Who's Who* yet, Carstairs? Even after three years in Congress? Never mind – those who deserve labefaction always achieve it in the long run.'

LABILE *a.* Unstable, liable to change. Essentially this is a technical term from the realms of chemistry, but it has been appropriated by social scientists who operate on the principle that the use of the esoteric term instead of the familiar will lend their writings an aura of scientific prestige (see *paradigm*). The term is thus used to refer to personality or emotion. It is, as it happens, rather nicely suggestive of a combination of *labial* (of the lips; involving compression of the lips) and *nubile* (marriageable – generally referring to the physical condition of young women). Rather a pity, then, that the real meaning is temperamental, moody.

LABROSE *a.* Thick-lipped. (See *abecedarian insult, an.*)

LACHRYMATORY *n.* A little bottle for keeping tears in. Typically a phial of glass or pottery, with a mouth shaped to fit over the eyeball. Sometimes decorated with a picture of an eye. 'And now, viewers, in the face of these allegations, the President is taking out his lachrymatory . . . he's putting it to his left eye . . . the suspense here is enormous . . . yes, he is in fact crying into the lachrymatory!'

LACONIUM *n.* Superior Person's word for a sauna.

LAEVOROTATORY *a.* Counterclockwise. A useful alternative for withershins (q.v.) when your family and friends finally work that one out. 'What do you mean, how do you turn it on? It's a tap, child, a tap – laevorotatory, laevorotatory, of course.'

LALLATION *n.* Unintelligible baby talk. 'Denise, I *must* introduce you to Sandra. You two talk the same language – I know you'll get on marvelously. Stand back, everyone, and let the lallation begin!'

LAMELLAR *a.* Made up of thin scales or flakes. Perhaps a polite way to refer to your friend's unfortunate dandruff problem.

LAMIA *n.* A female demon or bloodsucking undead vampire. 'I think Lamia would be a nice name for the

Harrisons' new baby, don't you, darling? Why don't you suggest it? They're too suspicious of me now.'

LANCEOLATE *a.* Shaped like a lance-head – about three times as long as it is broad, and tapering more gently toward apex than base. Sound like any of your friends?

LANGUESCENT *a.* Becoming tired. Somehow the languidity implicit here bespeaks an altogether superior form of tiredness – a world-weariness, perhaps, brought on by the sheer profundity of your reflections upon the late-night party scene from which you grow impatient to depart. 'Alas, Sybil – time for me to go now; languescence has set in, I'm afraid.'

LANUGINOUS *a.* Woolly, covered with down. 'Son, sit down. I'd like to have a word with you. As you grow, certain things happen to your body, and I notice that already your cheeks are becoming lanuginous. That is why your mother and I have decided to present you with this electric razor. Use it wisely.'

LAPACTIC *a.* An aperient, or laxative. 'What would you like for starters, Colonel? Whisky, gin, soft drink . . . something lapactic, perhaps?'

LAPIDATE *v.* Stone to death. When your mother's well-meaning but interventionist crony Mrs. Planterbox remarks, for the fourteenth time, what a pity it is that your children spend all their time reading instead of having a *proper* hobby, you explain that they used to take an interest in lapidation but have had difficulty in finding a suitable subject – perhaps she might find the time to oblige?

LAPILLUS *n.* A tiny pebble thrown out by a volcano. 'And what lapillus can we expect to emerge from the ferment of your mighty intellect tonight, Herr Doktor?'

LAPPING *n.* The act of privily dropping an object into your lap while seated at a table performing close-up magic. The author not infrequently performs lapping, quite unintentionally, with scrambled eggs – an entirely different effect.

LAPSUS CALAMI *phr.* A slip of the pen. To be distinguished from, but, if at all possible to be used in close conjunction with, **LAPSUS LINGUAE** *phr.*, a slip of the tongue, and **LAPSUS MEMORIAE** *phr.*, a slip of the memory. In short, the Superior Person's way of referring to his own mistakes. Perhaps the famous mistake of Joshua Reynolds, in painting a picture of a man wearing a hat while holding another hat in his hand, could be described as a *lapsus memoriae*. Certainly the mistake made in the so called 'Wicked Bible,' which gives the seventh commandment as 'Thou shalt commit adultery,' was a notable *lapsus calami*. But what sort of *lapsus* was Dr. Johnson's definition, in his famous dictionary, of 'leeward' as meaning exactly the same as 'windward'? Or the American college-student's assertion in an exam paper that 'Louis Pasteur discovered a cure for rabbis?' The musicologist Nicolas Slonimsky produced a whole book full of mistakes in judgement made by eminent music critics. What sort of *lapsi* are the following? 'There has not been an Italian composer yet more incapable of producing a tune than Verdi.' '*Rigoletto* has hardly any chance of remaining in the repertoire.' 'Tchaikovsky's *First Piano Concerto* is as difficult for popular apprehension as the name of the composer and includes long stretches of what seem a formless void.' 'Chopin effects the crudest modulations; while listening to his music it is hard to form the slightest idea of when wrong notes are played.'

LAPSUS PICTORAE *phr.* An expression invented by the author to fit such errors as the following. Next time you see the famous John Wayne movie *Stagecoach*, which was of course set in the nineteenth century, keep your eyes peeled and at one point you will see tyre tracks in the sand. In *It Happened One Night*, Clark Gable leaves his hotel room at 2.30 A.M., drives around New York, writes a story for his newspaper and returns to his room, where the clock still reads 2.30 A.M. In *The Black Knight*, starring Alan Ladd and, needless to say, set in the Middle Ages, one of the ladies of the court turns her back to the camera and reveals that her dress is secured with a zip fastener. In *The Wrong Box*, set in Victorian times, note how many TV aerials you can see on the roofs of houses.

LARGHISSIMO *adv.* Very slowly indeed. The ultimate largo in music. 'If you're really going to try to explain Chinese Checkers to Ryan, take it slow, won't you? His brain works . . . how can I put it . . . larghissimo?'

LATEBRICOLE *a.* Living in holes. Or, if you prefer, in what modern town planners and urban managers increasingly refer to as 'medium density residential facilities.'

LATERITIOUS *a.* Brick-like in colour or general appearance. 'And now a word about the gloom. From the day that my daughter first brought Brad to our house, we have always found him to be lateritious to a fault. . . .'

LATESCENT *a.* Becoming obscure or hidden away, as old-world courtesy in a teenager.

LATIBULIZE *v.* To hibernate. Function of a teenager during that part of the morning when papers are being brought in, cats being fed, garbage cans put out, digital clocks being reset after overnight power failures, etc., etc.

LATIFEROUS *a.* Bearing or containing latex. 'Ah, the latiferous ones approach,' you say, looking out the window at the Halloween trick-or-treaters with their rubber monster masks.

LATIFUNDIAN *a.* or *n.* Rich in real estate. 'If you *must* be multicultural and marry an ethnic person, Lavinia, for heaven's sake be realistic and choose a latifundian.'

LAY FIGURE *n.* It is important to understand that this is not the same as 'layman,' i.e., nonprofessional or nonclerical. A lay figure is a jointed wooden figure of the human body, used by artists for draping material on. Hence it has come to mean an unimportant person or nonentity, or a fictional character who has not been realistically fleshed out. 'Well, we've heard what the experts think about it. Now let's have the views of a lay figure. Gilbert?'

LAZARETTO *n.* A hospital or house for the victims of plague or other quarantinable diseases (originally leprosy). Yes, yet another nice term for your brother's bedroom.

LEMAN *n. Paramour* (q.v.); lover; inamorata (or, for that matter, inamorato – but the female sense, of mistress, has for some reason become the more common in recent times). May be pronounced lemon, leeman, or even, according to one of the author's sources, layman. The first and third of these pronunciations offer obvious opportunities.

LEMNISCATE *n.* A figure of eight drawn lying on its side. An occult symbol for eternity and the mathematical symbol for infinity. But which infinity? The number of odd numbers or the number of all numbers?

LENITIC *a.* Living in quiet waters. The aspiration of the *kakorrhaphiophobiac* (q.v.) lexicographer.

LENTIGINOSE *a.* Freckled. 'Long accustomed to the healthy, open-air life, her beauty is exceeded only by her lentiginosity.'

LEPID *a.* Charming, elegant, amiable. While watching your butterfly-hunting cousins gassing and impaling their catch for the day, you could perhaps engage them in light conversation, in the course of which you might express genteel surprise that lepidopterists are themselves so rarely lepid.

LESION *n.* The Superior Person's word for a scratch, cut, bruise, abrasion, sore, or pimple.

LESTOBIOSIS *n.* Living by furtive stealing; specifically a feature of the ant world in which two species live side by side and one lives by furtively stealing the food collected by the other. Nonplus the kids with this one when they're having their usual fight over the ownership of a packet of chips.

LETHOLOGICA and **LETHONOMIA** *n.* The former is the inability to recall the right word, the latter the inability to recall the right name. The reader who suffers from either (or, like the author, both) of these conditions should practice saying, 'Excuse my lethologica/ lethonomia'; this is distinctly preferable to saying, 'It's on the tip of my tongue . . .,' but, unfortunately, also distinctly harder – in fact, almost impossible for one who suffers from the condition(s) in question.

LEXIPHANIC *a.* Given to the use of pretentious terminology, such as the word *lexiphanic*.

LEX LOCI *phr.* The law of this place. 'I know that hitting your younger brother over the head with an omelette-maker is consistent with *lex talionis*, Evita, but in this house the *lex loci* prevails, and that explicitly rules out omelette-maker attacks.' (*Les talionis*, of course, is the law of retaliation.)

LIBRATE *v.* To oscillate, or swing from side to side before coming to rest. Action of a swinging voter. 'No use asking Adrian; put a simple question to him and he goes into a libration frenzy.'

LIED *n.* Song. German, and therefore, some think, Superior word, but it simply means song, and nothing more. When discussing the *Winterreise* with one of your more pretentious friends, make a point of referring always to the 'songs' which make it up. Ignore the pitying looks. Incidentally, one of the loveliest Schubertian-style lieder known to the author is that by Lord Berners, the distinguished English composer, entitled *Red Roses and Red Noses*. In it, Berners poses the question: which is the better – red roses or red noses? – and comes down in favour of the latter, in the beautiful final lines:

> 'Red noses last a lifetime,
> Red roses but a day.'

LIGNICOLOUS *a.* Growing on wood. 'Short back and sides for the young fellow, Mrs. Paramore? Always best when the hair is lignicolous.'

LIMACEOUS *a.* Sluglike, having to do with slugs. 'Keep your hands to yourself, you limaceous endomorph!'

LIMICOLOUS *a.* Living in mud. 'Looks like those limicolous Kingsley kids are on the way over – better get the hose out.'

LIMINALITY *n.* That part of a *rite de passage* (i.e., an event such as marriage or coronation, marking the transition of a member of society from one state to another) when the moment of transition arrives. 'Father, in the name of liminality I claim the right to join you in your pre-prandial libations.'

LIMOPHOITOS *n.* Insanity brought on by lack of food. A condition occurring in older teenagers after about ten o'clock at night, causing them to do strange things after the rest of the family have gone to bed, such as eating eight slices of cheese on toast while watching rap videos.

LIMPOPO *n.* A river, otherwise known (for obvious reasons) as the Crocodile River, in southern Africa. Alternatively (without the initial capital), the avocado, a pear-shaped tropical fruit, otherwise known as the alligator pear. This usage derives not from the connection between Crocodile River and alligator pear but from the writings of Kipling, whose phrase 'the great, grey, green, greasy Limpopo' is so exactly indicative of the nature of the fruit. The avocado had just been introduced into London at the time Kipling was writing his *Jungle Book*, and his description of the Limpopo is said to have been devised as a private joke for the amusement of two friends in whose presence he had first sampled the fruit in question and found it quite disgusting.

LINGULATE *a.* Tongue-shaped. 'The doctor said my tongue was lingulate, and there wasn't anything he could do about it – then started laughing. Do you think it's wise to keep on going to him?'

LIPOSTOMY *n.* Atrophy of the mouth. Useful term for cursing an overly loquacious sibling: 'May you have lipostomy ere nightfall!'

LIPPITUDE *n.* A bleary-eyed condition. Goes well with *lucifugous* (q.v.) in descriptions of morning-after symptoms.

LIXIVIATE *v.* To leach, i.e., to make a liquid percolate through a substance. 'Like me to lixiviate your coffee, Marigold? No? Oh, well, Instant for you, then – percolated for everyone else, eh?'

LOGANAMNOSIS *n.* A mania for trying to recall forgotten words. Do you remember *lethologica* – inability to recall words – from earlier in this book? Well, you wouldn't, would you, if you suffered from it. But in any event the present word goes rather beyond that; loganamnosis is the compulsive perseverance of a lethologiac to summon up that elusive memory – that maddening word that's 'on the tip of my tongue.' Most people give up after a few minutes; the loganamnostic reduces himself or herself to a neurotic case study in the attempt. And of course, as we all know, it's only when you finally stop trying to remember that you suddenly do remember. Another example of the divine overseer's sense of humor.

LOGORRHEA *n.* Excessive and incoherent talking. 'Who on earth can we seat next to Mrs. Maudsley? And in any case – is logorrhea contagious? Would it be safer to put her at the foot of the table?'

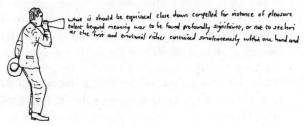

logorrhea

LOGOTYPE *n.* Never say 'logo.' The Superior Person always uses the full rather than the shortened form, the original rather than the modernized.

LONGANIMITY *n.* Suffering in silence over a period of time, while brooding on revenge. 'That's okay, Mom; I accept your decision with complete longanimity.'

LORICATE *a.* Having a hard, protective crust or shell. 'Are you going to go to the Simpsons' barbecue without makeup, or fully loricate?'

LOXODROMICS *n.* The art of oblique sailing. They do it deliberately? 'The wharf's out here in front of us, Ashleigh – not over there to the left.' Could be used, perhaps, as a corrective during family driving instruction.

LOXOGONONSPHERICALL *a.* I have no idea what this word means. It is one of the many bizarre *neoterisms* (q.v.) of Sir Thomas Urquhart, a seventeenth-century cavalier whose fortunes were destroyed by the Revolution and who devoted much of his life to the writing and publication of works reflecting his knowledge of esoteric lore and learning and in particular his highly creative approach to the English language. The word here instanced is from Urquhart's 1644 trigonometrical treatise *Trissotetras*, which is described by the *Encyclopaedia Britannica* as 'impenetrably obscure.' One of the entries in the glossary of this work reads: 'Cathetobasall, is said of the Concordance of Loxogononsphericall Moods, in the Datas of the Perpendicular, and the Base, for finding out of the Maine question.'

LUBRICITY *n.* Lasciviousness, lewdness, oiliness. A marvelously nasty word. Can be used nonpejoratively to mean smoothness, or slipperiness, e.g., of fate – but why waste such an insinuative word on such mundane uses?

LUBRIFACTION *n.* The process of lubricating, or making something slippery. 'Shall we retire to your gynaeceum for a little mutual lubrication, my beloved? After which, who knows?'

LUCIFUGOUS *a.* Avoiding daylight. A botanical term. 'I'm afraid John's not up yet, Mrs. Applecore; he overindulged somewhat last night, and the poor dear is distinctly lucifugous this morning.'

LUCRIPETOUS *a.* Money-hungry. Goes rather nicely with *nummamorous* (q.v.). Both words are suitable for muttered aspersions upon the motives of used-car salesmen, estate agents, funeral directors, and their ilk, when in their presence.

LUCTIFEROUS *a.* Sad and sorry. Suggested conclusion for your primary school homework essay: 'And so we all returned, luctiferous, from our day at the beach.' Primary teachers use only *The Typist's Pocket Dictionary, Simplified Version*, so she'll never find out what you meant.

LUCUBRATION *n.* Laborious intellectual effort; alternatively, a literary composition of a heavy-handed, overly elaborate nature, produced by dint of much burning of the midnight oil. Definitely pejorative in impact, even without allowing for its faint overtones of certain intrinsically unpleasant words such as *lugubrious* and *lubricious*.

LUDIFICATION *n.* Derision. 'Why not send some of your poems in to the paper, darling? Do you good to get a little ludification.'

LUMBRICOID *a.* Like an earthworm. 'I respect your aspirations as a bodybuilder, Gilbert; but as a lover you're just too lumbricoid.'

LUMINARY *n.* A person of great intellectual or spiritual stature; one who spreads the light of truth and beauty around him. As, for instance, the late Albert Schweitzer. Note that not all dignitaries are luminaries, and not all luminaries are dignitaries.

LUNATION *n.* The period of time between two reappearances of the new moon. In other words, pretty close to a month; hence the Superior Person's word for that period. 'See you in a couple of lunations, Mason!'

LUPANARIAN *a.* Pertaining to a brothel. 'Sorry, Reverend, but Billy just feels he's a little too old now for the Boy Scouts. But if it's any consolation, he's thinking of becoming a lupanarian.'

LUPINE *a.* Having the characteristics of a wolf. Everyone is familiar with the use of *feline, canine,* or *leonine* to describe human traits; in practice, *lupine* may well be more useful, as may *vulpine* (foxlike) and *hircine* (goatish).

LURDANE *a.* Dull and lazy. 'Ritchie's results this term were every bit as good as might have been hoped. His lurdanity seems, if anything, to grow with the years – something few of us would have thought possible.'

LUSTRATION *n.* Ritual purification by ceremonial washing or sacrifice. Literally, illumination or making shiny. A nice grandiloquism for spring-cleaning.

lustration

LUSUS NATURAE *n.* A freak of nature; an abnormality. Literally, a sport of Nature. 'And now, fellow pupils, it is my privilege to welcome, on behalf of the student body, our most distinguished alumnus – a *lusus naturae* if ever there was one – Colonel . . .'

LUTULENT *a.* Muddy, thick, or turbid. A good word for term reports and staff appraisal statements. 'Quentin's thought processes are as lutulent as ever . . .'

LYGOPHILIA *n.* Love of darkness. A condition experienced in its most powerful form immediately after one has received the electricity bill.

LYPOPHRENIA *n.* A vague feeling of sadness, seemingly without cause. Mondayitis on Friday.

M

MACARONIC *n.* Every British schoolboy knows A. D. Godley's little poem which begins: 'What is this that roareth thus? / Can it be a motor bus? / Yes, the smell and hideous hum / *Indicat motorem bum!* . . .' The Superior Person also knows that the proper name for this kind of poem is *macaronic*; that is, a poem of a burlesque nature in which a modern vernacular language is intermixed with Latin words or inflections. The derivation appears to be from *macaroon*, which formerly meant not only the sweet biscuit of that name but also (and indeed more so) a coarse, doltish buffoon – or, as we would say today, a crazy mixed-up kid. If you are lucky enough to come across your *galootish* (q.v.) nephew Clint engaged in the consumption of a macaroon, you could quietly make a cryptic observation about the persistence of cannibalism in modern society.

MACERATE *v.* Soften by soaking. 'Oh, Mother, it really is *too* much; Richard's at it again – I wish you could stop him. I can't get into the bathroom. The door's

191

locked, and he's been in there for half an hour now; I'm sure he must be macerating.'

MACHICOLATION *n.* An opening at the top of a castle wall through which boiling oil or missiles could be cast down upon a besieging force. The act of so doing.

MACHICOLATE *v.* To construct these openings. 'I see you've had your hair machicolated as well as colored this time, Kimberley – well done!'

MACKLE *n.* A flaw, stain, or blurred impression. In printing, to mackle is to print in such a way as to produce a blurred or double image. When you come across something which has been mackled in the printing, put it aside and get it out later to use as a test piece when your dear old uncle is boasting about his new reading glasses. Speaking of macklish words, one is irresistibly reminded of the old Scottish saying *many a mickle makes a muckle*. I had always assumed this to mean that many small amounts, if combined, make a large amount; but Webster informs me that *mickle* means a large amount and *muckle* means a large quantity. In other words, many large amounts, added together, make a large quantity. Come to think of it, a true statement.

MACROLOGY *n.* Long and tiresome talk; a *nimiety* (q.v.) of words. A macrologist is thus a bore. When cornered by such a one at a party, you firmly steer him, still talking, to the nearest professor of organic chemistry. 'I'd like you to meet one of our leading macrologists,' you say, and leave the two together, having just given the good professor the impression that he has just been introduced to a specialist in a new field of microbiology.

MACTATION *n.* The killing of a sacrificial victim. 'In welcoming Dr. Fairbrother onto the dais tonight, I want to say that his Office of Meteorological Science can only do so much to help protect us from the ravages of bad weather, of the kind we have all been experiencing lately. The floods may have washed away your crops, your houses, and in many cases dearly beloved family members. But that is not Dr. Fairbrother's fault. His office did not make the floods. In any case, I feel sure that after tonight we can all look forward to a brighter future, and after the speeches we will of course be cementing this happy expectation with our age-old ceremony of mactation, in which we will be asking Dr. Fairbrother to play the traditional central role.'

MACULATION *n.* Being covered in spots. Condition of a leopard or a teenager.

MADEFY *v.* To dampen, wet, or moisten. You arrive, somewhat bedraggled, at the dinner party being given in your honor by your fiancée's mother, having been caught in the rain en route. She commiserates with you, but you brightly respond before the assembled group: 'Well, it could have been worse; I'm madefied, but at least I'm not *macerating* [q.v.].'

MADERIZE *v.* To become flat in taste through absorbing too much oxygen while maturing (normally said of wines). 'Okay – who didn't screw down the top on the soda this time? It's maderized again.'

MAESTOSO *adv.* (In playing music) majestically, nobly. 'Here comes your father, children. Ah, it's his *maestoso* walk tonight! Has he been made a Team Leader at the office? Or has he got a refund on the shirt he bought that was the wrong size?' The use of the standard musical directions for domestic situations has never been fully exploited, and offers all kinds of possibilities. '*Prestissimo, prestissimo!*' when endeavouring to get all three TV-watching children to the dinner table. '*Piano, piano!*' to the same group when you are answering the phone. And so on.

MALNOIA *n.* A vague feeling of mental discomfort. At last – the word we all wanted, to describe the way we feel five minutes after waking up in the morning when we realize that we are about to recall yesterday's unresolved problems.

MALVERSATION *n.* Not, as might seem, an evil conversation, but improper or corrupt administration, especially when in a position of trust. Literally, bad behavior. 'Now, ladies, this is the first confectionery committee meeting for the year, so let's get on with the agenda and leave the malversation till later.'

MAMMIFEROUS *a.* Having breasts. Strictly speaking, all mammals, whether male or female, but, needless to say, more commonly applied in relation to the latter. Like *steatopygous* (q.v.), a word that is not likely to be readily grasped by the unprepared listener. You have arrived at a seaside resort for a bachelor's holiday with your mother; en route to the hotel your taxi passes the local headquarters of the Young Women's Christian Association. 'Excuse me, Mama,'

194

you say excitedly, 'but I think I have spotted some specimens of the mammifera' – and, seizing your butterfly net, you leap out of the cab and send it, complete with mother, on ahead of you.

MANDIBULATE *a.* Pertaining to an insect with jaws designed for chewing. Suitable term for one of those continuously gum-chewing sportsmen. Why do they do it?

MANDUCATE *v.* To chew or eat (with figurative overtones – to 'make a meal' out of something; to worry away at it). 'I will say no more about your behavior last night, Daniel; it has already been the subject of more than adequate manducation by your mother . . .'

MANGELWURZEL *n.* Truly a word to revel in. Roll it round your tongue and belabor your fellow dinner guests with it at every opportunity – that is to say, whenever anything remotely like a root vegetable is served. 'How many of you know that the mangel-wurzel, or more properly the mangold-wurzel, from mangold (beet) and wurzel (root) is a variety of beet cultivated for cattle food?' you might amiably inquire, looking up and down the table and holding aloft on fork's end a piece of sweet potato.

MANQUÉ *a.* Having not achieved a condition pretended to, desired, or deemed suited for. Said of an individual who has failed (for want of opportunity, capacity, volition, or endeavor) to attain a position or role for which his affinity is now apparent from his ersatz performance or from his obsessive speech or behavior. Note that the term does not mean (as might have been supposed from its French derivation) simply the absence or lack of the quality in question. It implies a desire for it, and a longing or regret for what might have been. Thus every forty-year-old layman, but no forty-year-old priest, might be described as a voluptuary manqué.

MANUMIT *v.* To release from servitude, as for example to free a slave. 'Manumission! Manumission!' you cry as your last-born finally leaves home.

MARCHPANE *n.* Never say *marzipan*; always say *marchpane*. The two words are identical in meaning. *Marchpane*, the less common and therefore the preferable one, is derived from the French; *marzipan*, from the German.

MARCID *a.* Exhausted, withered, wasted away – even decayed. Hence the Marcidity Allowance, which is available to civil servants with more than thirty years' substantive service.

MARITODESPOTISM *n.* Ruthless domination by a husband. Can such things be?

maritodespotism

MATRIX *n.* Like *structure* (q.v.) and *parameter*, a term whose constant transmigration between the physical and the social sciences has led to all kinds of misuse and confusion. The primary meaning of *matrix* is a womb, or mold, in which something is engendered – the derivation is from the Latin word for mother. A secondary meaning, in mathematics, is a square or rectangular array of symbols. When a social scientist uses the term in any other sense, always ask immediately: 'Pardon me, but when you say "matrix," do you really mean, in this context, "parameter"?' When he uses the word *parameter* in any sense other than one of its technical mathematical senses, immediately ask: 'Pardon me, but when you say "parameter," do you really mean, in this context, "matrix"?'

MATTOID *a.* Mentally unbalanced with regard solely to a specific subject. 'Wayne and Clark are so sensible in every way; but get them talking about Judy Garland . . .'

MATURATIVE *a.* Conducive to suppuration, as for instance to the formation of pus in an abscess. 'Thanks for the socks, Sis. It's what I really wanted for my birthday. I don't know – living with you sometimes seems so . . . maturative.'

MATUTINAL *a.* Happening in the morning. A nicely ambiguous remark: 'I often think of you as I'm having my matutinal.' Matutinal what?, the hearer, having looked up the word itself, then wonders. And rightly so.

MEDULLA OBLONGATA *n.* The backside of the brain, where it tapers off into the spinal cord. Claimed by plausible neurologists to be a kind of main junction where nerve pathways cross and change direction. Claimed also to be the seat of control for breathing, circulation, and swallowing. Certainly the seat of a distinctive form of pounding agony induced by the consumption of large quantities of tequila the night before. Alternatively (but now obsolescent), a musical term meaning 'with accompaniment played on the medulla.' The medulla was a specially muted lute, developed in the sixteenth century by the notoriously underhanded troubadour Felix von Furchteviel, from whose name comes our word *furtive*.

MEGAPOD *a.* Having large feet. Useful if you wish to show consideration for the feelings of a police officer, while keeping the conversation on a factual level.

MEGRIM *n.* Archaic, and therefore Superior Person's, word for migraine.

MEMBRANACEOUS *a.* Like a membrane; thin, translucent, papery. 'I admire Arthur greatly for the way in which he has presented his case. His arguments, as always, are membranaceous. . .'

MENDACILOQUENT *a.* Speaking lies. Congressmen please note: if you say this quickly enough, on the floor of the House, when characterizing another Congressman (and God knows, in that environment you'll have plenty of occasions for so doing), the Speaker just might let you get away with it.

MENSEFUL *a.* Considerate, neat, and clean. A good one for the Personals: 'Menseful lady wishes to meet ditto gent, view discreet exchange of courtesies.'

MENTHACEOUS *a.* To do with the Mentha genus of fragrant perennial herbs of the mint family, including peppermint and spearmint. 'Menthacity is no substitute for sobriety, Nathan. What did you have more of – the martinis or the peppermints?'

MEPHITIC or **MEPHITICAL** *a.* Stinking, noxious, *noisome* (q.v.). Strictly speaking, foul or poisonous exhalations from the earth or other low-level source. See Frazer's account of the worship of mephitic vapors in *The Golden Bough*, from which the following: 'The ancients regarded the vents from which they [i.e., noxious vapors] were discharged as entrances to the infernal regions. In Italy the vapors were personified as a goddess, who bore the name of Mefitis. She had a temple in the famous valley of Amsanctus in the land of the Hirpini, where the exhalations, supposed to be the breath of Pluto himself, were of so deadly a character that all who set foot on the spot died. The pool is now called Mefite and the holes Mefitinelle. On the other side of the pool is a smaller pond called the Coccaio, or cauldron, because it appears to be perpetually boiling. Thick masses of mephitic vapor, visible a hundred yards off, float in rapid undulations on its surface. The exhalations given off by these waters are sometimes fatal, especially when they are borne on a high wind. But as the carbonic acid gas does not naturally rise more than two or three feet from the ground, it is possible in calm weather to walk around the pools, though to stoop is difficult and to fall would be dangerous.' *Mephitic* is thus a term that should not be applied to an aroma that is met with well above ground level, such as your lanky cousin Gilbert's aftershave lotion, but rather to the effluvia encountered during your annual clean-out of the grease trap behind the garage, a chance encounter with a dachshund, or a trip in an elevator with a short person who is smoking a pipe (see *suffumigate*).

MERACIOUS *a.* Unadulterated, full-strength, pure. 'I'll say one thing about Bellamy – whatever other people say about him – you have to admit that all his sins are meracious ones.'

MERKIN *n.* A pubic wig for women, or, to quote Grose's *Dictionary of the Vulgar Tongue*, 'counterfeit hair for women's privy parts.' Do not ask the author to explain this. The lexicographer's duty is merely to record. To others remains it to remark, with Ambrose Bierce, 'Can such things be?'

MERRYTHOUGHT *n.* Wishbone. A delightful archaism.

MERYCISM *n.* It sometimes falls to the lot of the lexicographer to apprise his readers of strange and fearful things. Merycism is human rumination, a medical condition sufficiently well-established to be dealt with in Gould and Pyle's *Anomalies and Curiosities of Medicine*. Not, of course, rumination in exactly the same sense as applies to cattle and other animals that chew their cud, but *the rechewing of regurgitated food*. A distinguished physiologist, Brown-Séquard, even acquired this habit as a result of experimenting upon himself. Gould and Pyle quote the case of another patient, himself a physician and something of an epicure: 'after a hearty meal the regurgitation was more marked – food had been regurgitated, tasting as good as when first eaten, several hours after the eating.'

MESNE LORD *phr.* (Pronounced 'meany,' by the way.) A kind of middle-level person under the feudal system; someone who rents land from a superior lord while himself having a subordinate tenant. 'Daniel, I know that you pay your mother and myself a small token rent for your room, and that we in turn pay rent for the house; and I appreciate your desire to make your college course in medieval studies "come alive", as you so cogently put it; but *must* you always refer to me as your "mesne lord" when talking to your mother?'

METAGNOSTIC *a.* Beyond human understanding. Instructions for Assemble-It-Yourself furniture, the Menu function on your mobile phone, any Help program in any computer application, the International Date Line, etc.

METASTASIS *n.* Abruptly passing over a subject as though it were insignificant. 'Dad, I wish to raise with you the subject of my borrowing the car tonight. And can we discuss this without the usual metatasis on your part. . . .'

METEMPIRICISM *n.* The science of pure reason. As exemplified in the General Theory of Relativity, chess endgame theory, code-breaking, etc. For a pleasing example of metempiricism in action, consider this true story about Ramanujau, the self-taught Indian mathematician who was made a fellow of the Royal Society in 1918. Terminally ill in hospital with tuberculosis, he was visited one day by a mathematician friend who, for want of anything better to say, remarked that the number of his taxi, 1729, had seemed a particularly boring one. 'Oh no!' cried Ramanujau at once; 'it is a very interesting number. It is the smallest number expressible as the sum of two cubes in two different ways.'

METOCHY *n.* A zoological term, for the relationship between two different types of living creature that live closely together, tolerating but not helping each other. An example is the cohabitation of certain ants with certain other insects. Or in some cases, I am told, a spouse with a spouse.

METOPOSCOPY *n.* Judging character from the appearance of the face. A casual look in the bathroom mirror first thing in the morning will readily demonstrate the fallibility of this notion.

METROPHOBIA *n.* A morbid dread of poetry. It is believed that most cases can be traced back to a specific traumatic incident involving enforced exposure to the genre in concentrated form, e.g., a junior secondary school pupil being compelled to study a Shakespeare play or a Literary Editor being compelled to act as judge in a newspaper poetry competition. Among noted metrophobes of recent times was the lexicographer Ambrose Bierce, who, in defining 'incompossible,' wrote that two things are incompossible when the world of being has scope enough for one of them but not enough for both, giving as his example Walt Whitman's poetry and God's mercy to man.

MEZZOTINT *n.* A kind of engraving made by first roughening the plate and then either scraping away or leaving the rough surface, thus producing various shading effects in the final print. Knowledge of the word is necessary for an understanding of the ghost stories of M. R. James; but don't bother going into the Happie Valley Arte and Crafte Gallerie and asking to see their mezzotints, as this could lead only to confusion.

MIASMA *n.* Noxious atmosphere or emanations. The proper appellation for the air inside a pseudo-French restaurant; in genuine French restaurants garlic is used in only *some* of the dishes. A word wonderfully evocative of stupefying mists, curling heavily and dankly around. Useful not only on entering restaurants but also on looking into younger brothers' bedrooms.

MICROHENRY *n.* Unit of measurement of electrical inductance equal to one millionth of a henry. The author's sources do not make it clear whether the definition is applicable to any henry; presumably it is, but in the absence of a clear reference on the matter, he suggests to readers that they interpret the relationship as applying to an average henry. A microlambert, incidentally, is a unit of brightness, equal to one millionth of a lambert.

MICRONOETIC *a.* With minimal intellectual or cognitive content. 'As Dean of the Faculty of Micronoetic Studies, I welcome all of you to this first meeting of the Academic Board. Now, are we all present? Educational Administration? Environmental Studies? Landscape Design? Catering Studies? Communication Studies? Social Administration? Community Studies? Multicultural Education? Ethnic Studies? Alternative Living Studies? Intercultural Studies? Park Administration? Recreation Planning? Good – now the first item on the agenda is our draft proposal for a new postdoctoral qualification in Bisexual Economics. . .'

MINIMIFIDIANISM *n.* Having almost no faith or belief. Condition of a commuter wondering if the train will arrive on time; of a householder wondering if the power blackout will end before dinnertime; or of a parent wondering if a teenager will place his dirty clothes in the laundry basket rather than on the floor under the bed.

MINNESINGER *n.* A thirteenth-century German writer/singer of love lyrics. What the hell, let's be obvious with this one. Pronounce it mini-singer and use it when referring to *pyknic* (q.v.) tenors.

MINUEND *n.* The number from which another number (the 'subtrahend') is taken away in a subtraction sum. Everyone knows about quotients, divisors, and so on, but not many people know about the minuend or the subtrahend, so use these terms remorselessly at every opportunity.

MISAPODYSIS *n.* An intense dislike of undressing in front of another person. 'My psychiatrist tells me, Mrs. Haberdash, that I need a course of intensive repetitive conditioning therapy to cure me of my misapodysis. This can be done at home in the privacy of a bedroom; but the presence of another person is essential. Could you, perhaps, give up an hour of your time each night to help me with this?'

misapodysis

MISONEISM *n.* A dislike of the new and the changed. Experienced at its most extreme by computer users who have only just mastered the previous disc-operating system when the new one comes out.

MISSION STATEMENT *n.* Not, as might be expected, an invoice received from a religious establishment, but the latest pretentious term from the world of New Management. It means 'objectives,' and seems to be largely replacing the previously popular 'corporate plan.' The comings and goings of the modish terminology of the New Managers, and the array of documentation that the terminology reflects, constitute a potential field of study for a doctoral thesis. A 'Duty

Statement,' for example, is a job description worded in sufficiently elementary terms to enable a dimwitted candidate to apply for the job. 'Selection Criteria' are descriptions of job qualifications worded in sufficiently elementary terms to enable a dimwitted selection panel member to select the wrong candidate. And so on.

MITHRIDATIZE *v.* To gradually make immune to a poison, by the consumption over a long period of increasing doses. From Mithridates, King of Pontus from 120 to 63 B.C., who is said to have so poison-proofed himself. 'No, the spices won't worry me at all, Mrs. Krishnaswamy; after ten years of Maria's cooking, I'm completely mithridatized.'

MOFETTE *n.* A poisonous release of gas from a hole in the ground; or the hole from which the noxious vapors emerge. 'I just know that Nathan's smoking in the basement again! And why those awful Ethiopian cigars, instead of cannabis like a normal person! Talk about your ultimate mofette!'

MOIETY *n.* Strictly speaking, this means 'half' or at least 'one of the parts of something that has been divided into two.' In common parlance, however, it carries a suggestion of 'fair share.' (The common parlance referred to here is, of course, common parlance between two Supreme Court judges or two Professors of Linguistics; the term is not exactly an everyday one – but then that, after all, is why it's in this book, isn't it?) A cute little word. Nauseate your children even further, when carving the roast beef, slicing the birthday cake, etc., with an unctuous reference to your intention that each shall receive his or her moiety.

MOKADOR *n.* A napkin or handkerchief, more especially for tucking into the collar to receive food droppings. In short, a bib. 'Scrambled eggs this morning – better get out your mokador, darling!'

MOLENDINACEOUS *a.* Like a windmill. Mode of motion of two post-pubertal teenagers vying to be first to get downstairs, into the car, etc.

MOLIMINOUS *a.* Momentous; of great bulk or importance; laborious in the execution and of great consequence in the finished form. As, for example, the present book. Generally applied to objects or enterprises, but could be jocularly applied to your employer, your mother-in-law, your bank manager, etc., as appropriate.

MONANDROUS *a.* Having one male mate at a time. Note that it is quite possible to be both monandrous and promiscuous, depending on the length of the time in question. 'Is she promiscuous? Well, let's put it this way – it's a miracle she's monandrous at any one moment.'

MONOGLOT *n.* Someone who is fluent in only one language. 'I'm sorry, Janita, but I'll have to refrain from indulging in the jellied lambs' brains; I have this medical problem, you see – I'm a monoglot, and. . .'

MONOPLEGIA *n.* Impressive medical name for writer's cramp. Overtaken, now that the pen has been replaced by the computer, by osteoarthritis of the small joints – especially if, like most authors, you use only two fingers.

MONSTRANCE *n.* The ornamental receptacle which is used to display the consecrated host to the congregation. Passing over the obvious opportunities for jokes about monsters and TV talk-show hosts, the responsible lexicographer can only point out that the derivation is the same as that of 'demonstrate' (*monstrare*, to show) and invite the reader to develop his or her own whimsical use for the term. *Use*, please note, not *usage*; it is amazing how many people think the two words having the same meaning. The one means what it says – use – and the other means commonality of use. Unfortunately, the Big Is Better syndrome (see *pressurize*) is constantly pushing us to use the bigger of the available variants for any term, regardless of such considerations as nicety of meaning.

MONTICULOUS *a.* Having small projections. From 'monticulus' – a small rise or elevation. A suitable and, ultimately, necessary alternative for *papuliferous* (q.v., pimply); your adolescent son is bound to find out sooner or later what you mean by that one.

MOROLOGY *n.* In speech or writing, being deliberately foolish or nonsensical as a means of achieving a desired effect. A technique not often employed by the present author, who ordinarily makes his effects by being *accidentally* foolish or nonsensical.

MOROSIS *n.* Imbecility. 'Why Belinda, the way you've done up the lounge room is just wonderful! It has this quality of . . . what the Portuguese call "morosis," I think. No one but you could have done it!'

MOUNSTER *n.* Old-fashioned form of 'monster.' 'So good that young Lavinia is learning to ride a horse now. Look at them now; what a pair they make – mount and mounster.'

MOUNTEBANK *n.* Spectacular charlatan. One who, in olden times, mounted a banco, or bench, to attract the attention of his audience. A little-known synonym is *saltimbanco* – the derivation being based on the same principle, *saltatio* being the Latin for a jump or leap. The difficulty of forming new words as easily as this today can be gauged from the fact that the charlatan who wishes to display his wares now does not mount a bench, but solicits a guest appearance on a daytime television talk show.

MOZETTA *n.* A kind of cowled coat worn by prelates in the Catholic Church. 'One thing I always say – it's not a proper pizza without mozetta.'

MUCILAGE *n.* The Superior Person does not use gum, glue, or paste. He or she uses mucilage.

MULIEBRITY *n.* The quality of being womanly; softness, femininity. The female equivalent of virility. Not to be confused with *mulishness*.

MULTILOQUOUS *a.* Very talkative. Goes well with *macrologist* (q.v.). *Pauciloquous* is the antonym.

MUMBLECRUST *n.* A toothless one; more figuratively, an old beggar. 'And another thing – I'm fed up with having those mumblecrust relatives of yours around the place at all hours!'

MUNDUNGUS *n.* Bad-smelling tobacco. Not, as one might expect, from *dung,* but from *mondongo* (Spanish for tripe). An archaism largely unknown today, but worth reviving as a synonym for pipe tobacco. When your pipe-smoking colleague enters your room, you say: 'Ah, still using the old mundungus, eh?' He cuts his visit short in order to go and look up the word while he can still remember it. Meanwhile you turn to your office copy of this book, to find a suitable word for his next visit.

MURCID *a.* Slothful, shirking work or duty. 'Well, Grandpa, when I leave school I plan to do a university course while working part-time. In the medium to longer term, of course, I aspire to full-time murcidity.'

MUSCID *a.* Pertaining to a housefly. 'He's an irresponsible muckraker. His behavior is positively muscid.'

MUSOPHOBIA *n.* The morbid dread of mice. Supposedly a condition of the female human, thugh not of any female known to the present author.

MUSQUASH *n.* A muskrat. 'So, you're a vegetarian, Bronwyn? Perhaps then you'd like a little musquash with your pumpkin?'

MUSSITATION *n.* Murmuring, grumbling. The sounds of a sulking teenager.

MYCOID *a.* Like a fungus. Appearance of (*a*) unwashed socks found under teenager's bed after three weeks, or (*b*) unshaven face of teenage daughter's first boyfriend.

MYCOPHAGY *n.* The eating of fungi. 'Mushroom soup, anyone? What, no mycophagists here?'

MYSOPHOBIA *n.* The morbid dread of contamination, e.g., from contact with dirt. 'We simply must have a heart-to-heart talk with Amphibia. Being a little fastidious about entering Liam's room is one thing; but this thing she has about spraying all of us with bleach aerosol whenever she comes into the family room – it's mysophobia gone mad.'

mysophobia

MYSTAGOGUE *n.* One who instructs in mystical or arcane lore and doctrines. Originally one who prepared candidates for initiation into the Eleusinian mysteries or other secret religious rites of the ancients. Nowadays, perhaps, one who demonstrates electronic organs in music shops.

211

MYTHOMANIA *n.* Pathological and continued lying in which the person concerned actually believes his or her own lies. It is thought that many cult leaders, politicians, and alternative healing practitioners reach this stage of affliction.

MYTHOPOEIA *n.* The deliberate and knowing creation of myth. 'Well, we've heard your account of what happened at the office Christmas party. So much for the mythopoeia. Now – let's have the real story!'

NACKET *n.* Superior Person's word for a tennis ball-boy.

NAPALM *n.* Everyone now knows what napalm is, but did you know that the word is an abbreviation of 'naphthenate palmitate'? Of course you didn't. Nor does your neighbor – the one with the three German shepherds in his back yard. 'Yes, I've noticed the dogs seem to be very restless after dark these days, Bill. Have you tried naphthenate palmitate? I hear it's very good for that sort of thing.'

NAPIFORM *a.* Shaped like a turnip. (See *abecedarian insult, an.*)

NARAPOIA *n.* A mental illness in which the sufferer believes that he is following someone, and that people are out to do him good. The credit for this delightful *neoterism* (q.v.) does not rest with this lexicographer, but with a science-fiction writer whose name, alas, I can no longer recall.

NASUTE *a.* Having an acute sense of smell. Do your best to arrange a blind date for such a person with a *tragomaschaliac* (q.v.).

NATATORIUM *n.* An indoor swimming pool. 'If and when your brother surfaces from his seclusion in the bathroom and joins you at the TV, kindly inform him that the receptacle in which he has been so audibly disporting himself is a bath, not a natatorium.'

NATTERJACK *n.* A curiously warty, pop-eyed toad, with a bright yellow line down its back. The word is useful for the simple Insult Concealed.

NAUMACHIA *n.* A mock naval battle presented as a spectacle in ancient Rome. In modern times, a nice grandiloquism for water polo.

NAUPATHIA *n.* The recommended grandiloquism for seasickness. (See also *kinetosis*.)

NECESSITARIANISM *n.* A highfalutin word for determinism, i.e., the doctrine of inevitability of action resulting from a combination of hereditary and environmental influences. The opposite of the concept of free will. This puts the children of two necessitarianists in a peculiarly favorable position. 'Yes, Mama, I know that I hit little Eric over the head with the vertical grill, and that he did lose consciousness for a moment, and, yes, that in falling he did break an ankle and also your Spode tureen. But Mama, as a necessitarianist you will appreciate that none of this is the result of an act of free will on my part. Indeed, it would seem that you and Papa, as my progenitors and the creators of my developmental environment, have a heavy responsibility to bear for what has happened. . .'

NECRENCEPHALUS *n.* Softening of the brain. Superior insult word.

NECROMIMESIS *n.* A morbid mental state in which the sufferer believes himself to be dead. Not as common as the reverse condition, in which the sufferers believe themselves to be alive.

NECROMORPHOUS *a.* Feigning death to deter an aggressor. This would explain a lot about the behavior of counter staff in government departments.

necromorphous

NEFANDOUS *a.* Unspeakable, unutterable. Usually associated with a noun indicative of wickedness: nefandous villainy, nefandous lechery, nefandous pipe-smoking, etc. The author prefers to associate it with *nefarious*, and speak of nefandous nefariousness. This is even more confusing than it sounds, because the etymology of the two words overlaps. The former comes from the Latin *ne* (not) and *fari* (to speak), and the latter from the Latin *ne* (not) and *fas* (divine law) – but *fas* itself is in turn related to *fari*. You might like to take time out to explain this to the listener when you use either word – especially if he is a pipe-smoker, since the chances are that before you have finished he will simply go away.

NEOPHOBIA *n.* The morbid dread of anything new. The nineteenth-century writer Samuel Rogers once said that whenever a new book came out, he made a point of reading an old one. A sentiment shared by the present author. When *Angela's Ashes* came out, I at once read *The Tenant of Wildfell Hall*.

NEOTENY *n.* An indefinite prolongation of the period of immaturity, with the retention of infantile or juvenile qualities into adulthood. Classic condition of the sports commentator, the lexicographer, and of course the schoolteacher.

NEOTERISM *n.* That which is new, and especially the invention of new words, or a particular newly coined word (the latter being also known as a *neologism*). For example, when Sir Thomas Urquhart (see *loxogononsphericall*) published his translation of Rabelais, he enriched the text by expanding a list of nine animal sounds to seventy-one, including the curking of quails, the nuzzing of camels, the smuttering of monkeys, the charming of beagles, the drintling of turkeys, the boing of buffaloes, the coniating of storks, the gueriating of apes, and the crouting of cormorants.

NEPENTHE *n.* Something that brings forgetfulness of sorrow and suffering. The perfect brand name for a new liqueur.

NEPHANALYSIS *n.* The analysis of cloud patterns. 'One day, Sis, you must do some nephanalysis on that stuff you spray on your hair; might be something in there to control the Bronze Orange Bug.'

NEPHELIGENOUS *a.* Producing clouds of smoke. From the Greek word for cloud. A suitably stern epithet for a pipe-smoker. Nephelology is the study of clouds. A nephelolater is an admirer of clouds. A nephelosphere is a vaporous, cloudy envelope surrounding a heavenly body. 'Ah, I thought I recognized your nephelosphere,' you say to Gloria as she enters the room, fresh from a session with her hairspray.

NEPOTATION *n.* Prodigality; extravagance, squandering one's money on riotous living. 'Well, Headmaster, since you ask, it had always been my ambition to go in for nepotation when I leave school; but in the light of my examination results I suppose Quantity Surveying *would* be more appropriate.' Not to be confused with nepotism, which is favoritism to relatives – originally fondness for nephews, specifically papal fondness for illegitimate sons euphemistically referred to as nephews and advantaged by the bestowal of papal patronage in various ways.

NESCIENCE *n.* Lack of knowledge, ignorance. A word of which – unlike *prescience* (foreknowledge) – most people are nescient. Hence useful for the Insult

Concealed. 'My dear, I can only marvel at the extent of your nescience.'

NIDDERING *a.* Infamous, base, or cowardly. Or, one presumes, all three at once. A difficult combination to achieve, outside of the halls of Congress.

NIDIFICATE *v.* To build a nest. You settle down in the quietness of the theater to enjoy the opening dream sequence of *Wild Strawberries*. From the seat in front of you comes an insistent crackling and rustling of candy wrappings. 'Usher!' you call out in a loud voice, 'I think the woman in front of me is nidificating in her seat!'

NIDIFUGOUS *a.* Leaving the nest while still young. 'You're so lucky that Nicol and Mallory were nidifugous. If only I could say the same for Cyprian – especially now that he's started collecting punk ephemera.'

NIKHEDONIA *n.* The pleasure and satisfaction derived from the anticipation of success. A harmless indulgence, and a prudent one too, since success comes only to some but nikhedonia is freely available to all. 'Off to golf so early, darling? Hadn't you better have your little nikhedonia session first? You know how badly you play when your gummata are troubling you.'

NIMBUS *n.* In ancient art, a disc or plate, often golden, sometimes multicolored, placed vertically behind the head of a person of special sanctity or dignity, as a badge, so to speak, of honour. The *halo*, which is normally a ring hovering horizontally over the head but may also take the form of a general radiance around the head, carries a similar significance. As does the *gloriole*, i.e., the circle of light around the head of pictured saints. Originally a symbol of power in the pre-Christian world, the nimbus was widely adopted in Christian art in the Middle Ages. When the rest of the family are seated at the dinner table, try making an entrance while holding one of your wife's best decorated china plates behind your head, so that, when questioned, you can explain that this is your nimbus. If not questioned, of course, your little jape will have failed embarrassingly, and all you can then resort to is a feeble: 'Well, who's for a game of *nurspell* [q.v.]?'

NIMIETY *n.* Excess, extravagance, surfeit. The adjective is *nimious*. According to Webster, Coleridge said: 'There is a nimiety, a too-muchness, in all Germans.' In modern times, perhaps American tourists might be substituted for Germans; but, be that as it may, Coleridge's *mot* does lead us to the possibility of using *nimious* in the sense of 'too much.' 'Really, Roger, you simply are nimious.'

NIPHABLEPSIA *n.* Snow blindness. 'Oh, the niphablepsia! The niphablepsia! I know confirmation dresses are supposed to be white, but . . . I'm blinded! I'm blinded! I don't think I'll be able to go to the service!'

NIPPERKIN *n.* An amount of liquor approximately equal to half a pint. 'Who, me? Oh, I'll have . . . just a little nipperkin of scotch, thank you.' Alternatively, you could ask for a nipperkin of nippitatum, which is an exceptionally good and strong ale.

NIPTER *n.* Ceremony of washing the feet on Maundy Thursday in the Eastern Orthodox church. Hang on . . . Maundy Thursday comes only *once a year!* On the face of it, this would seem to be a body blow to the cause of multiculturalism.

NOBILIARY PARTICLE *phr.* One of those prefixes such as *de* or *von* which, before a personal name, indicate noble ancestry. Remarkably useful to add to one's name when making a booking at a London hotel. In his book *The Rights of Man*, Tom Paine referred to the nobility as the 'No Ability.'

NOCENT and **NOCUOUS** *a.* Two never-used words with the same meaning – harmful. A moment's reflection will reveal that they provide the basis for those much more common words *innocent* and *innocuous*. It is comforting to discover that our civilization has found more use for the latter two terms than for the former two. On the other hand, it has found more use for *uncouth* than for *couth*. Perhaps this simply means that, for deep-laid psychological or linguistic reasons, we have a natural preference for the use of words which have been negatived by prefix. If so, the author may have high hopes for the success of his own neologism, *unundulating* (q.v.).

NOCTAMBULATION *n.* Superior Person's word for sleep-walking, otherwise known as somnambulism. The latter being a wonderful item for spelling tests, by the way; the first *m* gets them every time, possibly because of the wide currency of the Italian form *sonnambula* in the title of Bellini's opera.

noctambulation

NOCTIFLOROUS *a.* Blooming at night. 'We just have to face the fact that our daughter is noctiflorous. We'll have to try for the family Christmas photo in the window of opportunity between her leaving her bedroom tonight and getting out the front door.'

NOCTIVAGANT *a.* Wandering by night. An undoctored cat; or the large huntsman spider that appears on a different ceiling each morning. 'Sorry, Brett, I just don't know where Lisa is this evening; she's become rather noctivagant since she got her driver's license.'

NODOSE *a.* Knobbly, knotty. The noun is *nodosity*. When you express concern over Uncle Henry's *genual* (q.v.) nodosity, you are in fact merely commenting upon his knobby knees.

NOESIS *n.* The activity of the intellect in the process of cognition. 'Jimmy showed more effort this term, and did well in sports, leadership, and honest endeavor, but his subject marks remained low. He should not be too discouraged by this, since he is doing as well

221

as can be expected for someone without the advantage of the usual noesis.'

NOISOME *a.* Noxious, smelly, nasty. Note that this is definitely *not* a synonym for *noisy*. Much quiet satisfaction can be derived from putting your head around the door of your younger brother's room, saying, 'It's rather noisome in here, isn't it?' and hearing him turn down his stereo as you go on your way.

NOLENS VOLENS *phr.* Latin phrase meaning 'whether unwilling or willing,' and of course the origin of the common English phrase 'willy-nilly,' the oddity being that in the latter case the two components of the phrase are mutually transposed. So, in future when expressing this concept, don't say 'willy-nilly'; say 'nilly-willy.' This will confirm your reputation as a tiresome eccentric and at the same time enable you to correct your well-meaning correctors.

NOMOLOGY *n.* The study of laws and lawmaking. Also that branch of any specific discipline which deals with its laws, e.g., the nomology of physics. But what is the nomology of nomology called?

NONE *pron.* Not any. The interest here lies in the question, much debated in the past, of whether the word is singular or plural. The argument used to be that since *one* was singular, and since *none* was derived from *no one*, then *none* should have a singular verb. In practice, of course, it is used equally if not more freely with a plural verb. In any event, the argument is absurd, since the word refers neither to a single entity nor to multiple entities; it refers to a nullity, and hence calls for the development by a creative linguist of an entirely new conjugative inflection. Unfortunately, 'creative linguist' is an *oxymoron* (q.v.).

NONFEASANCE *n.* Failure to perform some action which ought to have been performed. (Cf. *malfeasance*, official misconduct, and *misfeasance*, wrongful exercise of authority.) 'You're looking just a trifle inimical tonight, oh my best beloved. Pray tell – have I committed malfeasance, misfeasance, or nonfeasance?'

NONPLUS *v.* To confuse or disconcert. A likeable word which ought to be used more often than it is. One of the more nonplussing things about it is how it came to mean what it does. It comes from the Latin *non plus*, i.e., 'not more,' and the derivation appears to be from medieval scholastic disputations when the out-argued disputant was said to have arrived at a non plus. Be that as it may, a nice way to nonplus your friends is to pronounce the term as 'nun-ploss.' It may prove possible to persuade the more gullible among them that this is the traditional eighteenth-century pronunciation. Of course, on the other hand this may serve merely to reinforce your already growing reputation as a boring old fart with a penchant for tedious whimsy.

NOSISM *n.* Collective egotism; group conceit. 'Perhaps, Prime Minister, if your ministerial colleagues could group themselves more closely around you – that's right, shoulder to shoulder – we want everyone to be in the photo – perhaps with your arms on each other's shoulders – that's right – wonderful – we want to bring out the solidarity, the nosism, of the Cabinet as a whole . . .'

NOSOPOETIC *a.* Producing disease, unhygienic; infected. 'Ah, how perfectly nosopoetic!' is the proper exclamation for you to employ when the wealthy Pimplewickers, of whose possessions you are already insanely jealous, proudly show off to you their new fishpond/seaside cottage/sunken garden/bathroom tiles/Samoyed dog/Abyssinian cat/antique Persian rug, etc., etc.

NOSTOLOGY *n.* The study of second childhood in extreme old age. 'Mom, do you know what Dad's doing? He's been buying all these comics, and I caught him writing away for a skull ring and a pair of Magic X-Ray Spectacles! And he keeps saying he's a nostologist!'

NOSTOMANIA *n.* An unduly powerful or excessive nostalgia. 'Nostalgia ain't what it used to be; it used to be nostomania.'

NOSTOPATHY *n.* A morbid dread of returning to one's home. A more useful contribution to philology would perhaps be a word for a morbid dread of someone else returning to one's home.

NOSTRIFICATE *v.* To accept as one's own. 'Don't lean too far over the edge of the monkey pit, children; they are all too likely to nostrificate you.'

224

NOTAPHILY *n.* The collecting of bank notes, as a hobby. (Curiously enough, the author himself pursues this hobby, specializing in present-day Australian dollar denominations. Readers who may be in a position to help him extend his collection are very welcome to do so; he knows you will appreciate that he pursues this interest for love, not money, and is unable to pay for any items that you may wish to volunteer.)

NOT A PROBLEM *phr.* This phrase, which is currently much in vogue with car salespeople, insurance agents, and their ilk, means more or less 'that's a real problem you've thrown at me, man, and I'll need time to come up with some ploy to gloss over the difficulty.'

NOUMENON *n.* The transcendent, unknowable, mystical essence of something, in contradistinction to the *phenomenon*, an objective entity which may be directly perceived by the senses. Walk into your teenager's poster-bedecked bedroom when he or she is out and empty your mind of all other thoughts for a moment, and you may gain some idea of the concept.

NOVERCAL *a.* In the manner of a stepmother. 'Mother, I think you're perfectly beastly about this curfew thing. Just because you can't relate to Luke's innovative body-piercing. You're just so . . . so *novercal!*'

NOYADE *n.* Mass execution by drowning, as in revolutionary France. The technique was invented by a 'monster of ferocity' (to quote Maunder) named Carrier, and involved some one hundred and fifty people being shut up in the hold of a ship, which was then scuttled in the Loire. This was called, rather delightfully, 'Carrier's Vertical Deportation.' 'Have a good old noyade, now,' you cry out to the Seventh Grade as they depart in the school bus for their swimming lesson. Knowing your penchant for esoteric vocabulary, they smile tolerantly and turn their full attention to the task of *defenestrating* (q.v.) the phys. ed. teacher.

NUCIVOROUS *a.* Nut-eating. 'I see that Andrew's idea of putting out some hors d'oeuvres for our guests is to set out a dozen bowls full of assorted nuts. Not surprising, I suppose, given that he's surrounded at the office by people who are either parrots or apes.' (Raising her voice:) 'What time are the nucivores arriving, darling?'

NUGACITY *n.* Triviality, futility. 'Why not ask Boris and Deirdre? Add a touch of nugacity to the evening?'

NUGATORY *a.* Of no value, trifling, insubstantial, pointless. Unfavorable criticism of the present book could properly be so characterized.

NULLIBIETY *n.* State of being nowhere. A word for which it would at first appear difficult to conceive any practical use; but no incomprehensible word can be completely useless. 'And in conclusion, Stafford, on behalf of everyone here, may I heartily wish you an unimpaired nullibiety.' Or: 'Yes, when there's a job to be done around the house, I know I can rely absolutely on Stafford's nullibiety.'

NULLIBIST *n.* One who denies the existence of the soul in space. 'Now that we're in orbit, Teresa, you will appreciate that as a confirmed nullibist I have no sense of moral obligation, and will not have any until re-entry in three days' time. So how's about a little you-know-what, cookie, or would you rather I farted in your oxygen supply?'

NULLIFIDIAN *a.* or *n.* Without religious faith; one who is without religious faith. Useful when confronted by religious proselytizers at your front door. If you admit to them that you are an agnostic or an atheist, they will merely redouble their efforts to convert you; but a smiling statement that you are a nulli-fidian will send them away content, if somewhat baffled.

NUMEN *n.* An internal spirit or power that gives life and/or guidance. 'Leave your father alone for a few minutes, you children – can't you see that his numen is weakening?'

NUMINOUS *a.* Divine. Like a deity in human form. You may wish to so characterize your beloved – but in that event first make sure that she knows what it means. Best to buy her a copy of this book right now, in fact.

NUMMAMOROUS *a.* Money-loving. From the Latin *nummus*, a coin. (See also *lucripetous*.)

NUMMULAR *a.* Coin-shaped; pertaining to the possession of money. Given the two meanings, on being introduced to your daughter's latest hopeful, you

might say to your wife, 'Well, he's certainly nummular – but is he nummular?'

NUNCHEON *n.* A noon drink. 'I'll just leave the accounts
till this afternoon if you don't mind, Miles; I find
that I'm running late for a nuncheon appointment.'

NUNCUPATIVE *a.* In legal matters, oral rather than written. (Be it noted, by the way, that 'verbal' is not the
same as 'oral.' All language, whether oral or written,
is verbal.) 'Yes, I do seem to recall saying something
about a substantial monetary reward if you got
straight *A*'s this term; but Leonard, we're talking a
nuncupative undertaking here, I think, aren't we?
And you know what that means?'

NURSPELL *n.* I give here the scholarly J. W. Mollet's definition of *nurspell* in full: 'An old English game like
trap, bat and ball. It is played with kibble, a nur and
a spell. When the end of the spell is struck with the
kibble, the nur rises in the air, etc.' *Etcetera?* What is
this etcetera? This man should be writing instructions for changing computer settings.

NUTATION *n.* The act of nodding; more specifically,
habitual or constant nodding of the head. 'Hickmott
would be a very sound choice to head your Department, Minister – always gives full value – state-of-
the-art nutation, day in, day out.'

NUTRICISM *n.* A form of symbiosis in which one of the
two organisms involved is nourished or protected by
the other without making any reciprocal contribution. Parenthood, presumably.

NYCTERENT *a.* One who hunts by night. A dog looking for a loose-lidded garbage can to push over and disembowel spectacularly. A garbage can owner looking for a nycterent dog. A lovesick teenager looking for another lovesick teenager.

NYCTITROPIC *a.* Turning in a certain direction at night. 'Brendan's nyctitropic. Put him outside at night and he turns in the direction of the nearest bar.'

NYCTOPHOBIA *n.* The morbid dread of night. Question: would it be possible for a nyctophobic to suffer also from *photophobia* (q.v.)? Think about it.

NYCTOPHONIAC *a.* Able to give voice only at night. The neighborhood dog that remains miraculously silent all day but becomes remarkably voluble after midnight.

NYMPHAEUM *n.* A nymph's shrine. Today, a daughter's unguent-bestrewn dressing table.

NYMPHOLEPSY *n.* *Not* a convulsive condition of nubiles, but a passionate longing for something unattainable. A sufferer is a *nympholept*. The condition is named after the supposed result of looking upon a nymph, an act which, according to legend, produced a frenzy of enthusiastic emotion in the looker-upon. In modern parlance, you could use the term to refer to the passion of a vintage-car enthusiast for an impossibly expensive Bugatti; or of a bibliophile for a Shakespeare First Folio; or, let's face it, of a voluptuary *manqué* (q.v.) for a nymphomaniac.

OBAMBULATE *v.* To wander or walk about in an aimless fashion. The motion of a male spouse in a Sunday morning flea market or a female spouse in a department store. 'For heaven's sake, where's your father got to now? He's gone obambulating again, just when it's time to go home.'

OBDORMITION *n.* The technical term for that familiar physical condition – the 'going to sleep' of a limb when pressure on a nerve has caused a tingly numbness. 'Waldemar is the only person I know who gets obdormition of the brain.'

OBEX *n.* Any device that can hold a door shut, such as a lock, a latch, a bolt, or a crossbar. 'I don't care how much it costs; if Daryl is going to be alone in the house after school, I want an obex for the door of my room.'

OBJURGATE *v.* Chide, scold, upbraid vehemently. The third of the three great principles inculcated in young ladies by finishing schools: Conjugate, Subjugate, Objurgate.

OBLATION *n.* In canon law (see *canonical age*), any property that is given to the Church. Oddly, there seems to be no word for property given by the Church, as for example to the poor. In Shaw's play *Captain Brasshound's Conversion*, one of the characters expresses alarm at being in a Moslem country, saying that Moslems believe that they will go to heaven if they kill a Christian. 'Don't worry,' replies another character, 'in England the people are Christians, and believe that they will go to heaven if they give their money to the poor – but they don't do it!'

OBLIQUITY *n.* Deviation. 'Tried any new obliquities this week, Simon?'

OBLONGITUDE *n.* Believe it or not, the state of being oblong. The 'g' is pronounced 'j.' 'You've done it at last, Mrs. Mummery; a cake with real oblongitude!'

OBLOQUY *n.* (i) Public condemnation, and/or the ensuing disgrace; (ii) opprobrious language. A word that hangs uncertainly between *odium* and *opprobrium*, leaning more toward the latter but sometimes simply meaning scornful and accusing language. The author would try to set forth a sentence using all three, for illustrative purposes, were it not for the odium, the obloquy, the opprobrium, and indeed the objurgation that would be his lot if he succeeded only in effecting an obfuscation.

231

OBNUBILATION *n.* A state of consciousness in which the mind is clouded over and the thinking processes vague. 'I know it's only just after breakfast, darling, and we can't expect obnubilation to have entirely dissipated yet, but do you really think you should be going to the office wearing your pyjama pants under your designer slacks?'

OBSOLAGNIUM *n.* Waning sexual desire due to age. A mythical condition invented by the young folk, who, already chafing from the knowledge that their elders have more power, more experience more savoir faire, more knowledge, and more money than they do, feel obliged to postulate some equalizing disadvantage. Bad luck, kiddies. Not only do we get more of it than you, but for us it's safer as well.

occultation

OBTUND *v.* To blunt, dull, or deaden. 'And now, dear colleagues, as the evening comes to a close, to thoroughly obtund all our conviviality, all the exchanges of ideas and enthusiasms that we have shared tonight, here is our final speaker, the Chairman of the Board, Sir Maurice himself!'

OCCULTATION *n.* Being hidden from view, or lost to notice. An astronomical term, referring specifically to the extinction of a heavenly body's light by the intervention of another. Such as Miss U.S.A. inadvertently or otherwise stepping between Miss Sweden and the camera.

OCHLOPHOBIA *n.* The obsessive fear of crowds. The most understandable of phobias.

ochlophobia

OCULOGYRIC *a.* Eye-rolling. 'Attention all male children in this household above the age of ten! Your mother is inquiring about the origin of certain muddy footprints found on the living-room carpet. Report to your mother at once, and be warned – whilst total frenzy has not yet occurred, the oculogyric phase has already commenced!'

ODIUM *n.* The burden of the distastefulness of a particular act. Generally borne or incurred by a person associated with the act in question. Not to be confused with *opprobrium*, the disgrace incurred as a consequence of the act. The difficulty of dissociating the two meanings lies in the fact that the two penalties they represent are generally incurred at the same time, through the same act, and both involve the disapproval of others. The emphasis in the case of *odium*, however, is upon the intrinsic hatefulness of the act itself; in the case of *opprobrium*, upon the actual reproaches incurred. There is generally a time-sequence element involved also. As you prepare to fling the tomato at the old lady in the wheelchair, you are already steeling yourself to bear the odium of the act; as you fling it, you incur the odium; the opprobrium of the bystanders follows a split second later.

ODONTALGIA and **ODONTIASIS** *n.* Toothache and teething, respectively. Your own odontalgia, or your child's odontiasis, might usefully be mentioned when excusing yourself from coming into the office until later on in the morning. But not too bluntly. Say, in a diffident and strained tone of voice: 'I'm having a spot of my old trouble again, I'm afraid – you know, the, er . . .' (here lower your voice to a confidential whisper) '. . . odontalgia. I'd sooner the others didn't know, incidentally.'

OENOMEL *n.* (i) A beverage made of wine and honey; thence, (ii) something that blends strength with sweetness. A female wrestler, perhaps?

OLEAGINOUS *a.* Oily. The personal manner of actors appearing in television commercials for banks and finance companies.

OLIGOPHAGOUS *a.* Eating only a few particular kinds of food. This is the recommended word for use in those embarrassing situations when your hostess serves up for your four-year-old son a main course consisting largely of something which is *anathema* (q.v.) to him. As soon as you sense the *alliaceous miasma* (q.v.), you say, apologetically: 'I'm a little embarrassed to have to confess this, but I'm afraid he has an oligophagous condition; I wonder if you have any dry biscuits – or perhaps something else a little, er, plainer?' Used with sufficient finesse, this technique can lead to his being presented with a plateful of sausage rolls.

OLIGOPHRENIA *n.* Feeblemindedness; extreme mental retardation. (See *abecedarian insult, an.*)

OLIGOTROPHIA *n.* Lack of nourishment. Alleged condition of the teenage human male even after regularly consuming one family-sized pizza, six slices of buttered toast, one giant-size packet of potato chips, and one quart of chocolate milk, in between and in addition to any two normal meals.

OLLA-PODRIDA *n.* A Spanish mixed hash of meat and vegetables, or indeed any incongruous combination of leftovers from the bottom shelf of the fridge. Literally, 'rotten pot.' A suggested addition to your *Who's Who* entry, under Hobbies: 'Playing the harpsichord; collecting early Oriental porcelain; and making olla-podrida fritters at dead of night.'

OMBROPHILOUS *a.* Capable of withstanding heavy and continuous rain. For example, tropical vegetation. The correct epithet for a preschool child who has been got up for the day by his mother in gumboots, a knee-length raincoat, a rain-hat, and a miniature umbrella.

OMNIPHAGOUS *a.* Eating everything. One of the great experimental omniphages was William Buckland, the first Professor of Geology at Oxford University. He ate hedgehog, crocodile, and mole meat, and even a bluebottle fly, the taste of which he considered the most repulsive he had ever experienced. Once when lost on a dark night during a ride to London with a friend, he dismounted, scooped up a handful of earth, smelt it, and immediately declared 'Uxbridge!' The Archbishop of York once proudly showed Buckland a snuff box containing the heart of Louis XIV, which the Archbishop had bought from a tomb-robber when in Paris during the revolution. Remarking, 'I've eaten many things, but never the heart of a king,' Buckland seized the heart and swallowed it on the spot.

ONEIRODYNIA *n.* Nightmare. 'If it turns out to be a girl, have you thought of giving her one of those lovely, mellifluous, ancient Greek names? Lydia, say, or Persephone? Or perhaps . . . Oneirodynia?'

ONERABLE *a.* Nothing to do with 'honorable.' Instead, a variant form of 'onerous,' i.e., burdensome or troublesome. 'I see you've invited the Colonel. He's an onerable old stick, isn't he?'

ONIOMANIA *n.* An irresistible urge to buy things. The condition is generally found in association with penury; where it is not, it soon will be, especially as oniomaniacs, like *thermanasthesiacs* (q.v.), often marry each other.

ONOMASTICON *n.* An ordered list of names. 'Mom, Hugo's in his bedroom, using the phone book as his personal onomasticon again! Can't you do anything about it? It's just disgusting!'

ONTOLOGICAL *a.* Having to do with the science or study of essence or being. The ontological argument for the existence of God, as developed by Anselm, is that the very concept of a perfect being leads inevitably to the existence of that being, since a nonexistent perfect being's perfection would be made imperfect by its nonexistence. The same argument may, of course, be used to prove the existence of the perfect hamburger, though it was not so used by Anselm. There are two reasons for equipping yourself with this word. First, to armor yourself psychologically against the pretensions of existentialists – progressive theologians, educationists, and their ilk – who use the term indiscriminately, waving it over their monologues like a magic wand that is supposed to turn words into arguments. Secondly, to pepper your own conversation with it, for the purpose of obscuring issues, impressing undergraduates of the

237

opposite sex, and confusing social scientists. Thus: 'Ontologically speaking, . . .' (this can lead into virtually *any* remark); 'there's a certain ontological force about what you say, I admit, but . . .'; etc., etc.

ONYCHOPHAGY *n.* Nail-biting. 'With those remarks I conclude my address tonight on the issues facing you at this election. In a few minutes my opponent will take the floor – but before he does, I want him to know something. I have proof positive, in the form of this video recording, which I have in my hand – a video shot with a concealed camera – that this man, who puts himself forward as a suitable candidate to represent you in the halls of Congress – this man, this very same man, regularly indulges in onychophagy. I have arranged for the video to be shown on the large screen behind me, at the conclusion of his speech. That is all. Over to you, now, Mr. Hilary. Don't forget your lines.'

ONYMOUS *a.* Not anonymous. A rather sweet little word: 'And I'd appreciate it if you'd stop sending me onymous letters!' you call out after your unwanted suitor as he walks away down the crowded main street, crestfallen from your latest rebuff.

OPERCULUM *n.* Organ of a plant or animal that acts as a covering or lid. Could be used to describe the hat worn by one of those men who *never* go anywhere, or do anything, hatless. Plainclothes policemen are traditionally operculiferous. An even more extreme case is that of the man who wears his hat while actually driving his car. Be warned: it is an observed fact that operculiferous drivers are dangerous. More so

even than pipe-smoking drivers. If you notice that
the driver of the car in front of yours, or behind it, is
both operculiferous and pipe-smoking, then pull to
the side of the road immediately, and wait until it is
safe to proceed.

OPHELIMITY *n.* The primary meaning is 'the ability to
please sexually'; but there is also a secondary meaning, 'the ability to please generally' – a useful ambiguity which should allow you to gain a certain
degree of quiet enjoyment from the use of the term.
(See *orexigenic*.)

OPHIDIOPHOBIA *n.* The morbid dread of snakes. As
distinct from the ordinary common or garden dread
of snakes – particularly in the common or garden.

ophidiophobia

OPISTHENAR *n.* Back of the hand. In pronouncing, the
stress is on the *pis*. 'Mom,' you cry out from the

239

bathroom at a quarter to seven in the morning, when she is only just beginning to wake up, 'I've got a nasty little red sore on my opisthenar.'

OPISTHOPOREIA *n.* Involuntary walking backward. Apart from walking up the down escalator, it is hard (though amusing) to conceive a case of this. How would the sufferer ever get to work in the morning? And, much more worrying from the sufferer's point of view, how would he get home?

OPOPANAX *n.* Aromatic gum resin used in perfumery. 'Lucille has opopanaxed the third floor again – she's been up there only five minutes, and eleven people have already come down with hay fever.'

OPSABLEPSIA *n.* Not looking into another's eyes. In some cultures a sign of disrespect or evasion; in others a sign of respect and deference. Make what you will of this.

OPSIGAMY *n.* Marriage late in life. All things considered, probably a better fate than *opsiproligery*, which is the ability to have children late in life.

OPSIMATH *n.* One who learns late in life. From the Greek *opse* (late) and *manthano* (learn). Useful when writing out report cards. 'Timothy's results in English, History, Mathematics, Geography, Science, Physical Education, and Effort were, admittedly, a little disappointing, even for him; but at this stage he certainly has all the necessary grounding to seek to make a future for himself as an opsimath.'

ORARIAN *n.* Dweller by the seashore. Goes well with *otiant* (q.v.).

ORCHIDECTOMY *n.* Not, as you might think, an operation to cut out your orchids, but an operation to cut out something even more important. Orchidectomy is castration. Perhaps a florist, in dealing with unpleasant customers: 'A thousand apologies, monsieur et madame, that we have no Yugoslavian peonies; perhaps by way of compensation I could offer madame, with the compliments of the firm, this petite corsage, and monsieur, perhaps' (here waving the pruning shears), 'a leetle orchidectomy?'

OREXIGENIC *a.* Whetting the appetite, especially the sexual appetite. 'Morning, Miss Wesley,' you say as you pass her desk; 'orexigenic *and* ophelimitous this morning, I see!' You are quite safe. She will be able to find neither of these two words in the *Secretary's Handy Desk Dictionary*.

ORGULOUS *a.* Proud, haughty, showy. 'The decorations are marvelous, Cynthia dear! How perfectly orgulous of you!'

ORISMOLOGY *n.* The explanation of technical terms. Such as orismology.

ORNAMENTS RUBRIC *phr.* A rubric (i.e., a direction for the performance of divine worship, originally printed in red) relating to the vestments which the officiating ministers should wear. 'Finlay, you know perfectly well that when we visit Aunt Martha, the ornaments rubric for the day specifically prohibits

241

the wearing of a T-shirt embroidered with the slogan "Shit happens." '

OROGRAPHY *n.* In physical geography, the study of mountains and mountain systems. As you pack the ski gear into your friend's car, you assure your mother that this is for your compulsory unit in Orography III.

ORTHOBIOSIS *n.* A hygienic and moral lifestyle. 'Well, your qualifications and career history seem very relevant. How is your health? No arthritis, no orthobiosis, I hope?'

ORTHOGRAPHY *n.* Spelling correctly. The great nineteenth-century critic Sainte-Beuve once offended a journalist, who immediately challenged him to a duel. Sainte-Beuve accepted the challenge, saying: 'As the challenged party, I have the right to choose weapons. I choose spelling – you're dead!'

ORTHOPTEROUS *a.* To do with insects; insectlike. 'Now look here, you orthopterous creep. . .'

ORTHOSIS *n.* The correction of a neurotic state. 'Poor dear! He/she has tried chiropracty, homeopathy, naturopathy, *and* iridology – and I remember telling him/her in the first place that all he/she needed was a little orthosis.'

ORTHOSTATIC *a.* Pertaining to standing upright. 'What a dilemma for Nicholas! Orthostatic coma! Still, I suppose it must be some consolation to Marge to know that she's married to a medical miracle. . .'

OSCITANCY *n.* The act of yawning, or a state of exceptional drowsiness. 'Ladies and gentlemen, our guest lecturer tonight will be talking about "Great Moments in the History of Accrual Accounting." Prepare yourselves for an evening of pure oscitancy!' (**OSCITATION** *n.* Inattention. An overt display of lack of interest, with much yawning, etc. 'Go ahead,' you say encouragingly to the *aporial macrologist* (q.v.), 'I'm all oscitation!')

OSMOPHOBIA *n.* A morbid dread of odours. Such as those generated by a sufferer from *osmidrosis* (strong-smelling perspiration), especially if the osmophobe also has *osmethesia* (a strong sensitivity to odours).

OSOPHAGIST *n.* A fastidious eater. One who picks and chooses. Adolescent children are by nature and inclination osophagic, and moreover their respective osophagies are rarely coincident. Thus the need, in a two-adolescent family, for two different brands of sauce, two different methods of cleaning the silverware, two different ways of cooking the french fries, etc., etc. This is known as multiple osophagy, and increases exponentially with the number of children involved.

OSTINATO *n.* A musical term used to describe a repetitive and simple melodic theme which serves as an underpinning for the main line of music, as in the example of an ostinato bass. From the Latin word for obstinate. 'Thank you for taking little Bobbie on the school excursion today, Mr. Pomfrey. I know it's a long trip, but you'll find his singing away, there in the back seat, a charming accompaniment to the journey, I just know. His current favourite is "Baa Baa Black Sheep" – he loves it so much, he just won't stop. But you play whatever you want to on the radio, of course. He'll just provide the ostinato background.'

OTIANT *a.* Idle or resting. The author's dearest wish is to be an otiant *orarian* (q.v.).

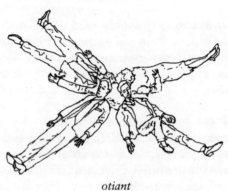

otiant

OTIOSE *a.* Serving no useful purpose. Alternatively: leisurely. Both meanings presumably come from the same Latin origin, *otium* (leisure) – in the former case no doubt via the intermediate concept of *idle*. The overtones of *odious, adipose*, and *obese* make this a useful word for unsettling the ignorant in casual conversation.

OUBLIETTE *n.* A dungeon, often in the form of a deep and narrow well, designed for the permanent incarceration of those whom it is desired to forget. From the French *oublier* (to forget). 'Out of sight, out of mind,' no doubt our medieval forebears (or at least those of them who owned castles) thought as the duke's tax-collector was lowered down the stone tube and the heavy iron lid clanged shut far above him. To modern ears, the word is not unsuggestive of some delicate item of Parisian millinery. 'Ah, I can just see you in a lovely little oubliette,' you rhapsodize to your sister when she finally emerges, fully made up, from the bathroom.

OUPHE *n.* (Pronounced 'oof'.) An elf, gnome, or goblin. 'Yes, Director, this is our kindergarten class, and here are all our little ouphes sitting at their little tables cutting out their little pieces of colored paper. Would you like them to sing to you?'

OUTSERT *n.* I love this word. A genuine printing term, meaning a folded sheet of printed paper which is wrapped *around the outside of* another folder section. In other words, the opposite of *insert*.

OVIFORM or **OVINE** *a.* Like a sheep. The movement or behavior pattern of a one-day golfing crowd.

OVIPOSIT *v.* To lay an egg. 'Hope the new book oviposits well and truly!' is your encouraging remark to the new author.

OXYMORON *n.* Extremely concise contradiction in terms, e.g., 'cruel kindness,' 'beloved enemy,' 'delicious sauerkraut.' One of those wonderfully named figures of speech that we all learnt about at school. (Remember metonymy? synecdoche?) It would be unreasonable to expect even the Superior Person to maintain a working knowledge of all these terms. The author suggests that one only be selected for memorizing and repeated use; his own favorite is *aposiopesis* (q.v.), which he once used to great effect at a dog-poisoner's biennial, when – but that is another story.

OZOSTOMIA *n.* Evil-smelling breath. Or so my source defines it. Not bad, you will note, not sour; but *evil*. How does breath smell evil? Is this the origin of the famous royal motto 'Evil be to him who evil stinks'? Or have I got that wrong?

P

PABULUM *n.* The means of nutrient for animals or plants. Food as a basic fuel, as distinct from any aesthetic or appetizing qualities that it may have. 'Ah, Lady Mountjoy, as always – you offer your fortunate guests pabulum – pure pabulum!'

PAIZOGONY *n.* Love play. 'I know this great little Italian take-out restaurant. Let's go down there first and then go to the drive-in and have some paizogony in the car.'

PALANQUIN *n.* A covered litter in which persons of importance were transported from place to place, borne by poles resting on the shoulders of two or four men. Given the height above road level at which the passenger sat, the nearest modern analogy is probably one of those urban four-wheel drive vehicles which sit alongside you at the traffic lights, blocking your view of the entire street. The analogy breaks down, however, when one considers the relative importance of the persons thus conveyed.

PALIMPSEST *n.* A manuscript whose original writing has been scraped off or treated in some way so that a second layer of writing can be superimposed on the document. When your sister's new friend, the budding poet, shyly seeks your comment on his latest effort, a free-form rhapsody on the coming of autumn, you read it, stare as though entranced into the distance for a half-minute, and then say slowly: 'You know, I think I see the basis for a marvelous palimpsest in this.'

PALINGENESIS *n.* A new or second birth into a higher form of being. Not quite the same as *resurrection*, but close enough to enable you to introduce a nice element of confusion into any theological discussion. The greatest claim to fame of the post-war American pentecostalist preacher William Branham was his resurrection of a fish. *Pentecost* itself is an interesting word, referring as it does to both Jewish and Christian festivals as well as to extremes of fundamentalist behaviour. And did you know that a *pentecostys* was a division of fifty Spartan soldiers?

PALINOIA *n.* The compulsive repetition of an act, over and over again, until it is performed perfectly. One of the classic forms of the condition is of course the dogged piano practice of the freckled ten-year-old next door who is preparing the infamous Minute Waltz for the local eisteddfod. The technical term for this is pianola palinoia, and the condition brought on in the listener is known as pianola palinoia paranoia. To be preferred is palinoiac *paraphilemia* (q.v.).

PALIURUS *n.* A Mediterranean thorny bush, with long, sharp spikes, sometimes called 'Christ's thorn' because it is said to have been used to make the crown of thorns that was placed upon the head of Jesus. 'Well done, Jaclyn, well done! Second place in the class spelling competition! Now let the orthographer be crowned with a wreath of paliurus!'

PANDAEMONIUM *n.* Commonly spelled 'pandemonium' and taken to mean a great noise and disorder; but actually the capital city of Hell in Milton's *Paradise Lost*. In the full knowledge of its original meaning, and *always* giving full value to the central diphthong when pronouncing it, you might so refer to the rumpus room, your youngest child's bedroom, etc.

PANDICULATION *n.* Stretching and yawning. 'This morning, right in the middle of my *ante-jentacular* [q.v.] pandiculation, . . .'

PANPSYCHIST *n.* One who believes that everything, whether animal, vegetable, or mineral, has a soul. Perhaps today's paradigmatic panpsychist is the young lady who gives her hatchback a Christian name and speaks affectionately of it by that name. On the other hand, there are also the people who play music to flowers. And the gamblers who harangue their dice. And the homemakers who stand at their front doors, shouting 'Grow, you bastard, grow!' at a newly seeded lawn. But perhaps the ultimate in panpsychism is a case known to the author – a person whose idealism was so unstinting that he once attempted to have a conversation with a certified public accountant.

249

PANTOPHAGY *n.* Omnivorousness, i.e. eating anything and everything. 'Sorry to have to say this about my brother, but I should let you know about him if you're really thinking of inviting him into your house. The fact is he's . . . er, well . . . I'm ashamed to say this but I suppose I have to . . . he's pantophagous.'

PANTOPHOBIA *n.* The morbid fear of everything. There had to be a name for it. Fortunately it hits most of us for only a few minutes at a time.

pantophobia

PAPULIFEROUS *n.* Pimply. Typical condition of a *groak* (q.v.).

PARACME *n.* The stage after one's peak, when decline and senescence set in. 'What an idea, Professor! You are indeed at the paracme of your powers!'

PARADIASTOLE *n.* A euphemistic half-truth. 'Gosh, dear, you look fabulous in your new dress – no really, I mean it – paradiastoles fail me.'

PARADIGM *n.* Model, pattern, or example. A pretentious and unnecessary word, normally found only in psychology theses. Never use this word yourself, but be prepared, when it is used by another, to lean forward intently, narrow your eyes, and say, 'Just a moment – do you really *mean* "paradigm" in *that* context?' When, somewhat bemused, he avers that he does, you merely raise your eyebrows and remain silent. With any luck at all, he will now have forgotten what he was going to say. Apply the same technique when confronted with *parameter, infrastructure, structure,* or *matrix* (q.v.).

PARALOGISM *n.* Illogical reasoning, the illogicality of which the reasoner in question is unaware of. 'Ah, Herr Doktor, how can I possibly hope to match you in paralogism?'

PARAMOUR *n.* Illicit lover. A rather beautiful word (from the French *par amour*, fairly obviously) which has undeservedly acquired a denigratory signification. Even the good Dr. Johnson seems to have regretted this, referring to it gratuitously as 'not inelegant or unmusical.'

PARAPHILEMIA *n.* Love play. When engaging a secretary, you tactfully ask each candidate at the interview whether she has suffered from any major medical problems; in the course of this you inquire gently: 'No paraphilemiaphobia, I hope?' She smiles blankly and shakes her head.

PARISOLOGY *n.* The deliberate pursuit of ambiguity in one's use of language. Like *charientism* (q.v.), an end to which this book is a means.

PARONOMASIA *n.* Wordplay of the punning kind, i.e., using similar-sounding (or identical-sounding) words with different meanings in close proximity to each other, for an effect of comedy, balance, or cleverness. *Paronomasiac* is an appropriate grandiloquism for punster, as well as for anyone with a penchant for messing around with words.

PAROREXIA *n.* A perverted appetite, or craving for strange foods. Supposedly the condition of gravid females, but more classically the condition of (*a*) the adolescent human male ('Don't be like that, Dad – haven't you ever seen a two-minute noodles and tomato sauce toasted sandwich before?') and (*b*) the gastronomic parvenu ('I've found this absolutely *wonderful* little Provençal restaurant – my dear, their marinated hedgehog in quince sauce with just a *little* more garlic than usual – delicious!')

PARTURITION *n.* Childbirth. For referring to bodily functions, there is a range of Latinate expressions which are uncommon enough to lend interest to your discourse without being so outlandish as to convict you of preciosity. Also recommended are *gravid* and *enceinte* (both to be preferred to *pregnant*), and *micturition*.

PASTIME *n.* Game, recreation. Derived, believe it or not, from *pass* and *time*. Every schoolboy knows of the French sundial inscribed on one side *L'amour fait* *passer le temps* and on the other *Le temps fait passer l'amour.*

PEASCOD-BELLY *n.* A false stomach worn under the clothing by Elizabethan men as part of the then fashionable use of sculpted underwear to convey an artificial impression of an exaggerated body shape. The peascod-belly was made by stuffing a whalebone or wooden frame with old rags, sawdust, bran, etc. There is an account of one unfortunate gallant whose peascod-belly caught on a nail as he was ceremonially advancing to make his obediences to Queen Elizabeth, with the result that its filling escaped and left him deflated literally as well as metaphorically in front of the whole court. Today, the concept of the peascod-belly can perhaps be used as part of a response to any unkind reference to your 'beer-belly.' Simply convert your unfortunate affliction into a fashion statement.

PECULATE *v.* To pilfer or embezzle. Etymologically quite distinct from 'speculate,' but many do both while under the impression that they are doing only the one or the other.

PEDAGOGY *n.* The science or art of teaching. Note that this is not a synonym for *teaching*; but, surprisingly, *pedagogue* indeed *is* a synonym for *teacher*. The word *pedagogue* is of some interest, in that its usage in England tends to be somewhat *pejorative* (q.v.) in *contradistinction* (q.v.) to its usage in French, there being connotations of pedantry in the English usage. The original derivation is from an ancient Greek term describing a slave who led his master's children to school. The modern-day teacher is, of course, the slave of the children, but may be allowed to lead them to a local cinema for the afternoon as part of an elective course in media appreciation.

PEDICULAR *a.* Lousy. The pronunciation is almost identical with that of *particular*. Hence (to your sister, after she has refused to let you use her electric shaver): 'I didn't know you were quite so pedicular.'

PEDUNCLE *n.* A stalklike appendage in a biological organism. Chambers defines it, mysteriously, as 'the stalk by which a sedentary animal is attached.' Attached to what? And what is a sedentary animal? A civil servant? And if so, what is the civil servant attached to? Best perhaps to leave these questions to older and wiser heads – which themselves have their own peduncles, incidentally, since a peduncle is also 'a tract of white fibres in the brain.' Be that as it may, this is a word that cries out for greater use in conversation. Talk to your friends about your peduncle. Ask them about theirs. Do your bit to increase appendage-consciousness in the community at large.

PEEN *n.* The wedge-shaped or thin end of a hammer head. A ridiculous word. (See also *garb*.)

PEJORATIVE *a.* Derogatory. Often describing the use in this manner of a particular word or phrase not in itself necessarily derogatory, and – just to make this definition harder to follow – often used in the context of an assurance that the word or phrase in question is *not* being used in its derogatory sense, e.g.,

'His approach was Machiavellian – I do not use the term in its pejorative sense.' This is the example *par excellence* of a Superior Word. The author has encountered few people who use it freely in normal conversation, but it is a word that the listener knows he has seen somewhere, knows he is not quite clear about, but feels he ought to be. For maximum effect it should be used glibly and casually, without special emphasis.

PERADVENTURE *adv.* The Superior alternative to *perhaps*.

PERIPETY *n.* A sudden and dramatic reversal of fortune – normally from good to bad. 'Ashleigh has chosen voluntary redundancy, from the limited choices available to him, and in making this farewell speech I know that those of you who have worked with him for so long and, ha, ha, enjoyed his unique management style, will join with me in wishing him complete peripety from this point on.'

PERISTALSIS *n.* The contractions of the alimentary canal in the process of digestion. 'How fitting,' you might say to the avant-garde composer after the premiere of his latest threnody for guitar, cowbells, and synthesizer; 'how fitting were those peristaltic rhythms for that last, for want of a better word, movement.'

PERISTASIS *n.* The complete environment of a living organism, including all the procesess vital to its life. 'This really is your peristatis, isn't it?' you inquire wearily of your teenage son as he reclines on the couch before his array of digital audio and video pleasure machines.

PERNICKETY *a.* Finical (always to be preferred to the more commonly used 'finicky'), fussy, fastidious. Not many people know that this word was invented by A. A. Milne when searching for a rhyme for 'rickety' in a humorous poem about an impoverished king. (You don't get this sort of information in the American Heritage Dictionary.)

PERNOCTATION *n.* In ecclesiastical usage, an all-night vigil. Literally, 'passing the night.' *Compernoctation* could thus be a useful neologism for 'spending the night together.'

PETALIFEROUS *a.* Having petals. 'Nice dress – so petaliferous.'

PETARD *n.* Small explosive device, used by military engineers in medieval times to undermine castle walls, break down drawbridges, etc. 'It is now rarely used,' says Webster, rather sweetly. From the French *peter* (to break wind). The man who knows his Onions (the Shakespeare glossarist – *Ed.*) will be familiar with the use in *Hamlet*, Act III, Scene 4 – 'For 'tis the sport to have the engineer / Hoist with his own petard.'

PETTITOES *n.* Pig's trotters. According to Johnson, used by Shakespeare as a contemptuous term for feet; but not so recorded in Onions. 'Ah, Samantha, you have the sweetest little pettitoes.'

PHANEROMANIA *n.* A compulsion to pick at a skin growth or imperfection. Is there *anyone* who doesn't suffer from this?

PHATIC *a.* Denoting speech which consists of noises rather than words, i.e., when emotions rather than thought are being communicated, as for example in baby talk or when a car owner is engaged in a miaowing dialogue with her cat. Sometimes also called 'idiot salutations.' Mode of communication much favored by grandparents.

PHILOGYNY *n.* The love of, indeed devotion to, women. The most understandable of idiosyncrasies.

PHONOMANIA *n.* Homicidal mania. One of those words that could be thought to mean anything but what it really means. Something to say when you are interrupted at dinner by a telemarketer selling a new phone billing offer. 'Ah, you're giving me a real case of phonomania! Why not give me your name and private address, and I'll call round one night!'

PHORONOMICS *n.* Kinematics, i.e., the science of motion. The cinema is called the cinema today because it began as the cinematograph, which was originally called the kinematograph, i.e., that which transcribes motions. This gives you the choice of annoying your film buff friends by speaking of the cinema as the 'kinema' or baffling them by referring to it as the 'phoronomograph.'

PHOTODRAMA and **PHOTOPLAY** *n.* Both words simply mean a motion picture, and were in common use in the early days of the kinematograph. Remarks such as 'Well, we went along to the cinema yesterday and saw a wonderful photodrama, starring an actor named Alberto Pacino,' will reinforce your reputation as a lovable eccentric.

PHOTOPHOBIA *n.* The morbid dread of light. You know – that thing of Dracula's. And of the computer generation.

photophobia

PIAFFER *n.* In the art of formal or ceremonial horse-riding for display purposes, a piaffer is a particular movement in which the horse is made to lift a forefoot and the diagonally opposite hindfoot at the same time and then slowly place them forward, backward, or to one side. Humans do this, though less gracefully, and call it line dancing. The Hubble telescope has searched to the farthest reaches of the known universe and has, I understand, failed to find a more boring form of animate activity than line dancing, so when next you find yourself a stupefied spectator as groups of strangely clad people prepare to lift their cowboy-booted feet in the closest to unison that they can manage, wait for a moment's silence and then call out, with feigned enthusiasm, in a loud voice: 'With a hey nonny nonny and a hot cha cha! Let the piaffering begin!'

PICAROON *n.* A vagabond. Someone who lives by his wits. A rogue. The suggestion, furthermore, is of a *lovable* rogue. A professional talk-show guest, a tax evader, a financial advisor, a politician's press secretary, et al.

PICAYUNE *a.* Trifling, paltry. Too small or insignificant to be worth consideration. A picayune was an early-nineteenth-century American coin of small value. 'Father, don't you think that my weekly allowance has become somewhat picayune with the passage of time?'

PIERIA *n.* A place in Thessaly, famed in legend as the location of the Pierian Spring, the fount of learning and poetry. Thus, from Pope's *Essay on Criticism*:

> 'A little learning is a dangerous thing;
> Drink deep, or taste not the Pierian Spring:
> There shallow draughts intoxicate the brain,
> And drinking largely sobers us again.'

The Superior Person should never quote a familiar maxim, such as the first line of the above, on its own – he should always quote the full context as well. Another useful way to give this word an airing is to say to your cousin Ralph, as he leaves for home after an interminable weekend: 'By the way, I see that you're still free from any signs of Pieria.' He leaves in faint bemusement, under the impression that you have congratulated him on his dental health.

259

PIGSNEY *n.* Believe it or not, a term of endearment used when addressing a girl. From the Saxon word for girl. Try it out on your inamorata; she will surely be charmed and delighted. 'Come, my little pigsney . . .'

PILGARLIC *n.* A poor, wretched, bald-headed man who presents a sorry spectacle. From *pilled* (peeled) garlic.

PILLIWINKS *n.* The thumbscrews. 'Okay,' you cry, after being compelled to play Scrabble so many times in succession that your host has at last succeeded in winning a round, 'now let's have some real fun! Who's for pilliwinks?'

PIMPERNEL *n.* For those of you who have always wanted to know what the famous 'scarlet pimpernel' really is: a plant of the primrose family.

PINUS RADIATA *n.* A common type of pine tree, otherwise known as radiata pine; with shrubs, trees, etc. the so-called 'scientific' name is always to be preferred, pronounced of course as Latin, not Anglicized. Thus 'i' is pronounced 'ee,' not 'eye.'

PIS ALLER *n.* A makeshift. Something that will do for lack of anything better. From *pis*, worse, and *aller*, to go. No relation to a *pismire*, which is simply an ant, and which in turn has no relation to *piss-ant*, a term mistakenly used by the ignorant as one of contempt when in fact it is a variant of *puissant*, i.e., powerful.

PISHOGUE *n.* A yellowish-white fungus, thought to be made at dead of night by a group of malevolent men and women, after a solemn invocation of the Devil, as a means of cursing a rival dairyfarmer's produce. A practice, and belief, still extant in the twenty-first century. This certainly explains the condition of the can of evaporated milk left opened and forgotten at the back of the refrigerator.

PISIFORM *a.* Pea-shaped. 'Nuff said?

PISTOLOGY *n.* The study of faith. Presumably it was as an exercise in pistology that the BBC recently questioned 103 English bishops, and discovered that only three believed in the Biblical version of the creation of the world, eighty doubted the story of Adam and Eve, and one in four did not believe that Jesus was born of a virgin.

PLASTRON *n.* A decorative addition to the front of a woman's dress, reaching from the waist upwards to the throat, or as near to it as the dress allows. Also a fencer's leather breastplate, and the bottom side of a turtle's protective shell. Similarly, a *plastrum* is the starched front of a man's evening shirt, or an iron breastplate in medievel armour. 'Would you mind putting your hand up my plastrum, Miss Lackenby, to straighten it out for me?'

PLAUSIBLE *a.* Seemingly reasonable; convincing on the surface, but . . . The word can be applied either to a statement or a person, as can its near-synonym *specious*; the marginal difference between the two words consists in the fact that *plausible* tends to be applied more naturally to persons, and *specious* to statements. The Concise Oxford Dictionary's definition of *plausible*, as applied to persons, reads in its entirety: '(of persons), fair-spoken (usually implying deceit).' What a world of disillusionment is embodied in those few words, torn as they seem to be from the soul of some careworn Oxonian lexicographer who sipped the wine of life and found it bitter.

PLEIONOSIS *n.* The exaggeration of one's own importance. The only disorder universal to humankind.

PLEIOSYLLABIC *a.* Having more than one syllable (more especially, having two or three). 'Definitely not a pleiosyllabicist!' is perhaps the safest comment you can make when asked your opinion of your sister-in-law's latest reflexologist.

PLENILOQUENCE *n.* Literally, a plenitude of talking. Excessive loquacity. There are two species of the genus, entitled the Senate and the House of Representatives.

PLENILUNARY *a.* Pertaining to the full moon. Useful for excuses. 'I'm awfully sorry, Cynthia – we'd love to come around tonight, but it's that time of the month again, I'm afraid, and we have to consider poor Quentin's plenilunary condition.'

PLETHORA *n.* Too many of a good or bad thing (cf. *surfeit*, too much of a good thing). The number of objects constituting a plethora varies. To the house-proud matron, a single cockroach in her kitchen is a plethora, since cockroaches are, to her, *anathema* (q.v.). Indeed, a house-proud matron is, by definition, someone with a plethora of anathemas.

PLURISIGNATION *n.* Multiple meanings simultaneously expressed in poetic language (as distinct from ambiguity, which implies a choice of alternative meanings). A worthy end, to which this book, one earnestly hopes, is a means.

PLUVIOMETER *n.* Superior person's word for a rain gauge. (See also *udometer.*)

PNIGEROPHOBIA *n.* A morbid dread of being smothered. The only real disincentive to union with a *viscerotonic* (q.v.).

POETASTER *n.* Ersatz and amateurish poet. The classic example in recent times was probably that of Simon Quinsy (see his biography, *Lank, Dank and Disgusting to Know*, by his lifetime friend and colleague the Hon. Roddie Smoothe-Lewis), whose heavily alliterative and strongly accented style, with its sudden descents from romance into realism, concealed what was seen even by his admirers as being, essentially, a total lack of meaning. All these features can be discerned in the following excerpt from the song cycle *Ear, Nose and Throat Ward*, on which he was working when he was first struck down by the appalling disease that was ultimately to take his life:

> 'O my marmoreal month of May,
> Twice-twisting, trembling in my tree,
> When will you wend your way away,
> At dismal dawning, or at about twenty-five
> past three?'

In connection with the second line of the above, it is perhaps worthy of mention that both Quinsy and

Smoothe-Lewis pronounced *r* as *w* – a trait inherited by Quinsy and probably passed on to Smoothe-Lewis during their collaboration on the ill-fated comedy version of *Sartor Resartus*.

POGONOPHOBIA *n.* A morbid dread of beards. As many *whilom* (q.v.) bearded ones can attest, the severity of this complaint is as nothing compared with the severity of its opposite number – the morbid dread by family members of a face from which a beard has just been removed.

POLIOSIS *n.* Premature greying of the hair. A puzzling concept – after all, what greying of the hair is *not* premature?

POLYPHAGIA *n.* Excessive eating. 'Ah, yuletide! Blessed season of joy! The Christmas tree, the decorations, the gifts, the carols, the sleigh bells, the *eructations* (q.v.), the polyphagia . . .'

PONOPHOBIA *n.* A morbid dread of work. Think about it. A civil servant could get a whole lifetime's sick leave out of this.

POPINJAY *n.* Empty-headed and pushy young *coxcomb* (q.v.). The emphasis here is on the brashness rather than the empty-headedness, and the image conveyed is of a garishly clad, interfering jabberer. The word is said to have originally described a target in the form of a parrot on a pole. Note the similarity to Papageno. One cannot help wondering who first had an idea so bizarre as that of using a parrot on a pole as a target. How, for that matter, was the parrot fixed to the pole? What did the parrot think of it? What, above all, was it a target for?

PORIOMANIA *n.* Wanderlust. A disease of cats, teenagers, and elderly ladies.

PORSONIAN *a.* An unashamed *neoterism* (q.v.) on the part of the author, referring to excessive indulgence in the cup that cheers. After Dr. Richard Porson (1759–1808), the greatest classical scholar in the age of classical scholarship, and a drunkard on a truly heroic scale. According to the historian Timbs, Porson was 'scarcely more ahead of his contemporaries in Greek than he was in drinking, in which his excesses were frightful.' He would drink anything, including ink, liniment, and once, in mistake for gin, a bottle of lamp oil.

POSTULANT *n.* One who seeks admission to a religious order. 'So – be it known that Mum and Dad seek admission to our game of Trivial Pursuit. Are the postulants ready to avow that they will not lose their temper when soundly beaten; that they will not seek to be reminded of the rules and procedure on more than five occasions per half hour; that they will not, on being informed that they have given an incorrect answer, use the words "I don't think that's right"; and that they will not exclaim, at the end of the game, "I don't know how anyone can be expected to know those questions – I've never heard of those pop singers"? They are? Then let the postulants be admitted.'

POTOMANIA *n.* Alcoholism, dipsomania, delirium tremens – three somewhat different things, be it noted, the word therefore raising the possibility that all three conditions could be experienced at the same time. (See *porsonian*.)

PRAGMATISM *n.* Mere expediency and low cunning. Formerly, a philosophical system adopted by a group of benevolent and forward-looking social reformers as the underpinning of their program for the enlightenment and advancement of society through educational processes that were creative, spontaneous, and equated the true with the good. *Sic transit gloria mundi.* An even earlier meaning of *pragmatical* (the common form of the adjective in the eighteenth century) was 'interfering and busybodyish.' *Pragmaticalness* was, according to Johnson, 'the quality of intermeddling without right or call.'

PRELIBATION *n.* Foretaste. The drink you have before you have a drink. And why not? Then there's postlibation too, of course. 'I can only repeat, Felicity – I have not had a single drink – merely a series of prelibations and of course the necessary postlibations.'

PRESCIND *v.* To cut off prematurely or abruptly. 'With Colonel Ferrier's concurrence, we will prescind his contribution to tonight's discussion. That okay, Colonel?'

PRESSURIZE *v.* Press. In future centuries, philologists will look back at the twentieth and characterize it as, verbally, the Age of Aggrandizement. What personal or societal traits this reflects is a matter for speculation by others; but certain it is that our natural tendency seems to be to create a noun out of a verb, and then convert the new noun into another and longer verb – a process which can be extended indefinitely. In the present case, the next step will probably be to replace 'pressure' with 'pressurization,' which will in turn come to be used itself as a verb. And so on. The Big Is Better syndrome has us by the throat.

PRESTIDIGITATION *n.* Sleight of hand. Literally, 'quick fingering.' 'My magic skills are getting better, Desirée; how about coming into my room for a little prestidigitation?'

PRETERMIT *v.* To pass over something, ignoring it or leaving it unattended to for the time being. 'Well, as Chairman I have to say that if Dr. Applehead feels so strongly about this agenda item, I think the rest of us would like to give him the opportunity, here and now, to pretermit it. Do you agree, Doctor?'

PRINK *v.* To deck out or smarten generally. 'Prink yourself up, Fotherway, or it'll be the worse for you.'

PROCACITY *n.* Petulance; impudence. Not to be confused with *precocity*. 'I think Natalie shows very considerable procacity,' you say earnestly to Mrs. Eastwacker after her narcissistic daughter has just beaten your own in the eisteddfod elocution finals.

PROCELLOUS *a.* Stormy, tempestuous. 'What sort of a mood is he in?' you are asked by the next candidate as you part from the official tester after your driver's license test. 'Procellous, distinctly procellous,' you reply, with a reassuring smile.

PROCERITY *n.* Tallness, height. 'I think you showed great procerity out there, darling,' you say proudly to your gangling teenager after she has just done her bit in the ballet class's end-of-term performance.

PROCTALGIA *n.* Pain in the backside. ('Rectalgia' means the same.) 'And this is our Corporate Resources Management Officer . . . I'm sorry, her name has just slipped my mind for the moment, but she's known to all of us, with the greatest possible affection, as Proctalgia.'

PROCUMBENT *a.* Lying or kneeling face down; prostrate. 'And another thing – I'd appreciate a little procumbency from you in future, Whittington.'

PROEM *n.* A prolegomenon, prolusion, prelude, introduction, foreword, or exordium.

PROLEGOMENA *n.* Introductory remarks, preliminary discussion. Much better than just saying *preface* or *prologue*.

PROLICIDE *a.* The killing of offspring. 'Oh . . . were you thinking of bringing the kids too, Carol? . . . Oh well, that's all right . . . No don't worry, *please* bring them . . . it's really all right . . . I'm sure I can arrange a little prolicide for them . . .'

PROLUSION *n.* A preliminary performance or attempt. A trial run or abbreviated effort, in preparation for the real thing. Thus a *matutinal* (q.v.) upbraiding by a spouse may be a mere prolusion for the full event at eventide.

PROPAEDEUTIC *n.* Preliminary study. 'The doctor said I'm allergic to propaedeutic, Mum, and I'm not to have any at night.'

PROSOPOGRAPHY *n.* The total description of a person – his or her appearance, personality, social status, family connections, qualifications, employment history, etc. The ultimate résumé. 'Candidates are asked to submit three copies of their prosopograph.'

PROSOPOPOEIA *n.* A rhetorical introduction of an imagined speaker or a personification of some abstraction or inanimate object. 'If these stones could speak . . .' 'As I stand here, tonight, I hear the voice of my late wife – pray God this is prosopopoeia and not one of my delusional states . . .'

PROTERVITY *n.* Petulance. 'Ah, Belinda, there is something so . . . so *young* about you . . . a kind of . . . how can I describe it . . . a kind of childlike . . . protervity . . .'

PROTOGENAL *a.* Pertaining to primitive creatures. 'Come on, we want your kids in the photo too, Cousin Sal! Line them up in front – that'll make the picture more protogenal!'

PROTOHUMAN *n.* or *a.* A primitive form of hominid, pre-dating homo sapiens. 'Well, Shannon's taste in boyfriends is improving. This latest primate of hers may be protohuman, but at least he's hominid.'

PRUNELLA *n.* A woollen cloth used both as a dress fabric and for the uppers of shoes. Also, a shoe made with prunella. Also, of course, a person's name, thereby providing a unique opportunity for wordplay in the event of such a person coming your way.

PSEPHOLOGY *n.* The alleged science of fortune-telling, the fortunes in this case being those of the megacephalic but micro-minded postures who periodically parade themselves before us, seeking political power, position, postage allowance, and pension. In short, psephology is the study of voting patterns at elections. Don't think too harshly of the psephologists. It's dirty work, but someone has to do it.

PSILOSIS *n.* Two different meanings: alopecia (i.e., baldness) and sprue (a tropical disease). In cursing an enemy, your imprecation could therefore include, as the climactic phrase, 'and *both* kinds of psilosis.'

PSITTACISM *n.* A string of meaningless, repetitive words. Literally 'parrot talk.' Superior person's word for New Age mantras and grandparental phaticisms. (See *phatic*.)

PUSILLANIMITY *n.* Faint-heartedness. (Note that this is not quite a synonym for *cowardice*.) Much used by Dr. Johnson in the eighteenth century, and in the twentieth by a learned *clerical* (q.v.) gentleman of the author's acquaintance, who is given to remarking on 'the difficulty of drawing the line between Christian meekness and pusillanimity.' This is the kind of remark which, suitable though it is for the Superior Person, should be used only once in a lifetime. Its repetition entails the risk of a repeated hearing by the same individual, with a consequent diminution of lexical credibility on the part of the speaker.

PUSTULANT *a.* or *n.* Causing pustules to appear; or a pharmaceutical that causes pustules to appear. 'And now, a little pustulant for Matthew?' you inquire avuncularly, as you offer the little chap a piece of chocolate.

PYKNIC *a.* (Pronounced the same as 'picnic.') Short and squat in build, with small hands and feet, short limbs and neck, a round face, and a domed abdomen. 'I see he has the true pyknic build,' you remark to Althea about her new and proudly displayed baby; 'strange – I thought that was always inherited. Heavens, I don't suppose. . .?'

PYRIFORM *a.* Shaped like a pear. But what *is* shaped like a pear – other than, of course, a pear?

PYROTIC *a.* Corrosive. 'No, the punch is non-alcoholic, I assure you. Jennifer has just put a little pyrotic in it, to stimulate the taste buds – that's all.'

QHYTHSONTYD *n.* Whether it's for fitting something into a seemingly impossible situation on a crowded Scrabble board, or nonplussing the smart alecks in a spelling competition, or meeting the challenge to produce yet another 'Q' word without a 'u' after the 'Q,' or discountenancing someone who claims she can pronounce *anything* . . . The meaning hardly matters, does it? But just to prove it isn't made up: qhythsontyd is an obsolete form of the rather better-known 'whitsuntide,' i.e., Whit Sunday, the seventh Sunday after Easter.

QUAB *n.* A very small fish; or something immature or unfinished. The latter meaning would appear to be a metaphorical derivative of the former. 'So they've made little Kenny head of the Department? Not surprised. He's a quab, but his *nutation* (q.v.) skills are awesome.'

QUACKSALVER *n.* Much to be preferred to the more usual, abbreviated form *quack*: an ignorant pretender to medical skills. A quacksalver was one who quacked, or chattered boastfully, about his salves, or healing ointments. The abbreviated form is fairly commonly used nowadays by the disrespectful as a synonym for *doctor*, for reasons unknown to the author. The use in such instances of the full form of the word would, it is suggested, help to avoid embarrassment in the event of its inadvertent use in the presence of one of the medical fraternity; indeed, a casual reference to one's quacksalver may well pass unchallenged in a roomful of doctors, who will probably assume that you are speaking of an item of domestic silver.

QUADDLE *v.* To grumble. To be a quaddler seems somehow to sound more amiable than to be a grumbler. 'He's a lovable old quaddler.'

QUADRAGENARIAN *n.* Someone who is between forty and fifty years of age. Since the word sounds to the uninitiated as though it means simply 'forty-year-old,' it is particularly suitable for use by forty-nine-year-olds as a self-descriptive.

QUADRIVIUM *n.* Everyone knows that in medieval times the seven liberal arts that composed the curriculum of educational institutions were divided into the four more advanced subjects (the quadrivium) and the three lesser subjects (the trivium). But how many of you can name the seven subjects? Or the seven wonders of the ancient world, for that matter? The quadrivium was made up of Arithmetic, Geometry, Astronomy, and Music; the trivium of Grammar, Logic, and Rhetoric. In the modern curriculum, Grammar, Logic, and Rhetoric have been replaced by Sports Studies, Media Appreciation, and Self-actualisation, thus giving the term 'trivium' a renewed level of significance.

QUADRUMANE *a.* Having four prehensile hands or feet, like a monkey. A muttered 'Quadrumane!' is a satisfying ladylike parting shot at your young brother as he leaves the room after an argument.

QUADRUPLICITIES *n.* One of the many quaint terms used by astrologers, this refers to the grouping of the twelve signs of the zodiac into three groups of four: the cardinal (Aries, Libra, Cancer, and Capricorn), the fixed (Taurus, Scorpio, Leo, and Aquarius), and the mutable (Gemini, Sagittarius, Virgo, and Pisces). Tell someone that you are aware of their quadruplicity; this is guaranteed to leave them vaguely unsettled.

QUAESTUARY *n.* Someone whose first and foremost objective is profit. A teenage son who will work in the garden only if paid to do so.

QUAG *n.* A boggy place, especially one that quakes underfoot. 'Simon! Come here this minute and clean

quag

up your room! Do you realize that the area around and under your bed is pure quag?'

QUAGGLE *n.* A quivering, as of jelly. 'And our special prize for the waltz competition tonight goes to Mrs. Broadbeem, for her unique Quaggle Effect.'

QUAINTISE *n.* A cunning little ploy or stratagem. One for the weekly executive group meeting: 'Well, Mr. Wetherby, what little quaintise do you have in store for us this morning, under Other Business?'

QUAKEBUTTOCK *n.* A nicely scornful word for a coward.

QUALM *n.* A sudden uneasiness, generally about some action or proposed action of one's own. Less intellectual and more intuitive than a *scruple* (q.v.) or a misgiving. In modern parlance, the degree of uneasiness implied is only moderate, but formerly the use of the term implied nausea or even pain. The present meaning lies rather beautifully midway between those of *queasy* and *calm*, but the apparently hybrid spelling is purely fortuitous and has nothing to do with either word. Normally one has qualms rather than a qualm. 'I must confess to having some qualms about our new advertising slogan, Fosdyke.' But in such a case, exactly how many qualms does the speaker have? The author believes he has the answer to this. He has always seen a qualm as being a small, round, jellylike object about five centimeters in diameter – i.e., a pocket-sized object. The number of qualms normally held about anything would therefore equate to the number of pockets in a man's suit; that is, about half a dozen. This theory also fits the observed fact that women generally have fewer qualms than men.

QUAQUAVERSAL *a.* Pointing or facing in every direction. In relation to rock formations, the term specifically means sloping down in every direction from a more or less central tip. You might so refer to your Uncle Enderby's cranial structure.

QUEER PLUNGERS *n.* Not a reference to the lubricious doings of androgynes; a queer plunger was a rather charming form of eighteenth-century con man or confidence trickster. The following definition comes from Grose's *Dictionary of the Vulgar Tongue*: 'Cheats who throw themselves into the water, in order that they may be taken up by their accomplices, who carry them to one of the houses appointed by the Humane Society for the recovery of drowned persons, where they are rewarded by the Society with a guinea each; and the supposed drowned person, pretending he was driven to that extremity by great necessity, is also frequently sent away with a contribution in his pocket.'

QUERIMONY *n.* Complaint. *Querimonious* is a synonym of *querulous*, but the former is to be preferred on account of its superior grandiloquence. Should one of your immediate family be in the habit of having regular faultfinding sessions on your personal appearance, your clothes, your manners, your habits, etc., you might find an opportunity to refer to such sessions as his or her *quotidian* (q.v.) querimony ceremony.

QUIDDITY *n.* (i) The essence of something; literally, its *whatness*; (ii) a quibble, or trifling nicety. One might say that the quiddity of a quiddity is its quirkish, quizzical, quibbling quaintness.

QUIDNUNC *n.* A gossip; a stickybeak; one who is forever anxious to know about everything that is going on. Literally, 'what now?' One is never just a quidnunc; one is an *inveterate* quidnunc. Interestingly, the term was for a time more commonly taken to mean a politician. Grose mentions a character named Quidnunc, a politician, in a farce called *The Upholsterer*. Not to be confused with 'quincunx,' an arrangement of five things in such a way that four of them are the points of a square and the fifth is in the center of the square.

QUIESCENT *a.* At rest for the time being; dormant; inactive. The odd thing about this word is not what it means but what it does not mean. *Quiesce* means 'to grow quiet or still' and by any normal process *quiescent* should mean 'growing quiet or still'; instead, it has a quite specific usage, referring as it does always to a condition that was formerly active, is now inactive, but will become active again in due course – such as the reader's *cardialgia* (q.v.), or his wife's *oniomania* (q.v.).

QUIETIST *n.* One who practices quietism, that is to say the doctrine that true exaltation of the spirit is attained only by self-denial and passive contemplation. When the fundamentalists call to discuss your belief in God and the coming Armageddon, just put your finger to your lips and hold up a simply lettered cardboard sign reading WE ARE QUIETISTS. Then smile benignly and close the door.

QUIETUS *n.* A blow or other action bringing about death; a *coup de grace*. As in *Hamlet*: 'his quietus make / With a bare bodkin. . . .' (a bodkin being a pin or other pointed instrument such as a stiletto). A suggestively gentle word for a grim thing. 'Time for your quietus now, children,' you gently say, as you usher your visitors' uncontrolled little offspring out of the lounge room; 'I have some lovely plastic bags for you to play with in the rumpus room.'

QUILLET *n.* A subtlety in argument. 'And what's more, in all the many speeches that Quentin has made over the years in the Senate, there has never been so much as a hint of personal vilification or the use of quillets to aid his case.'

QUIM *n.* The private parts of a woman (an eighteenth-century usage, possibly derived from *queme*, an obsolete word meaning 'pleasant, snug'). 'Ah, women,' you muse out loud, in the middle of your sister's bridal shower. 'I love them, for all their quims and fancies.' Alternatively, when you come upon your beloved apparently lost in reverie, you cry jovially: 'A *merkin* [q.v.] for your quim, my dear!' She assumes you to be using an esoteric variant of 'a penny for your thoughts,' and opens her heart to you.

QUINK *n.* The common brant (a kind of goose). Conversation Stopper No. 331: 'Did you know that the quink was the common brant?'

QUINT *n.* A pipe organ stop, which sounds at the interval of a fifth above the key depressed. In case you think that this is an odd name for an organ stop, here are some others: Amorosa (a hybrid flute stop); Bearded Gamba (a string stop 'of keen and cutting quality'); Chimney Flute (a half-covered flute); Clarabella (an open wood flute); Copula (I'm not saying what that one does); Corno Di Bassetto (basset horn – Bernard Shaw's *nom de plume* as a music critic); Gravissima (I had thought this meant a very pregnant lady, but according to my source it gives the organist 'an impressive bottom for his combinations'); Gross Quint (gross quint); Heckelphone (unaccountably, there appears to be no Jeckelphone); Krummhorn ('mournful and sedate'); Ludwigtone (sounding like Ludwig); Stentorphone (you've guessed it – very loud); Suave Flute (suave flute – would not be seen dead with Gross Quint); Tibia Dura (shinbone – no, only joking); Tuba d'Amour (love tube – keep well away from Copula); Viol Quint (vile quint – often seen with Gross Quint); and Zink ('pungent, nasal'). I have made up none of these names, many of which, incidentally, have an obvious potentiality of application to the world of human types. All of us know a few Zinks, for example.

QUINTAIN *n.* Something set in place to be tilted at. 'I don't know why you children have to keep pestering me while I'm cooking. There's your father out there on the sun lounger – let him be your quintain instead!'

QUIRT *n.* A braided leather riding whip with a short handle. 'A taste of the quirt, Leonie?' you politely inquire, offering her the hors d'oeuvres.

quirt

QUISQUOUS *a.* Perplexing, puzzling. 'How extremely quisquous!' you declare, as you pore over the chessboard.

QUODLIBET *n.* (i) A debating point; a nice point, or scholastic subtlety raised for disputation. One might almost say that the *quiddity* (q.v.) of quodlibet is the same as the quiddity of a quiddity. (ii) An impromptu musical medley.

QUONDAM *a.* *Whilom* (q.v.). Enough said?

QUOTHA! *excl.* (Pronounced 'quoather', by the way.) Exclamation indicative of surprise, with a slight overlay of derision. Much the same effect as 'Forsooth!' 'I came all the way from town by the mountain route, and the old car used one quart of petrol!' 'Quotha!'

QUOTIDIAN *a.* Everyday; recurring daily; ordinary, commonplace. Can also be used as a noun, meaning a daily allowance or allotment. 'Have you had your quotidian yet?' is a question that will leave a friend nicely bemused. *Diurnal* in one of its senses means the same, but in another means 'by day,' as distinct from 'by night' – the opposite of *nocturnal*, in fact; hence it is not necessarily a solecism to speak of a diurnal quotidian. To speak of a nocturnal quotidian is, of course, quite another thing.

R

RADDLED *a.* Most of us have heard this expression used of someone who is getting on in years and is in a confused state – meaning more or less 'old and silly.' But the actual meaning is, to quote Chambers, 'aged and worsened by debauchery.' From 'reddle' – red ocher, or coarse rouge, referring to the rouging of elderly roués' cheeks, particularly in the eighteenth century. Be not too unkind in the way that you use this knowledge.

RAMENTUM *n.* (Plural *ramenta*.) A tiny flake that has been rubbed or scraped off something. 'Mummy, it's disgusting! Luke has left his ramenta all over the vanity unit again! I want my own bathroom like you and Daddy have!'

RAMPALLION *n.* A bold, forward, rampant, or wanton woman; a woman who romps. An Elizabethan term. Thus Falstaff to Mistress Quickly, when she attempts to have him arrested: 'Away, you scullion; you rampallion; you fustilarian! I'll tickle your catastrophe.' (*Henry IV Pt. II,* Act II, Scene 1.) A suggested modern use: 'Mom, can I have a rampallion for my birthday?' (Incidentally, a *fustilarian* is a fusty-lugs, or beastly, sluttish woman; and a *catastrophe*, in the above context, is a posterior.)

RANARIUM *n.* A frog farm. 'Better smarten up, Fosdyke, or it'll be the ranarium for you.'

RAREE SHOW *phr.* A lovely old-fashioned phrase which should be used more often than it is. A raree show was a travelling showman's cheap little peepshow or bizarre exhibit, typically but not always carried in a box. When your daughter's new boyfriend, during his first dinner with the family, has finished showing off his skills of catching a pile of coins from his elbow, catching thrown peanuts in his mouth, turning both eyeballs inwards, and cracking his knuckles at will, you could clap your hands with simulated delight and thank your daughter for having brought such a raree show into the home.

RASORIAL *a.* Constantly scratching around in search of food, like a fowl (or a sister's boyfriend). Pronounced more or less in the same way as *risorial* (laughter-provoking) and *rosorial* (rodentlike; gnawing). 'I'm sorry if I sometimes seem ambivalent in my attitude to your mother, Natalie; it's just that I find it very hard to make up my mind whether I see her as essentially rasorial, rosorial, or risorial.'

RATIOCINATE, RATIOCINANT *a.* It's important to get these right. Oh, all right, it's not really. But it's knowledge that only you will have. Used as an adjective, ratiocinate means 'reasoned about,' whereas ratiocinant means 'reasoning.' Thus: 'Our business plan was ratiocinate enough, God knows, but unfortunately the ratiocinant beings who developed it were not very good at ratiocination.'

RAVEL *v.* No, not the composer's name. One of those few words which means exactly the same as its apparent opposite. (*Flammable* means the same as *inflammable*; *boned* means the same as *deboned*.) Believe it or not, to ravel something is to unravel it. 'Ravel the morning paper for me, will you, dear?'

REBARBATIVE *a.* Repulsive, off-putting, daunting. A relatively innocuous-sounding epithet, and therefore suitable for use in relation to food, children, or dachshunds when in the presence of hostesses, mothers, and dog-owners.

REBOANT *a.* Reverberating very loudly. 'Remember, children, this is a chapel of remembrance; when we're inside would you all please lower your voices to about reboant level.'

RECALESCENT *a.* Glowing with heat again, temporarily, at a certain stage of the process of cooling down from white heat. A fitting epithet for an elderly acquaintance who is making a fool of himself with a *poppet* or a *frippet* (q.v.), and having the time of his life in the process.

RECIDIVISM *n.* Habitual relapsing into criminal or otherwise antisocial behavior. As, for example, a neighbor's habitually letting his German shepherd run loose in the street, playing Scott Joplin records at full volume, or assaulting itinerant Mormons. Note the difference from *atavism*, which is the reappearance of a more primitive form of behavior; as, for example, a neighbor running loose in the street himself, playing Scottish country dance records at full volume, or *not* assaulting itinerant Mormons.

RECREMENT *n.* A bodily secretion that is reabsorbed. The obvious example – indeed the only one known to the author, who is not, and does not seek to be, well-versed in such matters – is saliva. Rather than speak of a nubile damsel, or a plate of steaming frankfurters, as making your mouth water, you could refer to yourself as experiencing an increment in your recrement.

RECUBATION *n.* Reclining in a near-horizontal position, as did ancient Romans at the banquet table. 'There'll be no recubation at *this* dinner table, young man! Sit up straight – and take off that baseball cap!'

RECUSANT *n.* One refusing staunchly to comply with some generally accepted rule or custom. The most appropriate modern application would be to that small but hardy band who refuse to be searched, labeled, unlabeled, interrogated, or otherwise bullied or humiliated on their entrance to, or egress from, supermarket-style chain stores. 'Leave me alone!' they cry in ringing tones, on being approached by the store security officers; 'Go away! Stop bothering me, you rude man!' The author, whose natural *pusillanimity* (q.v.) prevents him from being more than a recusant *manqué* (q.v.), bows before them in respect and admiration.

REDHIBITION *n.* The nullification of a sale because of a defect in the article sold. Something to say when the priest asks whether you will take this person to be your lawful wedded spouse: 'Are there redhibition rights on this contract? Only joking!'

REDIVIVUS *a.* Restored to life, or to full liveliness. Use *after* the noun, and preferably after an incongruously non-classical noun. If, for example, your name is Boggins, you might emerge from your shower, taken after a hard day's gardening, and cry to your wife: 'Behold! Boggins redivivus!'

REFOCILLATION *n.* Total refreshment; revival or revitalization. You stagger into the bar, collapse onto the stool immediately facing the *bathycolpian* (q.v.) barmaid, and gasp: 'Refocillate me!' Whether she understands or misunderstands you, there is at least some chance that you will achieve refocillation.

REGELATION *n.* Freezing together again, after having melted apart (as ice may, when it is subject to changing levels of pressure). 'So Jonquil and Bruce are together again, eh? Five years after their divorce – fancy that! Are they going to have a regelation ceremony?'

REJECTAMENTA *n.* Things that have been rejected, as being worthless. A delicate way for a young lady to refer to a former suitor – 'one of my rejectamenta.'

REMARKS, EXASPERATING *n.* (See also *bully for you!* and *stout fellow!*) '*You are very wise.*' This is recommended as an effective all-purpose response on any occasion when you have been out-argued, ridiculed, shouted down, or simply proved hopelessly wrong. It should be uttered in a quiet, dignified fashion and with an earnest facial expression. Its effect is multiplied if it can be used again within the ensuing few minutes.

'*You may well be right.*' For use in similar circumstances to the above. Should be used, however, with studied nonchalance and a gentle smile, as though you have decided that the other party will have to be humored.

'*Spare me your rapierlike wit.*' For use when a spouse or workmate has made a successful sally at your expense. A little touch of mock supplication in your tone will help with this one.

'. . . *for want of a better word.*' Use immediately following any exceptionally grandiloquent or esoteric term. 'You don't find Gilbert to be a little . . . er . . . *ultracrepidarian* [q.v.] – for want of a better word?'

REMIPED *n.* Having feet that are adapted for use as oars. May be of use as a substitute for *megapod* (q.v.) when in the presence of a policeman.

REMONTADO *n.* Someone who has fled to the mountains and renounced civilization. A ski instructor.

REMPLISSAGE *n.* Padding, i.e., needless filling, in literature. From the French, naturally. Not possible in a highly structured work of the present nature, but rampant in lesser forms such as the novel (which, as everyone knows, is merely a story with remplissage), the TV weather report, and the lawyer's bill of accounts.

RENIFORM *a.* Kidney-shaped. 'Kind of you to ask after me, Maurice. As it happens, I've just had some rather important news. Had a chat with my doctor, and it seems I have reniform kidneys.'

RENITENCY *n.* Reluctance or resistance. 'Don't worry, Dad; the idea of a weekly work assignment in return for my allowance is one that I can handle with complete renitency.'

REPLEVIN *n.* A legal term, denoting an inquiry the purpose of which is to restore to an owner goods that have been wrongfully taken away from him. As a literary term it refers to an inquiry intended to achieve a deserved reputation for a writer hitherto denied recognition. Join the Peter Bowler Replevin movement now! Send your petitions to booksellers everywhere!

replevin

REPTATION *n.* The motion of two plane figures (flat surfaces, you ignoramuses) when they are slid around against each other. A mathematical term which derives from 'reptile,' its alternative meaning being 'creeping like a reptile.' Hence the sense can reasonably be extended to characterize the locomotion of the figuratively reptilian. 'Our courses for encyclopaedia salespersons, insurance agents, investment advisors, and senior banking executives include basic accounting, business principles, communication, and reptation skills. . .'

REPULLULATE *v.* To sprout again; to recur, as a disease. The perfect verb with which to describe the reappearances of your beloved's young brother at the living-room door while you are engaged in an affectionate tête-à-tête with the young lady.

RESIPISCENCE *n.* Recognizing one's own error, or errors; seeing reason once again. 'I'm sure all of us look forward to your ultimate resipiscence, Jeremy.'

RESISTENTIALISM *n.* A fictitious philosophical system, created by Paul Jennings in the late 1940s, to account for the apparent harassment by inanimate matter of human beings. As for example in the failure of the car to start on the one occasion when it is vital that it does, or the jamming open of the zipper on your fly just when you are about to return from the toilet to the dais to give your speech at the convention. This raises the attractive possibility of creating other fictitious philosophical systems for domestic use. 'Sorry, darling, but your proposal that we break our trip here to spend time in the Craftie

Haven Hand-Painted Rusticware Centre is precluded by my long-held Destinationism; we must press on without delay!'

RESUPINATE *a.* Upside down as a result of twisting. 'So sad about Bannister. Been in politics only seven years and already suffering irreversible resupination.'

RETICULUM *n.* Any net-like structure. Well, what could be more net-like than a net? 'Ashleigh, you check the height of the reticulum while I go and get a *nacket* (q.v.). And who's brought the tennis balls?'

RETROBULBAR *a.* Behind the eyeball. Since this is (more or less) where the brain is, I suppose you could refer to an ideological adversary as being 'disadvantaged by a retrobulbar vacancy.'

RETROCESSION *n.* Retreat; returning a property to a former owner; and (of a disease) turning inwards into the body as distinct from breaking out, e.g., through the skin. The general sense is one of *extremity* of retreat. 'Have you seen Mum's face? Let's be there to watch when Dad comes in, and see how long it takes him to go into retrocession mode.'

RETROCOGNITION *n.* A form of extra-sensory perception in which the clairvoyant becomes aware of something that has happened in the past without having been told about it. 'Matthew, I feel an act of retrocognition coming on! You enter the room having been out all morning – and without having any empirical evidence to tell me this, I suddenly feel that I know with absolute certainty that you have spent the entire morning playing computer games at the mall!'

RETRUSION *n.* A displacement of the teeth toward the back of the mouth. 'If the Honorable Senator is so unhappy about my remarks, I would invite him to meet me afterward in the corridor, where I will be happy to give him a complete retrusion.'

retrusion

REVETMENT *n.* A sloping structure, of masonry, timber, etc., intended to act as a retaining wall to support a terrace, the bank of a river, the side of a railway cutting, or other swelling protuberance. 'Ah, Mrs. Zaftig, how I admire your revetment!'

RHADAMANTHINE *a.* Uncompromisingly just and completely incorruptible. From Rhadamanthus, a mythical Greek judge, and therefore an epithet normally reserved for persons in judicial positions. It is said, however, that there was once a rhadamanthine politician.

RHATHYMIA *n.* Carefree, indifferent, or light-hearted behavior. 'Now boys, this is a solemn ceremony; when the school chaplain gives his address, let's have some genuine rhathymia.'

RHINOCEROTIC *a.* According to the author's sources, this means 'pertaining to rhinoceroses'; but, since *rhinal* means 'of the nose' (see *dirhinous*), he cherishes the thought that an equally valid meaning would be 'using the nose, or nostrils, for erotic purposes.'

RHONCHISONANT *a.* This means snoring or snorting, but will sound a lot better than those terms when you put your self-description in the Personals.

RHYNCHOCEPHALIAN *a.* Pertaining to an almost-extinct order of lizardlike reptiles. The implication of this dictionary definition is that the creature in question is not a lizard, merely *like* a lizard. In that case, what is it? In any case, suitable as a descriptor for any of your acquaintances who are lizardlike and reptilian.

RHYTIDECTOMY *n.* A surgical operation in which the skin of the face is smoothed out and wrinkles removed. Commonly called a face-lift. 'Fancy meeting you after all these years, Meredith! I nearly didn't recognize you. And how wise of you not to have had a rhytidectomy, in spite of everything!'

RHYTISCOPIA *n.* A neurotic preoccupation with facial wrinkles. 'Elissa, how you've changed! Oh, I do hope you're not troubled by rhytiscopia!'

RICTAL BRISTLE *n.* A feather resembling a bristle which grows from the base of a bird's bill. A rather sweet name for your sister's boyfriend's incipient beard.

RICTUS *n.* A fixed gaping of the mouth, or grinning. *Rictus sardonicus* is the fixed grin on the face of one who has just died from strychnine poisoning, which induces muscular contractions; *rictus politicus*, that on the face of a Congressman who has just been confronted on live television with the news that he has lost his seat as a result of an unexpected swing during late counting of votes on election night; and *rictus excruciatus*, that on the face of the author when he suddenly realizes that he has forgotten the names of *both* of the two people whom he is trying to introduce to each other.

RIGIDULOUS *a.* Somewhat rigid; a little stiff. A tricky word, looking as it does so much like a misprint for 'ridiculous.' Not easy to say, either – try it, and you'll see what I mean.

RINDERPEST *n.* A malignant and contagious disease of cattle. 'I'd like to tell that child exactly what I think of him, but I can't decide whether he's got the rinderpest or whether he *is* the rinderpest.'

RISORGIMENTO *n.* A revival of artistic, liberal, or national spirit. However, in the hurly-burly of an Italian restaurant, it is almost always possible to convince at least one of your table companions that it is in fact a vegetarian pasta dish, and induce her to order it from a passing waiter.

RITORNELLO *n.* In music (or for that matter poetry), a short sequence that is repeated like a refrain. Literally, 'little return,' thus opening up the possibility of truth in investment advertising: 'Invest your money in our private scheme for Internet options futures! Ritornello!!'

ROBUR *n.* In ancient Roman times, a subterranean dungeon within a prison, used as a place of execution for criminals. Also called a *carnificina.* 'To the robur with you!' you cry, pointing down the steps to the basement.

RODOMONTADE *n.* Empty boasting and blustering; arrogant ranting, braggadocio. From Rodomont, a Moorish hero in Ariosto's *Orlando Furioso.* The nearest thing to a modern example that springs to mind is the televised prating of professional wrestlers, boxers, and politicians; but in at least two of these three cases there is an underlying suggestion of self-awareness and good humor that prevents the term being fully applicable. Note, incidentally, that *braggadocio* can be either the language that is spoken or the person who speaks it.

ROGATION *n.* A supplication to God; a prayer in which a specific request is made of the Deity. (From the ancient Roman term for the submission of a proposed new law to the people.) Sir Francis Galton, the great nineteenth-century scientist who invented fingerprints and eugenics, once carried out a statistical survey of the proportion of prayers which were answered. Another of his surveys was of the geographical distribution of good looks in Britain. (He

294

found that the prettiest women were in London and the ugliest in Aberdeen.) Galton wore his own Universal Patent Ventilating Hat, a top hat with a crown which could be raised by the action of a tube and a squeezable rubber bulb, thereby allowing the overheated head to cool.

ROINOUS *a.* Mean, nasty, and contemptible. 'I'll let Adrian speak for himself, and we'll all see just how roinous he can be.'

ROMERIA *n.* A festival held at a local shrine. 'Don't give me that stuff about obligatory attendance at a romeria! I know you're just going down to the bar to drink with your golf cronies!'

RONION *n.* A term of abuse for a woman, found in Shakespeare (*Merry Wives of Windsor* and *Macbeth*). The meaning is not entirely clear: Webster relates it to the French *rogne* (scab or mange) and suggests 'scabby, mangy'; but Johnson, more convincingly in view of Shakespeare's 'rump-fed ronyon,' relates it to the French *rognon* (the loins) and suggests 'fat, bulky.'

ROTURIER *n.* Someone without any rank or status in society. A peasant, a plebeian, a day-labourer, a schoolteacher, or a civil servant.

ROUNCEVAL *n.* Three quite different meanings for this one: a giant; a marrowfat pea; and a virago. Nice to be able to characterize something or someone with a term that is not just ambiguous but doubly so. 'A new book, eh, Lorraine? What a thoroughgoing rounceval you are!'

RUDERAL *n.* Thriving in rubbish or waste. A term from the world of plant life that has obvious potential for application to the animal world. 'She's had a truly ruderal career, you know – she's done well, first as secretary to a backbencher, then on the Minister's research staff, and now as executive assistant for the party leader.'

RUFOUS *a.* Coloured a dullish red or rusty reddish-brown. Reserve the term strictly for use in circumstances where someone named Rufus has just come in from working in the garden. Be patient. At least once in your life, this will happen.

RUGOSE *a.* Corrugated with wrinkles. 'Ah, Mrs. Sandal-bath, there must be many a woman half your age with a complexion not nearly as rugose as yours.'

RUPTUARY *n.* A commoner or plebeian. One of the few words that rhymes with 'voluptuary.' 'So glad you're in the insurance game now, Ernestine; it always seemed to me that you were suited for ruptuarial work.'

RUTILANT *a.* Glittering or glowing with reddish light. Your Uncle Arbuthnot's nose after a hard day's social intercourse.

S

SABIANISM *n.* The worship of heavenly bodies. Would the Miss World and Miss Universe competitions attract a little less opprobrium, perhaps, if they were to register as religious organizations, and call their adherents sabians?

SACKBUT *n.* A medieval instrument, not unlike a trombone. The term is derived from an old French word for a hook used to pull a man off a horse. Make what you will of this.

SAL VOLATILE *n.* Understood by the author to be the name of a young American film-star, of southern European descent, who made his name in the fifties doing bit parts in rock 'n' roll movies.

SAPID *a.* Flavorsome, lively, interesting. The opposite of *vapid*, and of *insipid*, but vaguely suggestive of both words and hence ideal for the Compliment Reluctant: 'I'm so glad you've invited Charles; I always find his conversation so sapid.' Or the Insult

Apparent: 'So Charles is coming, eh? Hmmm . . . do you think he'll fit in? His conversation is always so . . . sapid.'

SAPONACEOUS *a.* Soapy. Though the word comes from the objective realms of scientific and technological terminology, it could equally well be used metaphorically, in the sense of 'unctuous,' 'greasily ingratiating,' or 'Uriah Heepish.'

SAPOROUS *a.* Tasty, flavorsome. Like *saponaceous*, an objective scientific term that calls out for a more colorful usage. On being introduced to the couple who clearly regard themselves as two of the Beautiful People and who have just made their Impressive and Well-Timed Entrance, you exclaim admiringly: 'Ah, how perfect! The marriage of the saponaceous and the saporous!' Their evening is tormented by the necessity to remember the two words until they can get home and look them up in the dictionary; and when they do, they find themselves plagued by uncertainty as to which term you were applying to which person.

SARCOPHAGOUS *a.* No, not the stone coffin from which a muslin-swathed Lon Chaney practices *anabiosis* (q.v.), hand-first, to the dismay of a nearby Nubian or nubile. That is spelled *sarcophagus*, without the second *o*. The former word means flesh-eating, or carnivorous. Actually, the latter word is basically the same, despite its *o*-less condition, since it was originally a coffin used by the ancient Greeks which, because of the particular kind of limestone of which it was made, did in fact consume the

298

corpse, i.e., eat flesh. If you are a vegetarian, you might refer to your meat-eating acquaintances as sarcophagous.

SATRAP *n.* A petty or subordinate ruler with despotic powers within his own realm. An assistant principal, bus driver, dental nurse, head of a typing pool, hospital matron, motor-vehicle inspector, or headwaiter.

SAXICOLOUS *a.* Living or growing among rocks. A geology student.

SCIOLISM *n.* Superficial knowledge; a show of learning without any substantial foundation. 'As always, Herr Doktor, I bow to your superior sciolism.'

SCIOPHILOUS *a.* (Of plants) shade-loving; thriving in shady conditions. The plants that you and I always plant in full sun.

SCOPODROMIC *a.* Pertaining to the motion of a guided missile homing in on its target. 'You're not just putting the gingerbread men in the cookie jar, surely? Don't forget you-know-who's scopodromic qualities. What about the wall safe?'

SCOPOPHOBIA *n.* A morbid fear of being seen. 'Scotophobia' is a morbid fear of darkness. How appalling to suffer from both simultaneously! Think about it.

SCORDATURA *n.* An unusual tuning of a stringed instrument, intended to achieve a special effect. Convenient for use as a polite euphemism when invited to

299

comment on the violin playing of your host's ten-year-old. 'Hmm, interesting scordatura there – very interesting!'

SCRIPTORIUM *n.* The room in a monastery where books are written and copied. Superior Person's word for a study.

SCRIVENER *n.* A copyist of documents. One employed solely to copy out legal or financial documents by hand. A nineteenth-century occupation made famous forever by Melville's classic story *Bartleby the Scrivener*, in which the inoffensive Bartleby refuses any work other than copying, and quietly remains at his place of work while the work itself moves on, leaving him with nothing to do but die. An allegory for the age of micro-computers and multi-skilling. Honor Bartleby by refusing to use the term Carpal Tunnel Syndrome and insisting on referring to your condition instead as 'scrivener's palsy' – the old-fashioned term for writer's cramp.

SCRUPLE *n.* The common meaning, of course, is a feeling of reluctance or a hesitation, based on conscientious concern for a principle. In this sense, the word evokes conjecture about the precise number and nature of the scruples held in a particular instance. (See also *qualm*.) Whereas the author envisages a qualm as a small jellylike object carried in the pocket, he has always envisaged a scruple as being a small purple pretzel-shaped object caught in the hair. This also helps to account for the observed fact that women have more scruples than men. (See, again, *qualm*.) Be that as it may, there is a secondary (originally the primary) meaning for *scruple*: an extremely small unit of weight. This enables you to liven up a moribund party by declaring, during a quiet moment, that you know for a fact, and can prove, that Arabella has fewer scruples than Felicity.

SCUMBLE *v.* To lay a thin coat of opaque or nearly opaque color over a painted area with an almost dry brush, to soften the color or line of a picture. An endearingly unsophisticated word for such a sophisticated process. 'I'm sorry, he can't come to the phone; he's busy scumbling.'

SELF-ACTUALIZATION *n.* Self-realization. A term invented by contemporary educational theorists who envisage the liberated child opening like a flower before them as his natural instincts unfold and his own special talents and personality traits emerge and develop to their full in a free and open environment, untrammeled by outside interference. It is difficult to point to particular examples of the process in operation; but the life of Heinrich Himmler, or the growth of a cauliflower, appear to the author to fit the terms of the theory.

SEMPITERNAL *a.* The Superior Person's word for *eternal*. Strictly speaking, a somewhat tautological construction, deriving as it does from the Latin *semper* (always) and *aeternus* (eternal); but pleasingly archaic and rhetorical in flavor. Slightly confusing to the listener also: if your wife overhears you declaring a sempiternal affection for your secretary, you can always explain that the word you were using was *semi-paternal*.

SENESCHAL *n.* The steward or majordomo of a medieval mansion or cathedral. The school janitor, perhaps?

SERMOCINATION *n.* The practice of making speeches; the habit of preaching constantly. (See *stentorophonic*.)

SESQUIPEDALIAN *a.* Inordinately long (of words). Literally, a foot and a half long – hence, a word of that length. As a noun: an inveterate user of such words; a practitioner of the lore contained in this book; a *word-grubber* (q.v.).

SEXIST *a.* Tacitly assuming a conventional set of differences between the sexes. Not, as might appear at first sight, an active practitioner of sexual behavior.

SHANDYGAFF *n.* The full and proper name for what most people call a shandy. In the future, *never* use the abbreviated version; always the full. Know, too, that a shandygaff is properly not beer and lemonade, but beer and ginger beer. A young lady should always insist on the proprieties being observed in these matters.

SHIBBOLETH *n.* A doctrine or principle once held essential by a particular group or party but now seen as rather old-hat, if not abandoned altogether. It is probably a comment on the nature of life and mutability, rather than on etymological processes, that the original meaning was a password or other identifying sign, such as an opinion or style of dress, that distinguished the members of a particular group because of their unique attachment to it. Thus advocacy of the nationalization of industry was a shibboleth of the political left wing in former years in a sense quite different from that in which it is now their shibboleth. Just how important it was in earlier times to be on the right side of a shibboleth can be judged from the original usage in Judges 12: 5–6: '. . . and it was so, that when those Ephraimites which were escaped said, Let me go over; that the men of Gilead said unto him [*sic*], Art thou an Ephraimite? If he said, Nay; Then said they unto him, Say now Shibboleth: and he said Sibboleth: for he could not frame to pronounce it right. Then they took him, and slew him . . .'

SHITTLECOCK *n.* The true, proper, and original form of *shuttlecock*, from the Old English *scytel*, or bolt. Apparently fallen into *desuetude* (q.v.) in this form since the eighteenth century, for reasons unknown to the author. Its use in the original form is to be preferred, especially when playing badminton with your sister. (See also *bumblepuppy.*)

SHOULDERCLAPPER *n.* A Shakespearean term (*Comedy of Errors*) meaning a person who 'affects familiarity' but at the same time 'mischiefs privily.' Included here to give the author the opportunity of quoting from Johnson's superb definition.

SIALOGOGUE *n.* Something that stimulates the flow of saliva. 'Ah, Rachel, a quiet little dinner party like this, with just the two of us . . . and you the perfect sialogogue.'

sicarian

SICARIAN *n.* A murderer. More specifically, an assassin. 'You'll find 3B an interesting class this year, Carruthers. Very multicultural. There are some Lebanese, a couple of Croatians and Serbs . . . watch out for the two Irish kids – they're from opposite sides in Ulster . . . there's a Calabrian and a Sicilian . . . as for the others, they're mainly sicarians, I think.'

SIDERATION *n.* The use of green manure. 'Sorry to see you're having trouble with your complexion again, Candace. Collagen not working, eh? Have you thought of trying a little sideration?'

SILLABUB *n.* A dessert made mostly out of cream. A pleasing, eighteenth-centuryish term for the jar of creamed rice that you are obliged to open for your unexpected dinner guest. Metaphorically, sillabub is inane, inconsequential, or frothy speech.

SIMPLETON *n.* A person of little brainpower. There is a suggestion, too, of well-meaningness and gullibility. 'A democratic franchise of one simpleton, one vote'

(Shaw). The formation of the word by the addition to *simple* of *ton* (the latter perhaps an elision of 'the one'?) is pleasing, and suggests the similar formation of others, such as *feebleton, littleton,* etc. Grose suggests that *ton* is short for *Tony,* but gives no hint as to who the unfortunate Anthony, thus immortalized, may have been.

SITOPHOBIA *n.* Morbid fear of eating. Not common in its general form, but often encountered in its various specific forms, e.g., fear of eating your mother-in-law's garlic broccoli, fear of eating your small daughter's rock cakes, etc.

SKEUOMORPH *n.* An archaeological term to describe an object which has been made in such a way as to look like a similar one made in a different material; for example, a ceramic pot shaped and coloured to look like a bronze one. In today's households, a number of plastic articles, synthetic busts, etc. might be so described. 'So you've visited the Jarrods at last, eh? It's skeuomorph heaven in there, isn't it?'

SKULDUGGERY *n.* Dirty work. Common words sometimes have uncommon alternative forms and indeed meanings. These the Superior Person always prefers. Thus 'skulduddery' and its eighteenth-century sense of 'unchastity' will enable you to add a little life to this somewhat tired pejorative.

SLUBBER *v.* To smear or dirty something, or to wallow in something. Three-year-olds and politicians are good slubberers.

SLUBBERDEGULLION *n.* A glorious seventeenth-century term of contempt (found in *Hudibras*), apparently meaning a dirty, wretched slob.

SLUMGULLION *n.* A stew made out of meat and vege-tables. But also, be it noted, one of those wonderful words with a range of alternative meanings, all of them pejorative: a menial servant; a weak drink; fish offal; bluffer refuse; and the gunk at the bottom of mine sluiceways. 'Heavens, no, Bentley; in calling you a slumgullion I certainly didn't mean to imply that you were a cheap plate of food; look up the other meanings in a dictionary – I think you'll be pleasantly surprised.'

SMATCHET *n.* A small, nasty person, or a nasty child. 'Why, Carol – you've brought the twins! Gosh, when I see them together – smatchet and smatchet – I think I'm seeing double!'

SMEW *n.* A small species of merganser. Last-ditch-conversational-ploys-when-all-else-has-failed, No. 317: 'Did you know that the smew is a small species of merganser?'

SNOOD *n.* A band for the hair, formerly regarded in Scotland as a badge of virginity. Not a bad term, perhaps, for the headbands now modishly worn by macho sportsmen – most of whom are probably virgins anyway, if what I hear about steroids is correct.

SOFFIT *n.* An architectural term meaning 'the underside of an arch.' The possibilites for using the term (albeit with a little poetic license) in relation to the human body are too obvious – indeed, some may think, too indelicate – to be spelled out here.

SOLATION *n.* The liquefaction of a gel. 'Come in out of the rain, for heaven's sake, before solation sets in with that hairdo of yours.'

SOLIPSIST *n.* A philosopher who holds that only he himself exists, and that the external world exists only through his own conception of it. It is amusing to consider the spectacle of two solipsists at a philosophy seminar suspiciously eyeing each other and wondering which one of them is a figment of the other's imagination. The author prefers to use this term to describe any extremely self-centered person – one who is so wrapped up in himself that he behaves as though the external world does in fact exist only insofar as it serves his purposes. Thus, you are reclining on the golden sands, savoring the warm sun, the salt-sea breeze, and the gentle murmuring of the waves; the person who sits down beside you and turns on a transistor radio, which is tuned to a talk show, is a solipsist. You reach the top of a crowded escalator in a busy department store; the person on the step above you who, on stepping off the moving stairs, immediately stops dead, stands stock still, and looks around in a leisurely fashion, is a solipsist.

SOLMIZATION *n.* Using what would otherwise be nonsense syllables for the notes in the musical scale. Otherwise known as *solfeggio*; do, re, mi, fa, etc. 'You ask what I think of Lucille's singing, Mrs.

Weatherpost? Well, I honestly think she's reached the point where she could progress to solmization now.'

SOMETIME *a.* Former. As in 'sometime lecturer in Multicultural Studies at the Royal Military College.' A delightful archaism. Ideal for use in addressing envelopes to easily embarrassable friends: 'Mr. J. Smith, Esq., / Sometime Fellow in Ecclesiastical Parlance, / etc., etc.'

SOMNIFACIENT *a.* Conducive to the onset of sleep; having a hypnotic effect. Also *somniferous*, a slightly stronger expression of the same sense, meaning sleep-inducing or narcotic. A televised golf tournament, a line-dancing display in the mall, white goods comparison shopping, etc., etc.

SOPHOMANIA *n.* A delusional state in which the sufferer believes that he or she is a person of exceptional intelligence. Standard therapeutic procedure is for the sufferer to write a letter to the editor of a newspaper on a subject of current controversy; this invariably induces large numbers of other sufferers to write to the editor, telling the original sufferer what a fool he is. If therapy fails and the sufferer succumbs, he or she may be doomed to end his or her days as an economist.

SOTERIAL *a.* Pertaining to salvation. Thus *soteriology* is the doctrine of salvation. 'Harrison, you are the living refutation of soteriology.'

SPALLATION *n.* The splitting of the nucleus of an atom into many fragments as a result of high-energy bombardment. 'Hey, Bob, guess what – Mom's got Dad in the kitchen and she's giving him one of her lectures. He's reached the hands-over-the-ears-and-face-turning-red stage. I'd say spallation must be imminent. Let's go and watch.'

SPATIOTEMPORAL *a.* Having both space and time. 'Do we really need to invite the Harbingers? I mean – it's a small room, they're so big and so boring – so kind of . . . spatiotemporal.'

SPHRAGISTICS *n.* The study of engraved seals. The Superior Person should be equipped with as many such terms as possible so that he can make casual references to his familiarity with the most outré studies and pursuits. 'I remember, back in the days when I was reading sphragistics at Balliol, . . .' In this case, though, even the author does admit to *qualms* (q.v.) about the pursuit in question. The studies themselves would seem inoffensive enough, but the cruelty, the inhumanity of the original engraving process . . .

SPIRITUAL WIFE *phr.* According to Mormon tradition, my sources claim, a woman who has been married for eternity. In fact it only seems like that to her.

SPOONERISM *n.* We all know that this term describes the kind of metathesis (verbal reversals involving the transposition of initial letters or half-syllables) associated with the name of the Reverend William Spooner (1844–1930). But in fact most of the spoonerisms conventionally attributed to him ('our queer old Dean' instead of 'our dear old Queen' and so on) were never actually said by Spooner. One that is reliably recorded as a true Spoonerism occurred when he was leading prayers at New College, Oxford, and began by saying 'Darken our lightness, we beseech Thee, O Lord.' Similar errors can appear in print, and the publisher Kegan Paul, in his autobiography, admits to one that slipped past his proofreaders: a wild rock-strewn coastal plain, described by the author as being 'scattered with erratic blocks', came out in print as being 'scattered with erotic blacks.'

SPURIOUS *a.* Not genuine. This is not, however, simply a synonym for *fake*. The spurious have pretensions of a kind, but fall short of fulfilling them. 'The degree of accuracy implied in these statistics is spurious.' A lovely word to say aloud, flowing as it does off the tongue. Practice saying 'your prurience is spurious' – this could be a nicely ambivalent compliment for one of your friends.

STATISTICIAN *n.* As every schoolboy and several schoolgirls knows and know respectively, Dr. Johnson defined a lexicographer as 'a harmless drudge,' leading the present lexicographer naturally to the suggestion that a statistician be defined as 'a harmless drudge with an understanding of mathematical probability.' Be that as it may, the paradigm of the type is perhaps Charles Babbage, the nineteenth-century inventor of the calculating engine, who once took the trouble to write to the poet Alfred, Lord Tennyson about one of the poet's lines that had been troubling him. Tennyson had written this couplet:

> 'Every moment dies a man
> Every moment one is born.'

Babbage, in his letter to Tennyson, said: 'it must be manifest that if this were true, the population of the world would be at a standstill', and suggested to Tennyson that he revise the lines to read:

> 'Every moment dies a man
> Every moment one and one sixteenth is born.'

Speaking of Alfred, Lord Tennyson, by the way, the author wishes to state that in future he chooses to be known as Peter, Lord Bowler.

STAUROPHOBIA *n.* Pathological aversion to the cross or crucifix. Yes, this is it – the actual technical name for the condition which you have seen represented on the silver screen by countless actors lumbered with the task of portraying Dracula or other vampires and assorted evil spirits. This gives you the opportunity for much innocent byplay when you realize that the breast of your beloved is adorned by a pendant gold cross. With the standard *molendinaceous* (q.v.) arm wavings, baffled snarlings, and expressions of abject terror, you could recoil before the said cross, later shyly admitting to your staurophobia and stressing its standing as a recognized medical condition. And then, the cross removed, demonstrating your affection and gratitude with a little love-bite on the neck. . .

STEATOPYGOUS *a.* Fat-buttocked. Another excellent word for insulting without offending, especially as the listener is unlikely to be able to remember it long enough to look it up in a dictionary later, and is unlikely in any case to possess a dictionary that includes it.

STEGOPHILIST *n.* One whose hobby is climbing the outside of tall buildings. 'So you're suffering from fear of heights now, dearest? Hmm . . . have you thought of trying a little stegophily?'

STENTOROPHONIC *a.* Speaking very loudly. From Stentor, the Greek herald in the Trojan war, whose voice, according to Homer, was as loud as that of fifty men combined. There is always at least one stentorophone in close proximity in any public gathering where you are trying to enjoy a quiet conversation with a friend. 'Do we *have* to invite Mr. Wangensteen this time? I mean, it's bad enough having someone who's *sermocinatious* [q.v.], but when they're stentorophonic as *well* . . .'

STICHOMYTHIA *n.* A form of dialogue in which two speakers engage in a kind of verbal duel, each repeating part of what the previous speaker has said, but in a different sense. The example most frequently quoted is Hamlet's 'Mother, you have my father much offended,' in reply to the Queen's 'Hamlet, you have thy father much offended.' A somewhat better-known example, which protracts the conceit to unendurable length, is Abbott and Costello's 'Who's On First' routine.

STOCHASTIC *a.* Unpredictable in progression. In physics and probability theory, a stochastic process is a progression in which the next step cannot be predicted from the preceding steps. 'Oh look – Daddy's coming home at last, Mummy. He's getting out of the taxi . . . he's straightening up . . . he's putting the bottle away in his pocket . . . he's turning towards the house . . . now let the stochastic process commence.'

STOUT FELLOW! *n.* Exclamation indicative not of abhorrence of perceived corpulence, but of friendly admiration for a worthy act or statement. Thus, *A*: 'I was caned by my teacher every time I talked out of turn, and I believe that made me the man I am today.' *B*: 'Stout fellow!' Or, *A*: 'I am not prepared to sit idly by while this government ruins the country's economy.' *B*: 'Stout fellow!' This usage derives from what was formerly the primary meaning of *stout* (brave or resolute). The modern meaning is, of course, plump or tending to fatness; a fact which permits a nice degree of innuendo in the use of the above expression when it is addressed to people who are, in fact, slightly overweight.

STRAMINEOUS *a.* Strawlike, valueless. 'Such a pleasure to debate an issue with you, Herr Doktor. I always find your arguments so . . . stramineous.'

STREPHOSYMBOLIA *n.* A neurological disorder affecting the ability to read, in which a book may need to be read upside down to be understood. The author had already formed the opinion that some books are better read upside down; and the novels of Dashiell Hammett, he finds, can be enjoyed as much by reading the chapters in backward as in forward order.

STROBILATION *n.* Reproduction without sexual congress, as for example in jellyfish and tapeworms. 'How do you think Gerald came into existence? Strobilation? I mean – can you imagine Agnes and Simon actually . . . you know . . .?'

STRUCTURE *n.* Goering is debited with the oft-quoted: 'When I hear the word *culture*, I reach for my gun.' The author reacts in the same fashion to the indiscriminate use of the word *structure* to convey a range of half-formed and tenuous notions of an over-conceptualized nature, unrelated to constructional manner or form, the latter being the true sense of the word. *Structure* is *not* a synonym for words such as *theory, belief, argument,* or *concept.* The rule is simple: when the word is used in any sense other than that of its dictionary definition, interrupt the speaker immediately and say, 'What, precisely, do you mean by "structure" in this context?' After three such interruptions in the course of any one faculty soirée, you will either have been marked down as a future dean or politely invited to help with the canapés in the kitchen. The latter is, of course, the preferred alternative.

STRUTHIOUS *a.* Like an ostrich. A term of contempt for middle management.

STUPEFYING *a.* Inducing stupor. As, for example, the music of Scott Joplin, or a televised golf tournament. If used in a sufficiently favorable tone of voice ('How positively stupefying!'), it can be successfully confused in the listener's mind with *stupendous*.

SUANT *a.* Smooth, even, placid, agreeable, demure. If there is anyone out there who is both suant *and menseful* (q.v.), don't step under a bus – you are probably the last of your kind.

SUBAUDITION *n.* Not an audition for an understudy, but the act of reading between the lines or otherwise understanding a message that is implicit rather than explicit. Thus, when your beloved, speaking of something she has just cooked, sewn, knitted, or handicrafted, asks, 'Do you really like it, though? Tell me truly now – I want your honest opinion,' it is by an act of subaudition that you know that what she really means is: 'Tell me immediately that you like this very much; you may use superlatives if you wish, but please be convincing.'

SUBDERISORIOUS *a.* Mocking, but gently and with affection – as between friends or lovers. A needed word, describing as it does a particular quality for which there is no other satisfactory adjective. The attitude of the author's wife to his *nikhedonia* (q.v.) over the present book.

SUCCEDANEUM *n.* A substitute, resorted to when the real thing is not available. Normally an object (as, for instance, a baby's pacifier); but may be used of persons (as, for instance, by Walpole: 'In lieu of me, you will have a charming succedaneum, Lady Harriet Stanhope'). The latter is the model for the Superior Person to cultivate. The 'cc' is pronounced 'ks,' by the way; there is no feminine (or masculine) form; the plural is *succedanea*.

succedaneum

SUCCENTOR *n.* One who assists a precentor (a church choir leader). At the high school where you teach, when the pubescent Rochelle proudly informs you that she has been chosen as a cheerleader for the football season, you ask her, with your most irritatingly paternalistic smile, 'Will they take you on as a succentor first and then you work your way up to precentor?'; and, when she asks you what you mean, you tell her to ask her classics teacher (knowing full well that the school has not had a classics teacher since 1923).

SUCCINCTORIUM *n.* An embroidered band of cloth, worn hanging from the girdle by the Pope on solemn occasions. (Passing thought: what occasions involving the Pope are *not* solemn?) The Catholics' reply to the sporran. Unsettle your Scottish friend when he appears, bare-kneed but otherwise expensively clad for the big occasion, with a quiet query about his succinctorium hanging perhaps an inch or so too low?

SUCCUSSION *n.* Shaking. It is not widely known that Jerry Lee Lewis' *magnum opus* 'Whole Lotta Shakin' Goin' On' was in fact originally written as 'Whole Lotta Succussion Goin' On' but subsequently changed when the League of American Matrons objected to the term 'succussion' under the impression (mistaken, as it turned out) that it referred to an indelicate form of sexual congress.

SUDARIUM *n.* A cloth used for wiping sweat off the face, the most famous sudarium of all being the 'vernicle,' i.e., the veil or handkerchief of St. Veronica, believed to have retained miraculously the image of Christ's face when the saint wiped it for Him. 'And now Edberg and Becker leave the court to change ends, and . . . heavens! Edberg has lost his sudarium! This could be serious for the Swede, and . . . yes, Becker is offering Edberg the use of his own, but for some reason Edberg seems reluctant to accept it . . .'

SUFFUMIGATE *v.* To subject to smoke and fumes, more especially from below. Suffumigation is the process to which you are subjected in an elevator by a short person smoking a pipe.

SUGGILATE *v.* To beat black and blue; to bruise. When approached in the street for the twenty-third time by a jovial enthusiast soliciting money for a religious organization, you say, with an apologetic smile, 'I'm awfully sorry – I can't manage a cash donation at this time; but I could offer a suggilation, if that would do instead.'

SUMPTUARY and **SUMPTUOUS** *a.* The latter's meaning of luxurious, splendid, costly is well enough known, but the former is less familiar. It means 'having to do with the regulation or control of expenditure.' As Trent and Tabitha proceed down the aisle, you exclaim: 'Ah! The marriage of the sumptuous with the sumptuary!' When tackled on the matter, however, you decline to say which is which.

SUPEREROGATION *n.* Superfluity; something over and above what is needed. 'Works of supererogation' are good deeds over and above the call of duty. 'Verily, Mallory, the midwife who brought you into the world performed a work of supererogation.'

SUPEREXCRESCENCE *n.* Something growing superfluously. 'Sir, allow me to inform you that you are superexcrescent.'

SUPERNACULUM *n.* A liquor of high quality, fit for drinking to the last drop. 'It is a sad thing, Burnaby, that the custom of attending to one's religious devotions, upon arising in the morning and before retiring at night, has fallen into desuetude. In my own little way I try to compensate for that. I pride myself upon the fact that the sun does not rise upon a new day without my giving thanks with a supernaculum, in the privacy of my bedchamber.'

SUPERNAL *a.* Coming from on high. 'Supernal catch, lad!' you cry from your seat in the stand, as the outfielder just manages to pluck the ball out of the air. 'Supernal catch!'

SUPPOSITIOUS and **SUPPOSITITIOUS** *a.* As in the case of *abnegate, abrogate,* etc., the problem here is in grasping and retaining the difference in meaning. The former means supposed, assumed, hypothetical, conceptual, or notional; the latter means *spurious* (q.v.), phony, bogus, or ersatz. If at all possible, try to use both words in the one sentence, with a *very* straight face: 'I don't think we should dismiss Simon's standpoint out of hand; it's not necessarily supposititious just because it's suppositious, you know.'

SUSTENTACULAR *a.* Supporting or maintaining. (From the Latin *sustentare*, to hold up.) 'Ah, Mrs. Zaftig, we meet again! Goodness me, your revetment is indeed sustentacular today!'

SUSURRANT *a.* Gently whispering and rustling. Precisely descriptive of the surface noise emanating from your old long-playing records – or your new ones when your two-year-old has, in your absence, turned the treble control all the way up.

SYMPOSIUM *n.* Discussion of a set subject by a group of people, each of whom makes a contribution. Common enough a word in this sense, but what is less commonly known is its original sense – a postprandial drinking party, with dancers and music. Hence the usefulness of the word. 'Sorry to rush through dinner tonight, Mother; Ethel and I have to attend a symposium at eight o'clock.'

SYNCRETISTIC *a.* Seeking to identify common features of different belief systems, philosophies, or civilizations, and merge them into a single system. One can understand historians or theologians seeking to establish common elements in, for example, the Islamic, Judaic, and Christian traditions; but most modern historiographers would readily concede that no concept of syncretism can be considered sufficiently powerful to reconcile the existence of divine judgment with that of the television program *Candid Camera*.

SYNTONY *n.* The tuning of a specific transmitter and receiver into harmony with each other. Thus, syntonise: to put two pieces of wireless equipment into mutual resonance. 'Now that we're engaged, darling, do you think that before the marriage we should make sure that we can syntonise? It's a simple procedure that takes only a few minutes. We could do that now if you wanted to, right here in your bedroom.'

T

TABARD *n.* A medieval sleeveless tunic or jacket. A suitable archaism, perhaps, for a T-shirt? 'Do you have any Iron Maiden tabards?'

TABESCENT *a.* Wasting or withering away. (**TABEFACTION**: Emaciation.) Perhaps best used ironically, as with your Monday greeting for the bulimic co-worker who for many years has been growing more and more *globose* (q.v.). 'Glad to see that tabefaction has not set in over the weekend, Leslie.'

TABULA RASA *phr.* A clean slate. Commonly used metaphorically to describe the mind of a baby as being in effect a blank upon which the experiences of life will be imprinted over the years. Of course, you could also use it to describe the mind of a certain rather older person of your acquaintance; there'll be someone you know who fits the bill.

tabula rasa

TALARIA *n.* One of those wonderful words, like *caduceus* (q.v.), which denote a specific object seen relatively often in illustrations but maddeningly unnamable. The talaria are those little wings that you see on the feet or ankles of the fleet-footed messenger God Mercury (and sometimes Perseus and Minerva). Use in a love letter: 'Fly to me on the talaria of your love, O my beloved!'

TAPHEPHOBIA *n.* Morbid dread of being buried alive. 'No, not with you on top, Tabitha! I don't think I could handle that! I'm taphephobic, you see.'

TAPINOSIS *n.* The use of degrading diction about a subject. To some extent facilitated, I regret to admit, by this book.

TARDIGRADE *a.* Slow in movement. 'Hold it, children! That's a ladies' fashion boutique we've just passed; your mother has gone into tardigrade motion.'

TARSALGIA *n.* Pain in the foot. Perhaps, using a little creative philology, you could refer to the person of your choice as an arsalgia.

TARSORRHAPHY *n.* Stitching the eyelids together. It is sometimes the sad duty of the lexicographer to record the almost-unthinkable. In the present case, some relief may perhaps be obtained from the realization that here we have the ultimate spelling test for the smug super-spellers in your home or office.

TATTERDEMALION *n.* A ragged person whose clothes are always in tatters. To be preferred to *ragamuffin*, the nearest to an equivalent, because much less common and also because of the more equivocal etymology and signification of the latter. *Ragamuffin* in modern use is a ragged young scapegrace – a rather likable fellow whose escapades have a certain panache and whose worst sins are untidiness and recklessness. Formerly, the term meant much the same as *tatterdemalion* does now, a muff or muffin being a wretched or sorry creature and a ragamuffin thus being a sorry wretch in rags. As in *Henry IV Pt. I,* Act V, Scene 3, where Falstaff says, on his escape from the battle: '. . . God keep lead out of me! I need no more weight than mine own bowels. I have led my ragamuffins where they are peppered: there's not three of my hundred and fifty left alive.' Going back further still, however, the word may have had a much stronger meaning, being in fact, according to Webster, the name of the demon Ragamoffyn.

TAURIFORM *a.* Like a bull in shape, 'Ah, little Stephanie! Playing Mozart on the clavichord! And only nine years old! The experience would be perfect – if only she weren't so tauriform.'

tauromachian

TAUROMACHIAN *a.* Of or pertaining to bullfights. 'And are we to expect another tauromachian encounter when your mother visits us this Christmas, my dear?'

TAXONOMY *n.* In biology, the systematic classification of all organisms. Taken over recently by the social sciences as a piece of cant terminology useful for impressing the layman and for lengthening the curriculum of teacher training courses. Thus, where formerly we might have had, in botany, a taxonomy of blooms, we now have Bloom's Taxonomy of Educational Objectives. By the same process, we may shortly be confronted with Sudd's Taxonomy of

Ulterior Motives, Lindenblatt's Taxonomy of Unequivocal Statements, Simonson's Taxonomy of Snide Remarks, Ferrett's Taxonomy of Unexpected Reactions, Palethorpe's Taxonomy of Predictable Thesis Topics, Pelsart's Taxonomy of Inescapable Obligations, Runciman's Taxonomy of Buns, Wendelhead's Taxonomy of Impossible Dreams, d'Umbrella's Taxonomy of Foregone Conclusions, Friedlander's Taxonomy of Dubious Propositions, Bone's Taxonomy of Firm Criteria, Eiderdown's Taxonomy of Unfortunate Oversights, Bastable's Taxonomy of Political Campaign Tricks, Esterhazy's Taxonomy of Losing Poker Hands, Podder's Taxonomy of Missing Shopping Carts – and, of course, the present author's Taxonomy of Otiose Taxonomies.

TECHNOLATOR *n.* A person who is unduly worshipful of technology, gadgets, machinery, and the like. Everyone knows at least one technolator. He will play interminably with your broken sewing machine, radiogram, carburettor, etc., *without ever fixing it.*

TEGESTOLOGIST *n.* A collector of beer coasters. The species is normally male, falls within the age range of 19 to 23, and certainly does not know that it is so called.

TELEOPHOBIA *n.* A morbid dread of definite plans. 'I'm sorry, darling, but I have a medical problem that precludes any consideration of an actual marriage date. My teleophobia, I'm afraid – here's the doctor's certificate.'

TELESTEREOSCOPE *n.* An optical instrument which delivers to the observer the image in relief of a distant object. Yes, this is the Superior Person's name for those 3-D glasses you get at the 3-D cinema. Use the term casually, and once only, for maximum effect.

telestereoscope

TELODYNAMIC *a.* Relating to the transmission of power over a long distance. 'Telodynamics in action, darling; it's a long-distance call from your mother.'

TEMULENCY *n.* Inebriation, drunkenness. Another good one for sick-leave application forms.

TENEBRIFIC *a.* Making tenebrous, i.e., dark and obscure. 'Gee whiz, your lectures are tenebrific, Professor! No – it's true, we all think so – really tenebrific!'

TERATOSIS *n.* A biological freak, or monstrosity. Thence *teratism*, which means 'the adoration of the monstrous.' After your sister and her latest boyfriend have spent forty-three minutes on the telephone while you are waiting to use it, you remark admiringly upon the sheer extent of their mutual teratism.

TERGIVERSATE *v.* To equivocate; to change from one opinion to another repeatedly. 'Would you care to tergiversate over the menu now, dear?'

TERRAQUEOUS *a.* Living both on land and in water. A surfie.

TETRAGRAM *n.* A word with four letters. Note that the phrase 'four-letter word' is *pejorative* (q.v.), but that *tetragram* is not. Do what you can to remedy this situation.

TETRAGRAMMATON *n.* The Hebrew word for God, written with the four letters *YHVH*. The ideal personalized number plate for the Superior Person's car.

THANATOPHOBIA *n.* The morbid dread of death or dying. Ironic that it should be a *morbid* dread.

THAUMATURGE *n.* A wonder-worker, miracle man, or magician. *Thaumaturgus* was a term applied by the medieval Catholic Church to some of its saints, such as Gregory, Bishop of Neo-Caesarea, and St. Bernard, who was known as Thaumaturgus of the West. From this usage the term seems to have gradually descended to include in its coverage any kind of wonder-worker, including a conjuror or practitioner of legerdemain (i.e., sleight of hand). The nearest modern equivalent to the original meaning would seem to be the road-service mechanics employed by motorists' organizations such as AAA and the like.

THELYPHTHORIC *a.* That which corrupts women. The author's sources do not, unfortunately, identify the object so described; if any reader has one, perhaps he would be kind enough to send it to the author, enclosed in a plain wrapper.

THEODICY *n.* A theological theory that asserts God's justice in creating the world. (Despite all the evidence to the contrary, such as the existence of daytime television talks shows, Japanese drumming bands, etheric energy healing practitioners, etc., etc.)

THEOGONY *n.* The genealogy of a god or gods. For a pleasing effect of *tapinosis* (q.v.), refer to your sister-in-law's labors on the family genealogy as her 'ongoing theogony project.'

THEOMANIA *n.* A psychopathic condition in which the sufferer believes himself to be God. Clinical notes: Before administering sedatives or group therapy to the patient, the prudent psychiatrist will first ensure, by applying an appropriate test, that the patient's fixation does not have a basis in fact. For this purpose, crucifixion is *contraindicated* (q.v.), since a delay of three days is necessary to confirm a positive result, and in the event of a negative result the patient's condition will be terminal.

THERMANASTHESIA *n.* Inability to feel heat and cold. The use of this term might justifiably be adapted to signify insensitivity to the one *or* the other. Each of us knows someone who may be found rejoicing, coatless, in the bracing early-morning air of a late winter's day; and each of us knows someone who may be found huddled over the radiator, shivering, on a balmy spring evening. Fate has decreed that the two invariably marry each other. The lexicographer's contribution to their plight is that they may henceforth excuse their own condition, or commiserate with their helpmeet's, by the use of the above term.

THERMESTHESIA *n.* Sensitivity to heat. Long, long ago, before most of us were born, the virtuoso violinist Jascha Heifetz gave his debut recital in New York. In the audience, sitting together, were the already eminent violinist Mischa Elman and the great pianist Leopold Godowsky. It was a warm night, and during the interval Elman took the opportunity to remove his jacket, saying to Godowsky: 'Don't you think it's rather hot in here tonight?' Replied Godowsky: 'Not for pianists.'

thermanasthesia

THERSITICAL *a.* Abusive and foul-mouthed. 'I'd sooner you didn't bring the children this time, Gladys; if only I were as thersitical as they are I'd feel that I could relate to them better, but as it is. . .'

THIBLE *n.* (Pronounced 'thibble.') A spatula. You could get real mileage out of this one if you ever found yourself dealing with an apothecary named Sybil.

THIGMOTAXIS *n.* The movement of an organism in response to an object providing a mechanical stimulus. 'The cat's sleeping in my chair again, honey – pass me the broom and I'll try a little thigmotaxis.'

THINNIFY *v.* To thin, or thin out. Do not be surprised by this seemingly otiose extension of a simple word so adequate in itself. Remember how *press*, as a verb, became *pressure*, and *pressure* became *pressurize*?

THRASONICAL *a.* Bragging and boasting. 'The test results are back, Mr. Wheelwright, and let me say at once that you have absolutely nothing to be thrasonical about.'

THREMMATOLOGY *n.* The science of breeding domestic animals and plants. 'She's given up on her husband and kids, I hear, and is into thremmatology now. Says it's more rewarding.'

THURIBLE *n.* A censer, i.e., church vessel in which incense is ceremonially burnt. Superior Person's word for any device for the controlled inhalation of certain substances. A *thurifer* is the one who swings the censer during the ceremony. 'I'll just be down the backyard behind the shed with a few of my thurifer friends.'

THURIFICATION *n.* The act of burning incense, or of filling a room with the fumes of burning incense. From the Latin *thus, thuris* (frankincense). *Thuriferous* means 'producing or carrying incense.' 'I'm afraid we'll have to call in the drug squad again, Principal; the air in the prefects' room is distinctly thuriferous.'

TICKLER COIL *n.* A radio term. A tickler coil is a regenerative coil coupled in series with the plate circuit, used to intensify sound in a receiving circuit, through a feedback action. A true *technolator* (q.v.) might perhaps invite his beloved into his bedroom with an undertaking to show her his tickler coil.

TIFFIN *n.* A snack or light lunch. Deflate your socially pacesetting friends who have just been carrying on about this delightful new Chinese restaurant that has the most amusing *yum cha*, by saying brightly: 'Oh, that's a kind of tiffin, isn't it?'

TITTUP *v.* To frolic and generally kick up your heels, dancing or prancing along. A good word to introduce into your square-dance calls; but make sure to give equal emphasis to both syllables.

TITUBATION *n.* A disorder in bodily equilibrium, causing an unsteady gait and trembling. You might ruefully admit to being a trifle titubant the morning after the night before.

TITULAR *a.* Derived from the holding of a title; nominal. Thus the titular head of a country is usually the President, Prime Minister, Dictator, etc., as distinct from the effective head, who is usually his wife, cleaning lady, golfing partner, etc.

TOGGERY *n.* Collective noun for your togs, i.e., clothing. 'So – we're off to the beach and then on to the pictures. Everyone got their toggery?'

TOKENISM *n.* (i) The appointment of a female to a government committee; (ii) the appointment of a member of a minority group to a government committee. (See also *hypertokenism*.)

TOMENTOSE *a.* Densely covered with down or matted hair. 'For heaven's sake, Roger, get a haircut before you become totally tomentose.'

TONITRUOUS *a.* Thundering, explosive. 'And how are we tonight, my dear? Equanimitous or tonitruous?'

TOPECTOMY *n.* A surgical procedure in which the surgeon removes certain prefrontal cortical areas of the brain. 'Well, Rachel, I must say Shane looks absolutely wonderful since you're come back from overseas! He seems a new man! Tell me – did he have one of those Mexican topectomies?'

TORPILLAGE *n.* Electric shock therapy. 'Why not try some alternative medicine, dearest, to see if that helps? A little homeopathy, perhaps, some iridology, a course of torpillage?'

TORREFY *v.* To parch or scorch; to dry with heat. Your wife's hair dryer might perhaps be referred to as a torrefier.

TOXICOPHOBIA *n.* The morbid dread of poison. The story is well-known of the Roman emperor whose fear of being poisoned was so great that all his food was tasted before being passed to him. He succumbed when passed a dish of pre-tasted food so hot that it burnt his tongue, whereupon he called urgently for a drink of water. The poison was in the water. The moral: morbid dreads, useful though they are, do not necessarily protect you.

TRAGOMASCHALIA *n.* A condition in which the armpits are smelly. Fate has decreed that people with this condition always fall in love with people who are *nasute* (q.v.).

TRANSUBSTANTIATION *n.* Everyone is familiar with this term as signifying the transformation of bread and wine, during the Eucharist, into the body and blood respectively of Christ. A less well-known, but equally correct, meaning is a transformation of anything into something which is essentially different. Thus: 'Joel is actually wearing a tie to his graduation ceremony? And . . . what's this? Can it be? A suit? A suit *and* a tie? And he's shaved, actually shaved? I have seen it with my own eyes – a true transubstantiation!'

TREGETOUR *n.* A magician or juggler. In modern terms, a tax accountant.

TREMELLOSE *a.* Shaking like jelly. 'Your lactifera are tremellose!' you call out across the paddock to your large cousin Matilda as she performs an act of equitation. She assumes you to be warning her that her stirrup-leathers are loose.

TRICHOTILLOMANIA *n.* A condition in which the sufferer frenziedly tears his hair. 'Look at it this way, Mr. Birdworth; at least your baldness makes you immune to trichotillomania.'

TRILEMMA *n.* A problem situation in which there are not two, as in a dilemma, but *three* possible courses of action, each having its own disadvantages. Didn't know about this one, did you? You will find it depressingly useful in many life situations, including negotiations with auto repair shops, marital arguments (see also *zugzwang*), real-estate transactions, maternal visits, children's birthday parties, domestic budgeting, etc.

TRISTILOQUY *n.* A dull and depressing speech. 'And now, to really put a cap on the evening, we have the final speaker, one of our leading tristiloquists, Captain Arbuthnot. . .'

TROPE *n.* The figurative use of a word, and hence something well represented in the illustrative examples given in this volume. Also, less correctly but commonly used to mean any figure of speech. In that sense of the word, the Superior Person should familiarize himself or herself with all of the following figures of speech, and drop them casually into conversation at a moment's notice:

- *anadiplosis* repetition of an end at the next beginning: 'Though I yield, I yield gladly.'
- *anastrope* reversal of normal order: 'lexicographer supreme.'
- *asyndeton* omission of a conjunction between clauses: 'We loved, we laughed.'
- *brachylogia* omission of a conjunction between words or phrases: 'I have beauty, intelligence, wealth.'
- *diacope* repetition with a word between: 'Goddess, beautiful goddess.'
- *epanados* repetition but in reverse order: 'Must we leave? Leave we must.'
- *epanalepsis* ending a group of words with the same word that began it. As in the title of a 1926 silent Our Gang short: *Uncle Tom's Uncle*.
- *epanorthosis* addition to a correction: 'I love you – no, I adore you.'
- *hendiadys* expressing an idea with two nouns: 'Doom and gloom.'
- *hypallage* applying an adjective to the 'wrong' word: 'I had a sleepless night.'
- *litotes* affirming something by denying its negative: 'He's no slouch.'
- *metaplasmus* misspelling that still serves it purpose. See the signs on any fruit stall.
- *metonymy* substituting an attribute for the thing itself: 'I serve the crown.'
- *paradisastole* sarcastic euphuism as a means of disparagement, as in Ambrose Bierce's description of a monkey as being 'imperfectly beautiful.'
- *pleonasm* needless duplication of meaning: 'Illustrating example.'
- *polysyndeton* a surfeit of conjunctions. See any Hemingway story.

- *praeteritio* drawing attention to something by claiming to ignore it: 'I will make no mention during this campaign of my opponent's criminal record.'
- *prosthesis* tacking letters on to the beginning of a word: 'Bewail.'
- *syllepsis* relating the same word to two others in different senses: 'I swallowed my pride and an aspirin.'
- *synaesthesia* expressing one sensory experience by another: 'A heavy silence.'
- *synaloepha* combining two words with an omitted letter: 'Shouldn't.'
- *synecdoche* substituting the part of the whole: 'Ten head of cattle.'
- *tapinosis* belittling something or someone by sarcastic hyperbole: 'Well, here comes His Lordship!' (as your husband arrives on the scene).
- *zeugma* a verb governing two incongruous objects: 'She lost her heart and her purse.' (See also *syllepsis*.)

Why not have a 'Figure of Speech of the Month' for every month? Confound your friends with remarks such as 'I came, I saw, I conquered – ah yes – it's asyndeton month!'

In case the above brief guide to the world of the trope seems a little technical, let me assure you that a vastly more impenetrably esoteric field is that of prosody, which despite its name is not about the technicalities of prose but rather the technicalities of verse. Look into it at your peril.

TUBIFORM *a.* Shaped like a tube. 'Okay, tonight's family conference has been called with one agenda item only. We need to decide which of Paige's two aspiring suitors should take her to the prom. Which is to be – the tauriform or the tubiform?'

TUCK *n.* As is well-known, this is now a verb meaning to insert, but in the sixteenth and seventeenth centuries a tuck was a type of short sword or dagger. 'Just let me slip a tuck in here between the ribs,' you might caringly whisper to your most over-dressed competitor at the ballroom-dancing championships.

TURDIFORM *a.* Like a thrush in shape, the thrush being a bird of the family Turdidae.

TURGESCENCE *n.* Swelling or swollen; often with metaphorical connotations of pomposity. 'And now, it's that time of our meeting when we bow to the turgescence of our representative in the highest counsels of government. Ladies and gentlemen, I give you Senator . . .'

TURRICULATE *a.* Topped by a turret, i.e., by a small ornamental tower of the kind sometimes seen on top of a building. Add it to your armory of hairdo appraisal terminology.

TYPHLOSIS *n.* Blindness. 'And finally, I'd like to thank our long-suffering umpires and referees, who have given their time freely throughout the season to officiate at matches, week in, week out, often despite inconvenience – and even illness, as with Mr. Middlebroom, whose recurring typhlosis is well known to us all and has not made things any easier for him. It is a thankless task, and must ever remain so – especially in his case.'

U

UBIETY *n.* The state of being in a definite place – of having location or, so to speak, 'whereness.' Another of those well-nigh inexplicable words. Who or what would not have ubiety? 'This indefatigable ubiety of yours is a bit of a problem for us all, MacIndoe; could you manage to do something about it in the New Year?'

UBIQUITARIAN *n.* One whose existence is ubiquitous, i.e., who is everywhere. Said to be a characteristic of the God of pantheists, and for that matter of Christians; though somehow it does seem difficult to see the divine presence in the *Roseanne* show.

UDOMETER *n.* Another Superior Person's word for a rain gauge. (See also *pluviometer*.) If at all possible, use the two words in the one sentence.

ULIGINOUS *a.* Growing in muddy, oozy, or swampy places. 'Hmm,' you comment, after looking into your young brother's bedroom, 'I see Clive is going through another of his uliginous phases.'

ULLAGE *n.* The amount by which a liquid falls short of filling its container – whether because of evaporation, leakage, or any other reason. 'Well, old chap, since you were kind enough to bring along a bottle of truly excellent wine, I think I owe it to you to make sure you get all the ullage.'

ULOTRICHOUS *a.* Having short curly or woolly hair. Included here to give the author an excuse for introducing the following time-honored conundrum.

Question: 'Where do girls have short curly hair?'

Answer: 'New Guinea.'

ULTRACREPIDARIAN *a.* Going too far; overstepping the mark; presumptuous; intruding in someone else's business. 'Sir, you are an ultracrepidarian bounder.'

ultracrepidarian

ULTRAFIDIAN *a.* Going beyond faith. 'I suppose it would be ultrafidian to expect Lewis to arrive on time.'

ULTRAIST *n.* An extremist or radical in views or behavior. 'I think you'll like Jackson, Dad: he's an absolute ultraist, just like you.'

ULTRAMONTANE *a.* Beyond the mountains. Formerly, that faction within the Catholic Church which either lived north of the Alps, outside of Italy, and opposed the concept of papal supremacy, or lived south of the Alps, within Italy, and favored the concept of papal supremacy. Nowadays, more commonly used simply to mean situated beyond the mountains. As, for example, Palm Springs. Not to be confused with *ultramundane*, which means beyond the realities of earthly existence; unreal, unworldly. As, for example, Palm Springs. Not to be confused, also, with *ultra-mundane* (with a hyphen), which means excessively humdrum. As, for example, Palm Springs.

ULTRONEOUS *a.* Spontaneous. 'Have you done the preliminary research for your ultroneous remarks at the Annual Dinner yet, Percival?'

ULULATION *n.* A howling or wailing. The correct term for the sound of a discussion between a fully-grown female human and her mother-in-law on the subject of domestic management, occurring toward the end of a protracted visit by the latter to the former's place of residence.

ULUSCULE *n.* A little ulcer. When your academic acquaintance is showing off his technical expertise in bibliography by talking interminably about his majuscules and miniscules (which a normal person would call upper- and lower-case letters), you may find that you can suspend the flow of his expatiation with a passing reference to uluscules.

UMBLES *n.* Entrails of an animal, more especially those of a deer, but extended to cover any that are typically consumed as food. Thence the expression 'to eat humble pie,' i.e., 'umble pie,' this being the fodder reserved for those at the lowest end of the table. You already knew that, of course; but it may not have occurred to you to foster the use of the term in other contexts. Thus 'have some steak and umble [instead of kidney] pie,' or 'umbles [instead of liver] and bacon for breakfast today, dear,' or, if you really want to lower the tone on a social occasion, 'ah – my favorite – paté de umbles gras.' Often consequential upon umbles are *wambles* (q.v.).

UMBO *n.* The knob on a toadstool cap, a shield, or a seashell. A nicely deflating term for one of those woollen beanies that your trendy friends adorn their sconces with as the skiing season approaches.

UMBRAGEOUS *a.* Shady or shaded; quick to take offence, irritable. A nice double meaning. 'You're so umbrageous, Leigh. . . .'

UMBRIFEROUS *a.* Superior word for shady. 'Ah, my love,' you rhapsodize, 'let us retire to an umbriferous *dingle* [q.v.].'

UNASINOUS *a.* Being equally stupid. 'What a lovely marriage ceremony! So rare to see a couple so well-suited, so well-matched – so unasinous in every respect.'

unasinous

UNBELIEVER'S DEFENSE, THE *phr.* A technique
devised by the author to enable schoolchildren and
military personnel to avoid scripture lessons and
church functions if they wish. The method is not to
profess agnosticism, Hinduism, Buddhism, Islam, or
atheism – an approach fraught with incidental irrita-
tions – but to assert allegiance to a sect so little-
known or so obsolete that it can safely be assumed
that your school or regiment will not be able to provide the necessary specialist personnel for your pas-
toral care. Suggested as particularly suitable for this
purpose are the following sects:

The Abecedarians, who claimed that, since knowledge of the scriptures was passed on by the Holy
Spirit, it was wrong to learn to read. (Allegiance to
this sect can have obvious advantages in the school
situation.)

The Docetists, who believed that a mere phantom, not the real Jesus, was crucified.

The Monophysites, who believed that Christ's human and divine natures were one and the same.

The Muggletonians, who believed that the Father, not the Son, died on the cross, and that the Aaron of the Book of Revelation was Lodowick Muggleton, a seventeenth-century tailor.

The Nestorians, who believed that Mary should not be called the Mother of God, as she was the mother only of the human side, not of the divine side, of Jesus.

The Origenists, who believed that men's souls are created before their bodies.

The Quietists, who believed that man should occupy himself wholly with the continuous contemplation of God, to the point of becoming detached from influence by his senses or by the world around him. Especially suitable for use in the military world.

The Sabellists, who believed that God is indivisible but has three successive roles.

The Sandemanians or *Glassites*, who believed that justifying faith is no more than a simple assent to the divine testimony passively received by the understanding. Before you query the meaningfulness of this, know that Michael Faraday was one of their number.

The Southcottians, followers of Joanna Southcott, who announced when she was over fifty that she was about to give birth to a divine man named Siloh.

The Supralapsarians, who held that God put man into a position which made it inevitable that he would sin, and that his Creator would thereby have the opportunity of redeeming or punishing him.

UNCUS *n.* The hook with which the corpses of defeated gladiators were dragged out of the arena, or those of executed criminals from the *carnificina* (see *robur*). Suggested as a term for the hook on the end of a long pole with which music-hall performers whose acts were dying on stage were traditionally hauled off. 'Get out the uncus!' you arrange for everyone to cry in unison, halfway through the boss's speech at the office Christmas party.

UNDERGROPE *v.* To conceive or understand. Readers may wish to devise their own exemplary uses for this term, but are advised to keep them to themselves.

UNDINISM *n.* The association of water with erotic thoughts. Statistics show a national incidence of one sufferer per household. Think about it – which member of *your* family spends longest in the shower?

UNGUENT *n.* An ointment or salve, originally for anointing though nowadays more commonly medicated for application as a *cerate* (q.v.). A good conversation-stopper at the dinner table: 'Can anyone tell me – exactly what is the difference between a cerate and an unguent?'

UNGUICULATE *a.* Equipped with hooks, nails, and/or claws. 'So, Justin, you ask my advice as to whether you should marry Crystal. Well, she certainly has substantial investments and real property . . . but, let's look at it this way – she *is* unguiculate.'

UNGULATA *n.* The order of hoofed mammals. 'Look out! Get the plastic carpet protectors down! Here comes the ungulata!' might well be the cry as you observe your young son's football team moving purposefully in the direction of the kitchen door after training.

UNGULIGRADE *a.* Walking on hoofs. As a horse, a cow, the great god Pan, etc. 'Great boat shoes, darling! Love the extra height those platforms give you! Now you're truly unguligrade!'

UNIVOCAL *a.* Having only one meaning; or, said of several people expressing themselves with one voice. Rather ironic that a word which means 'having only one meaning' should itself have two.

UNNUN *v.* To defrock (metaphorically speaking) a nun. A delightful word in itself, and a formidable Scrabble weapon to boot.

UNTHIRLABLE *a.* Impenetrable. 'Say no more old chap – your logic is unthirlable.'

UNUNDULATING *a.* A pleasing neologism of the author's, meaning 'not undulating,' 'not wavelike in shape or motion,' i.e., flat. As for instance, 'the unundulating plains.'

URINIFEROUS *a.* Carrying urine. 'Behold, the uriniferous phial!' you cry triumphantly to your doctor as you emerge from the little room with your specimen.

URINOUS *a.* Looking like urine. One for the wine buffs. 'Ah yes, an excellent chardonnay, truly excellent! Medium-bodied . . . delightfully affectionate to the palate . . . not too fruity . . . lightly wooded . . . the cutest little varietal aroma . . . and urinous to a fault!'

UROPYGIUM *n.* The fleshy and bony prominence at the posterior end of a bird's body – the part of the bird to which its tail feathers are attached. Might be loosely used at the Christmas dinner table as a grandiloquism for the pope's nose. More loosely still, might be used in church as a cryptograndiloquism for the pope's nose.

URTICANT *a.* Stinging (like a nettle). 'Well, if you really need time out to "consider our relationship," as you so gracefully put it, why not go for a walk down the back paddock? It'll do you the world of good, too. Nice and urticant at this time of year!'

URUSHIOL *n.* A poisonous, irritant fluid; the active element in poison ivy. Something you could profess to have put in the salad dressing, leaving the others to look it up later.

USTION *n.* The act of setting fire to something, or the state of being set fire to. From the Latin *ustus*, past participle of *urere*, to burn. Pronounced 'usch'n'. Always to be used in preference to its longer synonym *combustion*.

ustion

USTULATE *a.* Scorched. The Superior Person's word for sunburned.

USUCAPTION *n.* The acquisition of property by right of long possession and enjoyment. Thus, in the average household, the bathroom is considered under common law to be owned, by right of usucaption, by the youngest female adult, and the telephone by the oldest female child.

USUFRUCT *n.* The right of using, benefiting from, and otherwise enjoying the fruits or output of someone else's property without damaging or diminishing the property itself. From the Latin *usus* (use) and *fructus* (fruit). A truly luscious word, if somewhat formidable to pronounce (*you-zoo-frukt*, with the emphasis on the *you*). 'May I hold your daughter in usufruct for the evening, Mrs. Galbally?'

UTRAQUIST *n.* One who partakes of the wine as well as the bread at communion. 'So that settles what we're all having for entrée and main course. Now, what'll we have to drink? Any utraquists among us? No? Well, we won't be needing the wine list, waiter – just a carafe of house water, please.'

UTTERANCE *n.* Great opportunity for a hidden double meaning here. Utterance of course means 'saying,' or 'something said,' but an archaic use of the term means 'the bitter end,' i.e., death, as in 'fight to the utterance.' 'James, I can't tell you how much I look forward to your utterance.'

UVULA *n.* The inverted cone of flesh hanging down from the soft palate at the back of the mouth. If your little soirée is being overwhelmed by the continuous neighing and trumpeting of the society matron brought along by your cousin Timothy, the interior decorator, you should quietly sidle up to her and, with conspiratorial confidentiality, whisper in her ear: 'I thought I should tell you – your uvula's showing.' At best, she can be expected to leave at once with Timothy; at next best, without him; and at worst, to spend at least twenty minutes locked in the bathroom examining her person in minute detail.

UXORILOCAL *a.* Living with one's wife's family. A suitable benison for a bride: 'May your husband be ever *uxorious* [q.v.] and never uxorilocal.' For a suitable curse, transpose the adjectives.

UXORIOUS *a.* Overly fond of a wife. The Concise Oxford Dictionary defines the meaning as 'excessively fond of one's wife'; but there does not appear to be anything in the etymology which excludes from the term's coverage the wives of others. However, if the conventional meaning is accepted, then, when next you are a wedding guest (and if you are a practicing exponent of the lore contained in this book, you had better make the most of it, since it may be the last time you are a guest anywhere), you quietly take the bride to one side, just before the happy couple is about to depart, and say to her: 'Jennifer, there's something you ought to know about Cyril. It's only fair to prepare you in advance for this. The fact is that you will find him extremely uxorious. I only hope . . .' (At this point you break away as if you have seen someone approaching and must on no account be overheard.)

VALETUDINARIAN *n.* An invalid – more especially one with a tendency to hypochondria. 'No, I'm sorry, we don't want to discuss the Bible on our front doorstep with two perfect strangers; in any case we're both valetudinarians – so good day to you . . . unless you'd care to make a donation?'

VAPULATION *n.* Flogging. Widespread ignorance of this word makes its use ('By God, old boy, I believe you deserve a vapulation for that!') quite safe even when addressing a Professor of English Language and Literature.

VARIETIST *n.* Someone whose attitudes or activities are not what most people would consider normal. Someone who chooses to be different. A *recusant* (q.v.) against the herd mentality, and to that extent the term is properly seen as complimentary. Thus, you are an eccentric; I am a varietist.

VARLET *n.* Low, menial scoundrel. One of a number of words of medieval origin, all indicative of unsavory status. Presumably the relatively large number of such words in existence is a reflection of the relatively high incidence of unsavoriness during the Middle Ages. Others that spring to mind are *lackey* (obsequious and servile hanger-on); *knave* (low-class rogue); and *caitiff* (base, despicable person). Note that knaves are always scurvy, i.e., thoroughly nasty, as is the appearance of one suffering from scurvy, one of the symptoms of which is scurf, or flaking skin, one of the instances of which is dandruff. Scurvy is a good descriptive for varlets, too, but not for lackeys. *Vassals* are also lowly creatures, but not as necessarily disreputable as varlets, lackeys, knaves, and caitiffs.

VASTATION *n.* Spiritual purification through the *ustion* (q.v.) of evil. 'Young man, be advised that I have performed vastation upon all those videotaped movies in your collection which have titles that include the word "blood" or the word "zombie." '

VATICINATE *v.* To foretell or prophesy. 'So tell me, darling, do your remarks about my employment prospects, now that I have been "let go," as the company so charmingly put it, constitute an act of true vaticination, or merely an attempt to add that extra edge to my dysphoria?'

VAVASOUR *n.* One who held his lands of a tenant in chief, i.e., the small farmer who rented his plot from the big farmer who rented his plots from the lord of the manor, whose ancestors had stolen it all from someone. In modern terms, the student who boards

352

in the backroom of the unit your daughter is renting. 'I'll pay you back on Saturday week, Daddy, when my vavasour pays her rent for the month.'

VECORDIOUS *a.* Mad, obsessive, senseless. The noun is *vecordy*. The general sense of the term is one of folly and dotage rather than of insanity. Useful for the Insult Concealed, especially in relation to the foibles of pet-fanciers, fishermen, golfers, stamp collectors, car-lovers, audio fanatics, sunbathers, lexicographers, train-spotters, bird watchers, joggers, oenologists, pedestrians, vegetarians, marching girls, film buffs, environmentalists, bibliophiles, mountaineers, *et hoc genus omne* (q.v.). 'No, darling, *of course* I'm quite happy for you to choose the color scheme. Just go ahead and trust your own judgment. I just know you can be relied on to come up with something utterly vecordious without any assistance from me.'

VELAMEN *n.* A veil worn by women, concealing the whole body as well as the head. 'Have you thought of wearing a velamen to the ball, Mrs. Underdown? It would really make you look your best, dear.'

VELLEITY *n.* A gentle volition; an almost passive inclination toward some act or objective. 'I sense within

velleity

myself a certain velleity to get up and go to work,'
you murmur to your semi-dormant helpmeet at
8:00 A.M., as the sunlight creeps slowly across the
counterpane (q.v.).

VELLICATE *v.* Twitch; or cause to twitch. 'There's no
need for all that vellication, Nathan; Mother doesn't
come here very often, and it's the only chance she
gets to listen to all her Scottish country dance
records on a really good stereo system.'

VELOCIPEDE *n.* A light vehicle propelled by the rider –
strictly speaking, by the rider's feet. A genuinely useful word, since it covers not only bicycles but also
tricycles, dinkies, toy cars, scooters, and the author's
VW. When your cul-de-sac is replete with pre-
schoolers and their older siblings, all pedaling away,
circling and recircling the macadam like so many
cruising sharks, you may properly refer to the scene
as exhibiting a *plethora* (q.v.) of velocipedes.

VENDITATION *n.* Displaying as if for sale. 'Have you
seen the dress that our daughter is proposing to wear
to the high-school ball, dear? She seems to have
graduated from ostentation to venditation.'

VENEFICIAL *a.* (i) Acting by poison, or poisoning;
(ii) acting by, or used in, witchcraft or sorcery, as for
instance a witches' brew; (iii) relating to the doings
of Venus, the goddess of love. The three meanings
come together when your beloved cooks you a meal
for the first time. The word is almost indistinguish-
able from *beneficial* if used casually in conversation.

VENERATION *n.* Profound respect and reverence. From the same root, ultimately, as *venereal* (i.e., pertaining to Venus). A piquant compliment to pay to an attractive member of the opposite sex is: 'Sir/Madam, you excite my veneration.'

VENERY *n.* (i) Sexual indulgence; (ii) hunting. A perfectly ambiguous word. While dining with a former duck-shooting companion and his wife, you could lean toward the latter during a break in the conversation and quietly ask: 'And is Athol still getting as much fun as he used to out of all that venery he went in for?'

VENTAGE *n.* A small outlet giving onto a confined space, as for example a fingerhole in some wind instruments. Just how far you go in applying this concept to the parts of the human body is up to you.

VENTOSENESS *n.* Flatulence; a tendency to suffer from wind. 'Maurice, you take elevator no. 1 – and remember, we're going to the eighteenth floor. Coralie, you'd better go with Maurice. Anyone else who's at all ventose? Okay, the rest of you come with me in elevator no. 2.'

VERACIOUS *a.* Of a truthful disposition. Pronounced exactly the same as *voracious*, i.e., of a greedy disposition. (See *ataxy*.)

VERBICIDE *n.* That which kills words or their meanings, i.e., a development or circumstance that destroys the common usage for a particular word or phrase. The obvious example in modern times is 'gay.'

355

Particularly unfortunate when, as in this case, the word so appropriated has a distinctive sense of its own and there are no obvious alternatives for that sense. So long, *Our Hearts Were Young and Gay* – you're history now.

VERBIGERATE *v.* To speak repetitively in totally meaningless language. A symptom of certain types of mental illness. And of readers who take this book too seriously.

VERECUND *a.* Modest, shy, or bashful. 'Okay, stop the partying for just a moment while I make an announcement! Step forward, Dimity! Lower the lights and turn the spotlight on Dimity, someone! That's right – now, here's what you've all been waiting to hear – Dimity is . . . wait for it . . . verecund!'

VERISIMILITUDE *n.* The appearance of being true. The display of characteristics strongly suggestive of authenticity. Note that verisimilitude is not quite the same as *evidence* of truth; it stops short. 'I concede, Baldwin, that this doctor's certificate lends, for the first time ever, I believe, a certain degree of verisimilitude to one of your sick-leave applications; but it would carry even more conviction if the handwriting was less legible and/or the word "flu" was not spelled "flew."'

VERMIAN *a.* Wormlike. 'Vermicular' means much the same, and 'vermiculation' is a state of infestation by worms, or transformation into worms. (Think about it for a moment. Yes, there's a horror film concept somewhere in every dictionary.) 'So you've been seeing her behind my back, you vermian little invertebrate. . .'

VERRUCOSE *a.* Covered in wartlike growths. Suitable for cursing under the guise of blessing. 'Bon voyage, Jacinta; may your path be smooth, your mind ever active, and your hands ever verrucose.'

VERTUGADE *n.* A *farthingale* (q.v.), i.e., a circular whalebone frame fastened around the hips – in former times a piece of women's underwear designed to provide a basis for extending the petticoat. Once tied around the waist it was impossible for the wearer to lower her arms, which she was therefore obliged to rest on the vertugade as if on a shelf. In England sometimes irreverently called a 'bum-roll.' Claimed by Rabelais to have been invented in a Spanish brothel for erotic purposes.

VESPIARY *n.* A nest of wasps. Jacinta's reply: 'May your workplace by day be as a humming hive, and in the evenings your house a vespiary.'

VETUST *a.* Venerable from antiquity, like the author.

VEXILLOLOGIST *n.* A student of flags. One of those people who can, and do, tell you when the flag of Montenegro is being flown upside down, and why the green bar on the Bulgarian flag is exactly the same shade of green as that on the flag of the old Austro-Hungarian Empire. There are people like this, just as there are people who know all about medals and exactly how they should be worn. There are *psephologists* (q.v.) too.

VIBRATIUNCULATION *n.* A slight shudder or vibration. As you stand beside the mechanic leaning over the engine of your car, you might say, 'It's just a little vibratiunculation, for want of a better word, that I get sometimes when starting on a hill.' Don't expect a reaction, though; he won't be paying any attention to anything you say anyway.

VIBRISSA *n.* A hair in the nostril. 'Well, bon voyage, Max; here's wishing you good health, a safe return, and lots and lots of vibrissae!'

VICISSITUDINARY *a.* Subject to constant change. 'Sorry, Brad – Simone's out with Owen tonight. And I think it's Craig tomorrow night. She's going through one of her vicissitudinary phases at the moment. Hang in there, man.'

VIDUITY *n.* Widowhood. 'Well, Benson, if you're considering your financial future, now's the time to look at insurance as an investment option. For example, I'm sure your wife would appreciate what we call a non-deferred viduity. . .'

VIGESIMAL *a.* Pertaining to the number twenty. 'As we all gather here to celebrate Daniel's twenty-first, it is chastening to remember that only a year ago this young man was – how can I express this without embarrassing him – vigesimal.'

VILLEGGIATURA *n.* A rural extended holiday or retirement. The aspiration of the lexicographer. A good word, which, spoken aloud in a dreamy manner, is extremely conducive to mental health.

VIOL *n.* Medieval six-stringed instrument; the predecessor of the violin, viola, and cello. Note that the viola is not a large violin; the violin is simply a small viola, since the word *violin* comes from *violino* (Italian, diminutive of *viola*). Note also that the cello is not a large viola; the proper term, which should *always* be used in its full form, is *violoncello* (n.b., *not* violincello), also from the Italian, being the diminutive of *violone*, or large viol. Got that?

VIRAGO *n.* A fierce, bad-tempered woman; a termagant. The derivation is from *vir* (a man). A virago is thus a mannish woman. The implication that being mannish is tantamount to being bad-tempered and violent seems to the author to be grossly discriminatory against his sex; he recommends, therefore, as the preferred expression, the virtual synonym *termagant*. The latter's derivation is much more fun. Oddly enough, it originally applied to men, not women. The term appears to have descended from *Tir-magian*, a Persian lord or god. The Crusaders apparently confused his followers with their enemies the Moslems, and this led in turn to *Termagant* becoming a stock figure on the medieval stage – a shouting, brawling, clubbing villain. (See *Hamlet*, Act III, Scene 2 – 'I could have such a fellow whipped for o'erdoing Termagant.') The transition of this figure into a stereotype of the brawling female is thought to be due to the fact that Termagant was traditionally represented on the stage in Eastern robes, like those worn in Europe by women.

VIRGATE *a.* Long, slender and straight. 'I'm bringing Celine over tonight, Dad, and I do not wish to hear the word "virgate" at any time during the evening – is that clear?'

VIRGINAL *n.* A small spinet without legs – a musical instrument used in Tudor and Elizabethan times. When next you call in at your neighborhood music store, choose the shop assistant who looks as though he/she knows least about music (this will not be easy – the competition will be pretty fierce); approach him or her with apparent diffidence, looking shiftily from side to side; cough quietly and say: 'Ah, excuse me – ah, I wonder if I might have – I don't see it on the shelves – ah, perhaps you have it under the counter – ah, a copy of the, er . . .' (Here you cough again, lean over the counter, and whisper), '. . . Fitzwilliam Virginal Book?'

VISCEROTONIC *a.* Having an amiable, comfort-loving temperament of the kind normally associated with endomorphy. (An endomorph is a person who by physical type is soft, rounded, and fleshy, and by psychological type warm and sociable.) 'Young gentleman wishes to meet viscerotonic millionairess; view comfort.'

VITELLINE *a.* To do with egg yolk. 'Ah, a truly vitelline restorative!' you exclaim, as you scoff your eggnog, the morning after.

VITIATE *v.* To weaken, degrade, or spoil. 'The impact of the Duke's address to the Conservation Society on the preservation of wildlife was somewhat vitiated by the circulation to members beforehand of a news report dealing with the great number of birds shot by the Duke during a sporting trip to the highlands.'

VITRESCIBLE *a.* Having the quality of forming a viscous, glassy layer when subjected to heat. Another suitable term for hairdo appraisal.

VIVANDIÈRE *n.* In former times, a woman who supplied food and drink to soldiers in the field. 'Ah, our vivandière cometh!' you cry, as your wife emerges from the kitchen with salad and punch for your backyard barbecue.

VOLE *n.* A kind of mouse. Alternatively, the winning of all the tricks in a deal when playing the card game *écarté* – hence the expression *to go the vole*, i.e., to risk everything in the hope of a big win. 'I'm going the vole on this one!' you cry, as you release the pet mice from their cage during your wife's bridge party.

VOMITORY *n.* In an ancient Roman amphitheater, the circumferential passage through which spectators reached the doors leading to the seating. The foyer to the dress circle, so to speak. As you display your home to a visitor, you could validly refer to the corridor between the children's bedrooms and the rec room as the vomitory.

VORLAGE *n.* A skiing term, vorlage being a stance in which the skier leans forward at an angle of less than a right angle to the line of ground surface. 'Hmm, he's in vorlage tonight,' you say, as the returning *pater familias* is observed approaching the front door, his tenuous maintenance of an angle from the perpendicular bespeaking a longer than usual stopover at Joe's Bar on the way home.

VORTIGINOUS *a.* Moving as if caught in a vortex, i.e., rotating toward a notional central point. Mode of locomotion of one suffering from the effects of *porsonian* (q.v.) *potomania* (q.v.).

VOUCHSAFE *v.* Deign to grant or offer. Literally, to guarantee, or vouch for the security of. Appropriately used in reference to such acts as giving your son his pocket-money, or his providing his services for thirty minutes' work in the garden. Should, if at all possible, be used in the same sentence as *eschew* (avoid, abstain from). Thus: 'Darling, if you could see your way clear to vouchsafe me the use of the car tomorrow, I think I can undertake to eschew any reference to the dents in the fender.'

VRIL *n.* A *neoterism* (q.v.) of ninenteenth-century author Edward Bulwer-Lytton, denoting a force of psychic vibrational energy of colossal destructive power. Seen by some of his modern readers as an inspired forecast of nuclear energy, but now thought to be a reference to premenstrual tension.

VULNERARY *a.* or *n.* Having a curative effect on wounds. 'A little vulnerary unguent for your shaving cuts, darling?'

VULPICIDE *n.* The killing of a fox *other than by hunting with hounds*; or one who does that. The italics are mine. A puzzling one indeed. This is the meaning of the term as given by both Webster and Oxford. Yet why should hunting with hounds be excluded from the definition? The implication would seem to be that there is a moral bonus, so to speak, in hunting with hounds; that this is an *ethical* way to despatch the wily Reynard, and that other methods are unethical. Yet what other methods are there? In what circumstances could the word vulpicide actually be used? 'I say, old chap – passed a fox on the way across the meadow this morning – got him on the head with a four iron!' 'You absolute rotter! You could have got out a few hounds and had them tear his throat out; but oh no, you just had to commit vulpicide!'

WADSET *n.* A Scottish legal term, a wadset being a pledge of some piece of property as security for a loan. A wadsetter is the one giving the loan and receiving the wadset. 'Be thou my wadsetter until payday, in recognition of which I leave with thee my entire collection of Scottish country dance music CDs.'

WAFTER *n.* A person who wafts, that is to say, floats gently along. *Wafture* is that which is wafted, as for example an odor. 'Hmm, the distinct fragrance of Athol's aftershave. Such a wafture surely precedes the wafter himself. Be ready to open the window.'

Wafter

WAMBLE *n.* A rumbling or similar disturbance of the stomach. A comforting word, which deserves to be more used. 'Was that my wamble or yours?'

WARISON *n.* One of those curious and useful words which have two meanings that are so different as to be all but diametrically opposed. In this case: a signal for attack; and a reward or other form of benign gift. 'You deserve a warison from me, Courtney; it shall come when you least expect it.'

WATTLE *n.* A fowl's jollop. But what, I hear you ask, is a jollop? A jollop is a wrinkled, brightly coloured strip of flesh hanging from the throat. When Dylan emerges from his daily preening hour in the bathroom, you peer at his face and then ask, with a hint of concern in your voice, 'Don't think me rude, but . . . is that a wattle growing on your left cheek?'

WAYZGOOSE *n.* A printer's annual holiday. My sources are silent on the matter of the timing of this holiday, but personal experience suggests that it is always taken on the day when, had it not been taken, your job would have been finished.

WEASINESS *n.* The quality or state of being given to gluttony. Succeeds queasiness lexicographically, but precedes it temporally.

WEDBEDRIP *n.* An agreement under which a feudal lord's tenant was bound to provide him, on request, with a day's reaping from the tenant's land. Instead of telling your workmates on Friday that you will be spending the weekend gardening, you could say that you have to carry out wedbedrip for your wife.

WEEN *v.* To suppose or think (that something is the case). Archaic terms beginning with *w* have a special charm, and should be used remorselessly. See *welkin* and *wistless*. Use all three in the one sentence if you can. (Do not write to the author telling him how you did this.)

WELKIN *n.* Archaic term for the sky, especially in the grand sense of the great vault of the heavens above. 'Ah, truly a wonderful welkin today, I ween.'

WHANGDOODLE *n.* A mythical bird that grieves continuously. As far as the lexicographer can tell from the limited source material available to him, this bears no relation to the somewhat mystifying title of the classic Howlin' Wolf number 'Wang-dang-doodle,' with its haunting refrain 'We're gonna pitch wang-dang-doodle all night long.'

WHIFFLE *n.* An unimportant person; someone more pretentious than significant. In short, a whippersnapper, i.e., a whipsnapper, a cracker of whips – someone who makes a lot of noise to no purpose.

WHILOM *a.* or *adv.* Former(ly); once, erstwhile. A pleasant archaism to use once in a while, particularly when in the company of those among your few remaining friends who are most irritated by your penchant for the antediluvian. 'Whilom, when I was but a callow youth . . .'

WHIMLING *n.* A weak, childish person. Don't knock it – whimlings have a lot of fun while strong, adult persons are worrying.

WHIPPERSNAPPER *n.* Intrusive young upstart. Someone younger, pushier, and callower than the author. Interesting that it is almost invariably preceded by the adjective *young*, even though the notion of youth is intrinsic to the noun itself. (See *codger*.)

WILLIWAW *n.* A sudden and powerful downdraft of wind moving violently down the slope of a mountainous coast. You could so characterize your father's post-prandial snores as he reclines, comatose, in his armchair before the television.

WINCHESTER GOOSE *n.* This Elizabethan euphemism means a swelling in the groin caused by venereal disease. It seems to have been a favorite with Shakespeare, who used it at least twice (*King Henry VI Pt. I,* and *Troilus and Cressida*). The interest is in the derivation, the expression having arisen from the fact that the brothels of Southwark were under the jurisdiction of the Bishop of Winchester. As your dinner companions *tergiversate* (q.v.) over the menu and the waiter becomes more and more unhelpful, you say to your escort: 'I wonder if these are all the poultry dishes they have – ask him if he has Winchester goose.' You then retire quickly to the powder room to avoid the ensuing confusion.

WISTLESS *a.* Slow to notice, not observant, inattentive. 'A little wistless tonight, I *ween* (q.v.), dearest?' (When he has not noticed your new hairstyle.)

wistless

WITHERSHINS or **WIDDERSHINS** *adv*. In an unfortunate direction. From the Middle High German *wider* (against) and *sin* (direction). In particular, either of two directions traditionally believed to be unlucky: a direction contrary to the apparent course of the sun; and counterclockwise. The former belief must have been inconvenient, to say the least, for dwellers on western coasts. The correct usage of the term in modern parlance is in relation to the course followed by your spouse in reversing the family car up the driveway.

WITLING *n*. A mere pretender to wit; a petty smart aleck. In response to a successful sally at your expense, you slap the offender genially on the back and exclaim: 'Ah, you're becoming quite a little witling, Nigel – we shall have to be on our guard against your little whimsicalities, shan't we?' The repetition of the word *little* helps to create the right effect.

368

WITZELSUCHT *n.* An emotional state characterized by futile attempts at humor. Too close for comfort, this one. Ten years I've been trying to win the Nobel Prize for Literature with these lousy definitions – even the BHP Award for Excellence, goddamit – even a Writer-in-Residence at a women's college in a small country town – anything – and what do I get? The Big O – and I'm not talking Roy Orbison here, I'm talking . . . [Editor's note: It would be kinder to draw a veil over the remainder of this quite lengthy, not to say rambling, item, which was the last one being worked on by Mr. Bowler before his unfortunate breakdown. Letters of encouragement, quantities of white chocolate, and negotiable bills of exchange may be sent to him by wellwishers, who are asked, however, in the interests of his ultimate recovery, not to include their own feeble attempts at humor in any covering letters.]

WOODIE *n.* Scottish humorous term for the gallows or the hangman's rope. Ah, those good old Scottish hangman's jokes – you don't hear many of them these days, do you?

WORD-GRUBBER *n.* One who is particular about fine points of verbal usage and who himself uses long and unusual words in everyday speech. An eighteenth-century slang term.

WRAPRASCAL *n.* A long, loose overcoat in common use in the eighteenth century. Today, Superior Person's word for the trench coat.

X

XANTHIC *a.* Yellow in color. 'Oh, Jessica dear,' you say, as you inspect the toilet bowl; 'been OD'ing on Mummy's multi-vitamin tablets again, have you?'

XANTHIPPE *n.* A shrewish, peevish, bad-tempered wife. From the name of Socrates' wife, said to have been such a one. Whilst at first it may seem surprising that the wise and good Socrates, of all people, should have had such a person as helpmeet, on reflection it seems less so. Imagine the effect on an initially happy and well-balanced young woman of being subjected daily to the Socratic Method – of having every detail of her housekeeping, her *oniomania* (q.v.), her personal behavior, etc., subjected to calm, friendly, benevolent, and relentlessly logical cross-examination. Perhaps the above word ought to be used instead to describe a wife who has to put up with a dry-as-dust egghead of a husband who never does anything she asks him to without first requesting that she define her terms and enumerate her alternatives.

XANTHODONTOUS *a.* Having yellow teeth. Included here only because of its interest to abecedarians, being the only remotely deprecatory adjective known to the author that begins with 'x'. (See *abecedarian insult, an.*)

XANTHOPSIA *n.* An ophthalmic condition in which everything appears yellow. Condition of a person wearing dark glasses purchased from the 'sale' section at the local gas station.

XENIAL *a.* To do with hospitality. 'And now, our genial host – I should say our genial xenial, I suppose. . . .'

XENIUM *n.* A present given to a guest. 'Always nice to come to the Tennysons', isn't it? And I suppose it's not fair to expect a xenium these days – the old xenial customs have gone out the window, eh?'

XENODOCHEIONOLOGY *n.* Love of hotels and inns. A passion shared by drunkards, womanizers, and Upwardly Mobile Young Managers, to whom Visible Movement is more important than staying in the office and getting on with their work.

XENODOCHIUM *n.* A building for the reception of strangers; a caravanserai. Yes, this is it. The Superior Person's word for a motel.

XENOGENESIS *n.* The fancied progeniture of a living organism completely different from either of its parents. A term invented by imaginative scientists of an earlier era for something that modern science declares to be impossible. Still, there is always hope.

When the gruesome Brett and Samantha break to you the news of their engagement, you either congratulate them in terms of their mutual compatibility or console them in terms of their looking forward to the possibility of xenogenesis – your choice of remark depending upon whether you wish to be ostracized by them after the wedding reception, or immediately. A further ploy would be to console them by referring to the possibility of parthenogenesis, which is reproduction without sexual union.

XENOGENOUS *a.* Due to an outside cause. '*Most* impressed by your clever son's matriculation results, Ivy! Fancy you and Gavin bringing forth such a genius! Absolutely xenogenous!'

XENOGLOSSIA *n.* The supposed ability to communicate with others in a language which you do not know. (A term from the world of so-called 'psychic research.') The impracticability of this concept is soon exposed if you attempt to talk with your teenager using some of the terms that you have heard him use in conversation with his friends. This will, however, at least afford him considerable entertainment, and you will be pressed, with much sniggering, to 'say that again' – something that he will never otherwise say to you.

XENOMANIA *n.* An obsessive mania for foreign customs, traditions, manners, institutions, fashions, etc. Nowadays this is called multiculturalism.

XENOPUS *n.* An African toad with teeth in its upper jaw, tentacles on the side of its head, webbed hind feet, and claws on its toes. Now don't say you didn't learn anything new from this book.

XERIC *a.* Extremely dry. The metaphoric use is suggested. 'How droll, Gregor, how perfectly xeric your sense of humour is.' Pressed for an explanation, you make an off-hand remark along the lines of 'from the Greek – you know – xerox, xeromorphy, xerophthalmia and all that – you know . . .'

XYLOID *a.* Woody. 'Little Robbie sure is his father's son, isn't he? Same happy smile, same hair color, same xyloid head. . .'

XYLOPHAGE *n.* An insect that eats wood. 'Do you have much trouble with xylophages in your hair?' might be a somewhat unsubtle Insult Concealed for use by a young *whippersnapper* (q.v.) against his elder sister, in retaliation for her monopolization of the bathroom for the purpose of perfecting her coiffure.

XYLOPYROGRAPHY *n.* Making designs on wood with a red-hot poker. Kids: use this word when your teachers ask you to fill in a career guidance form about what you want to do for a living. They won't have a dictionary that includes it, and they won't want to try to pronounce it in front of the class to ask you what it means. Make them suffer a little.

XYSTER *n.* A surgeon's instrument for scraping bones. 'Well, Agatha, if you're sure the doctors can't find anything wrong with you, why not try a naturopath? And ask them to give you a good going over with a xyster. Does wonders for your circulation, I'm told.'

XYSTUS *n.* An ancient Roman word, meaning the covered space in which athletes went through their physical preparations. The baths at Rome were furnished with large *xysti*, in which young men went through a number of exercises. A pleasingly archaic word for that feature of modern society, the gym.

YANKER *n.* According to Webster, an obsolete Scottish word for which there are, or were, three separate meanings: (i) a smart stroke or blow, (ii) an agile or clever girl, and (iii) a great falsehood, or whopper. How the three meanings relate to each other is beyond the author, but he suspects that it may have something to do with the great mystery of the Scottish kilt.

YARBOROUGH *n.* A hand of cards containing none higher than nine. If you ever get a hand with none *lower* than nine, you could always mutter something about bloody yarboroughs under your breath, on the off-chance that one of your opponents knows the term; and then, when the inevitable denouement occurs, exclaim that you never *could* remember whether it was higher or lower.

YATAGHAN *n.* A special form of Turkish scimitar in which the cutting edge of the blade has not one but two curves, one being convex and the other concave.

'Ah, Madam's taste in Persian carpets is beyond praise! As are Madam's skills in the ancient eastern art of price negotiation! Never before have I met a customer so eloquent, so persistent, so demanding of satisfaction! The many hours we have spent discussing the price and measurement of every carpet and every rug in my humble store are of inestimable value for me! As for this last difference of opinion between us on the price of this, my cheapest, smallest and most inferior rug – I could resolve it all now with one stroke of the yataghan – if Madam will permit?'

YAUL *v.* To deviate (in rocketry) from a stable course because of oscillation about the longitudinal axis. You *could* try this one on the traffic policeman, I suppose: 'It's not what you think, Ossifer. I'm not drunk. I'm just suffering from yaul, and therefore deviating from a stable course because of oscillation about my longitudinal axis. . .'

YCLEPT *a.* and **YESTREEN** *n.* and *adv.* These two words mean named and yesterday evening respectively. Two more of the author's archaisms, guaranteed to exasperate friends and relatives. For maximum effect, use in close juxtaposition to a modernism. 'Yestreen, as I was enjoying a television program yclept *Star Trek*, . . .'

YEAN *v.* To bring forth young. (As, for example, sheep or goats – a term from the world of animal husbandry.) But don't tell the ambulance people over the phone that your wife is yeaning; they may not have read the book.

YELLOW JACK *n.* The quarantine flag. 'Hoist the yellow jack!' you cry on first beholding the tell-tale pustules on your six-year-old's tummy.

YEMELESS *a.* Negligent. 'Well,' you say to the service-station proprietor as you pay for your grease and oil change, 'I suppose I can rely on your *younkers* [q.v.] in the service bay to have been every bit as yemeless as usual.' He nods and smiles uncomprehendingly and you go on your way with at least some sense of satisfaction in return for the emptying of your wallet.

YESTERFANG *n.* That which was taken at some time in the past. Your beloved's maidenhead; all the good seats in the grandstand; and the last bottle of really good champagne.

YETHHOUNDS *n.* A pack of phantom hounds pursuing a lady. From old English folklore. *Yeth* comes from heath. Also called wishhounds. Wisely is it said that the English have a word for everything. How this particular one first came into existence is a mystery to the author, even allowing for the penchant of the English for specialist hunting dogs (see *harrier*). There appears to be no equivalent term for a pack of phantom hounds pursuing a gentleman.

YEULING *n.* Walking around fruit trees praying for a good crop. Try it if you wish, but the author can only say that he has found swearing, abuse, and threats of extreme violence to be more effective.

YGDRASIL *n.* The gigantic ash tree which, according to Norse mythology, binds together with its roots and branches the whole of earth, heaven, and hell. Suggested as a pet name for that tree in your back yard – the one you want your husband to chop down before its spreading canopy brings total darkness to your clothesline, your herb garden, and your sunbathing spot.

YIRN *v.* To whine; to pout, or show petulance by facial grimaces. Pronounced the same as *yearn*. 'My husband is an idealist; he's always yirning for something.'

YISSE *v.* Desire, covet. On arriving at Colonel Carstairs's bridge party, you give his newly nubile daughter Amanda an *avuncular* (q.v.) pat on the head, saying to her father: 'Ah, I yisse this miss, I wis.' Knowing your penchant for childish wordplay, he chuckles politely and you head for the card table, already one trick up.

YLEM *n.* The primordial substance from which all the elements in the universe were supposed by early philosophers to have been formed. Thought by the ancients to have been water, by the moderns to be hydrogen, and by the Chinese to be monosodium glutamate.

YOUNKER *n.* Youngling, youth – more especially a male youth. Originally meaning a young gentleman, knight, or gallant, this word has gradually acquired a faintly pejorative signification, and now has connotations of callowness, inexperience, and even thick-headedness. (See *yemeless*.)

Z

ZAFTIG *a.* Desirably plump and curvaceous. Suitable for the Compliment Concealed. 'Ah, zaftig, très zaftig,' you murmur when your employer's wife enters the room.

ZARF *n.* A filigree metal holder for a hot coffee cup or glass. From the Arabic. One of those things they give you in coffee lounges to hold your steaming caffe latte in. But why on earth are they made of metal, which is after all such an effective conductor of heat? 'Excuse me, miss; I've just burnt my fingers on my wife's zarf – could I possibly have a vulnerary unguent?'

ZEDOARY *n.* A type of turmeric root that has the medicinal function of strengthening the activity of the stomach. 'Okay, everyone ready to order? We'll have six big burgers, five caramel sundaes, thirteen hash browns, five hot chocolates, eight medium french fries, seven blueberry muffins . . . and zedoaries all round, please.'

ZEIGARNIK *n.* A tendency to remember an uncompleted task. This is a term from the magic land of psychology, and describes a condition to which all of us are, to varying degrees, prone. With, of course, the notable exception of builders, who are immune.

ZEITGEIST *n.* The general intellectual, moral, and cultural level of an era. Thus, the zeitgeist of today's younger generation could be said to reflect the values of the conservation movement, equality of opportunity, the computer game, and the horror film.

ZELOTIPIA *n.* Morbid or fanatical zeal; jealousy. 'It's great to see a family where both daughters play the piano. So good for the young people to have something like that, isn't it? Just see what it does for them – you can see the zelotipia shining in their eyes!'

ZENANA *n.* That part of an Indian house in which high-caste women were sequestered. 'Mother, would you care to convey a message to my sister? She has retired to her bedroom in the usual high dudgeon, apparently in the belief that it is a zenana.'

ZIGGURAT *n.* In ancient times, a Babylonian temple with stepped terraces giving it a pyramidal shape, so that each storey was a little smaller than the one below it. 'So, how's the party fare coming along? Ah, gingerbread men, chocolates crackles, yes, donuts with pink icing . . . and do I see one of your mother's ziggurat cakes in the making?'

ZOANTHROPY *n.* A pathological conviction on the part of a human that he or she is an animal – or, more correctly, a nonhuman animal. 'Is Simon's zoanthropy improving at all, now that he's a sophomore?'

ZOIC *a.* To do with animals or with the life of animals. 'Yes, it's an interesting place to live. I think you'll like it after you've settled in. The atmosphere's very laid back. The neighbors are very friendly. They don't stand on ceremony; they'll pop in to see you all the time – and you'll find them truly zoic.'

ZOILISM *n.* Carping, destructive criticism. 'Ah, Miss Petherbridge, another solo from you on tonight's program, I see! If only I were free to convey to you the full extent of the zoilism that your playing inspires in me!'

ZONA *n.* In ancient times, a girdle that was used to gird up the skirts of a dress, in the interests of freedom of action. On solemn occasions the girdle was relaxed, so that the folds of the dress would hang down to the feet. During a marriage ceremony it was taken off altogether. 'Any chance of doffing the old zona tonight, babe?' might be a novel way of approaching an old subject.

ZOOERASTIA *n.* Sexual intercourse with an animal. As your office manager returns at the end of a lunch hour, red-faced and panting stertorously from the effects of his usual two-mile jog, you whisper to the new keyboard operator: 'Don't ask – it's just his hobby – zooerastia. Couldn't handle that myself, but it seems to keep him fit.' Sooner or later, she'll look it up.

ZOOPERY *n.* Experimentation on primitive animals. 'Still having trouble with 3B, Carruthers? Try a little zoopery – tell them they can watch a pornographic video when they've mastered the subjunctive.'

ZOOPHILOUS *a.* Animal-loving – a practice illegal in some countries. (Pray forgive the lexicographer his little facetiae – especially towards the end of the 'z's).

ZOOPHOBIA *n.* Morbid dread of animals. Could perhaps be applied to vegetarians across the dinner table ('No spare ribs, Kylie? I didn't know you were zoophobic'), though at the risk of a truly xeric comeback, since vegetarians' hunger for solid matter will certainly have led them to a reading of this book.

ZORI *n.* (pl.) The Superior Person's word for thongs, that peculiarly aestival form of footwear commonly employed for the purpose of jamming the wearer's foot underneath brake pedals, tripping him up in public places and upon acutely serrated seaside rock-formations, and rendering the sound of his coming and going akin to that of a flock of migrating ducks.

ZUGZWANG *n.* A state of play in a game of chess such that any of the various moves open to the player with the next move will damage his position. He is then said to be 'in zugzwang.' The term has obvious potential as a descriptive of certain stock situations of married life:

- Husband notices that floor is littered with assorted debris. If he (a) picks it all up, wife accuses him of regarding her as slovenly; if he (b) leaves it where it is, wife accuses him of never doing anything to help her around the house; if he (c) picks half of it up, wife accuses him of laziness. He is thus 'in zugzwang.'
- Wife notices gas gauge is on empty when husband is trying to start car. If she (a) asks him whether car has run out of gas, he will angrily tell her to shut up while he tries to listen to the motor; if she (b) says nothing, it will take him ten minutes to discover the cause of the trouble; if she (c) simply tells him that gas tank is empty, he will undergo severe loss of face and take it out on her for the rest of the evening. She is thus 'in zugzwang.'

ZYGOSIS *n.* The conjugation, or joining together, of two sex cells. Convince the shy couple that when they sit down with the priest to discuss the wedding ceremony they should check the zygosis occurs straight after the signing of vows.

ZZXJOANW *n.* A Maori drum. The recommended use is in Scrabble. The technique is to save up, at all costs, the letters *Z, X, J, O,* and *W* (or a blank that can be used in place of any you don't manage to acquire); to wait for a dangling *AN* on which you can build; and then to strike. The satisfaction to be derived from this single act altogether outweighs whatever chagrin you might otherwise experience through losing the game, as you assuredly will – even that experienced through losing six games in succession, if need be, before you can effect your coup.

Sources

The sources from which the words are derived include, as would be expected, various editions of the better-known dictionaries (more especially, Oxford, Webster's, Chambers, and Funk & Wagnalls) and also the following specific works:

Bombaugh, C. C. *Oddities and Curiosities of Words and Literature*. Dover, N.Y., 1961.

Byrne, Josefa Heifetz. *Mrs Byrne's Dictionary of Unusual, Obscure and Preposterous Words*. Citadel Press, Secaucus, N.J., 1976.

Drever, James. *A Dictionary of Psychology*. Penguin, London, 1958.

Haubrich, William S. *Medical Meanings: A Glossary of Word Origins*. Harcourt Brace Jovanovich, San Diego, 1984.

Hill, Robert H. (comp.). *A Dictionary of Difficult Words*. Signet, N.Y., 1975.

Johnson, Samuel. *A Dictionary of the English Language. Abstracted from the Folio Edition by the Author*. Allison et al., London, 1824.

Kupper, W. H. *Dictionary of Psychiatry and Psychology*. Colt Press, N.J., 1953.

Ogilvie, John (ed.). *A Supplement to the Imperial Dictionary: English, Technological and Scientific*. Blackie and Son, Glasgow, 1855.

Riley, P. A. and Cunningham, P. J. *The Faber Pocket Medical Dictionary*. Faber & Faber, London, 1977.

Shipley, Joseph T. *Dictionary of Word Origins*. Philosophical Library, N.Y., 1945.

The Family Bible Dictionary. Avenel Books, N.Y., n.d.

Tweney, C. F., and Hughes, L. E. C. (eds.). *Chambers Technical Dictionary*, Macmillan, N.Y., 1965.

Urdang, Laurence (ed.). *The New York Times Everyday Reader's Dictionary of Misunderstood, Misused, Mispronounced Words*. Weathervane Books, N.Y., n.d.

Uvarov, E. B., and Chapman, D. R. *A Dictionary of Science*. Penguin, London, 1951.

Weekley, Ernest. *An Etymological Dictionary of Modern English*. Dover, N.Y., 1967.

A NOTE ON THE TYPE

The text of this book is set in Linotype Sabon, named after the type founder, Jacques Sabon. It was designed by Jan Tschichold and jointly developed by Linotype, Monotype and Stempel, in response to a need for a typeface to be available in identical form for mechanical hot metal composition and hand composition using foundry type.

Tschichold based his design for Sabon on a fount engraved by Garamond, and Sabon italic on a fount by Granjon. It was first used in 1966 and has proved an enduring modern classic.